DIGITAL ASSETS & CRYPTO FOR INVESTORS

DIGITAL ASSETS & CRYPTO FOR INVESTORS

YOUR PRACTICAL GUIDE TO BUILDING A DIVERSIFIED PORTFOLIO

VANESSA GRELLET

Foreword by J. Christopher Giancarlo

WILEY

Published by John Wiley & Sons, Inc., Hoboken, New Jersey.

Library of Congress Cataloging-in-Publication Data is Available:

ISBN 9781394421053 (Cloth)
ISBN 9781394421060 (ePub)
ISBN 9781394421077 (ePDF)

Cover Design: Wiley
Cover Images: Wiley, Adisak Riwkratok/Shutterstock
Author Photo: Courtesy of YS Corporate

SKY10164832_080626

To my family, past and present.

CONTENTS

FOREWORD ix

INTRODUCTION: BEFORE YOU INVEST A DOLLAR xiii

CHAPTER 1
THE RISE OF DIGITAL ASSETS: ORIGINS, GROWTH, AND LEGITIMACY 1

CHAPTER 2
DIGITAL ASSET TECHNOLOGY AND USE CASES: HOW DIGITAL ASSETS WORK 37

CHAPTER 3
THE INVESTMENT OPPORTUNITY: ADOPTION, GROWTH, AND MARKET CYCLES 63

CHAPTER 4
INVESTING IN PUBLIC MARKETS: ETFs, SPOT, DERIVATIVES, AND EMERGING PRODUCTS 99

CHAPTER 5
INVESTING IN PRIVATE MARKETS: FUNDS OF FUNDS, VENTURE FUNDS, AND LIQUID FUNDS 139

CHAPTER 6
ACCESSING DIGITAL ASSET INVESTMENTS VIA SELF-CUSTODY AND DECENTRALIZED INFRASTRUCTURE 177

CHAPTER 7
YIELD OPPORTUNITIES IN DIGITAL ASSETS: GENERATING INCOME THROUGH STAKING, LENDING, AND LIQUIDITY POOLS 199

CHAPTER 8
PORTFOLIO DIVERSIFICATION: WHY DIGITAL ASSETS BELONG IN A MODERN PORTFOLIO 237

CONCLUSION: THE FUTURE OF DIGITAL ASSETS AND WHY IT MATTERS 263

LIST OF RESOURCES 265

NOTES 271

ACKNOWLEDGMENTS 281

ABOUT THE AUTHOR 285

INDEX 287

FOREWORD

"If you don't know where you are going, you will never get there!"

These were words of wisdom from a high school guidance counselor. The words and their logic have stuck with me throughout the course of a lifetime practicing law in New York and London, building a business on Wall Street, and serving as a senior government official in Washington. Scaling these heights came more through a sense of direction, rather than a detailed plan of action. Selecting the destination was the essential step in plotting the journey.

Knowing where you are going also applies to investing. Or more simply, having an investment framework in which to operate. In more than four decades in and around Wall Street, the most successful investors and traders that I have known were those who understood financial markets and had a comprehensive mental framework for how to invest in them. When it comes to crypto, few people have as clear and complete an investment framework as Vanessa Grellet.

Vanessa and I first met several years ago near St. Moritz. It was a sunny, but brisk January afternoon in Switzerland's snow-covered Engadine

Valley. Introduced by a colleague, we enjoyed a pot of Edelweiss tea in the cozy, Belle Époque grandeur of the grand lobby of the celebrated Suvretta House Hotel, host of the annual CFC-St. Moritz crypto conference.

With fading afternoon sunlight streaming through the tall windows onto the wood-paneled walls and comfortably upholstered sofas, Vanessa Grellet shared her extraordinary background. I learned of the significant roles she played at various leading crypto investment firms and her work driving the adoption of Ethereum-based products and establishing key initiatives such as the Enterprise Ethereum Alliance and the Blockchain for Social Impact Coalition. I was impressed with the range of Grellet's advisory and board roles with organizations like the Arts and Antiquities Blockchain Consortium and the Resolution Project. Mostly, I was struck by her grasp of the investment opportunities in crypto and her success in pursuing them.

Since that first meeting, Grellet launched Arche Capital, a firm that invests early in new businesses in the center of financial services, blockchain technology, and artificial intelligence. Included in the Arche investment portfolio are a broad range of companies that will undoubtedly shape the future of finance. Arche is the perfect vehicle for Grellet's keen eye for successful investment.

Grellet shares her investment framework in this book. She provides a brief but thorough history of crypto and blockchain innovation, explaining what it is and how it has become a durable, albeit volatile, investment asset class. She provides a thoughtful framework for engagement with crypto to realize its investment return.

Grellet is particularly effective in explaining how and why crypto and blockchain technology is a new architecture of finance, a digital network infrastructure changing the very way we record who owns what and who transfers what to whom. She shows how we are witnessing a wholesale transformation of the global financial system, in which blockchain technology "is changing how ownership is recorded, how value moves, and how transactions settle, often without changing the assets themselves."

Grellet explains that for investors, "the opportunity is to identify which digital asset technologies are becoming core financial infrastructure." The question is not whether change will happen, but which systems will emerge once it does. And, critically for investors, she examines how to invest in this digital network future of finance.

Before I served as a Commissioner and then Chairman of the Commodity Futures Trading Commission, the US Federal regulator of trading in many types of crypto, I spent almost 14 years on Wall Street as a senior executive of a fast-growing financial service firm. The firm's founder and CEO was a proven entrepreneur with a keen understanding of global financial markets. He also had a droll sense of humor. Often asked for his predictions on market trends, he would respond with an answer along the lines of: "I think the current market direction will remain for the present time and then it will gradually shift in a different trajectory for a while before going in a new direction, at first upward and then downward, or perhaps vice versa."

He would say this slowly with a serious face and, then gradually, the twinkle in his eye and the laugh lines around his mouth would betray a smile. Most often, his listener gradually got the point—no one, not even successful Wall Street professionals, can precisely predict the day-to-day direction of markets.

You don't need to have a crystal ball, however, to build a successful portfolio. But you do need to know where you want to go. The most successful investors set out with a clear destination despite market ups and downs.

If you want to invest in crypto and its underlying innovation, you will find a path laid out in this book.

Be not afraid!

J. Christopher Giancarlo

February 8, 2026

INTRODUCTION

BEFORE YOU INVEST A DOLLAR

Before you invest a dollar, you must decide what kind of investor you intend to be.

If you are holding this book, you are probably not searching for the latest hyped token or the fastest way to double your money.

You are likely asking a more consequential question: *How do digital assets, often referred to as "crypto," actually fit into investing, and do they belong in my portfolio at all?*

For more than a decade, digital assets have been framed as a binary choice. You either believe in the asset class, or you don't. You're either early or too late. You're either participating in a financial revolution or standing in its way.

That framing has generated enormous noise and remarkably little clarity.

This book begins from a different place.

It assumes you are not trying to make a philosophical or existential statement.

You are trying to make a financial decision.

WHY THIS BOOK EXISTS

Most investors encounter digital assets in the wrong order.

They see prices before they see structure. They hear narratives before they understand risk. They are shown opportunities long before they are shown trade-offs.

As a result, many first allocations to digital assets are made without a framework. And in investing, frameworks matter.

I came to digital assets from inside the traditional financial system. I was trained as a securities lawyer and spent several years at the New York Stock Exchange, working on strategic investments, public M&A transactions, and derivatives markets. That experience shaped how I see markets: as systems built on structure, incentives, regulation, and trust.

I discovered Bitcoin in 2013, long before institutions took it seriously, and I have lived through multiple market cycles since—periods of exuberance, collapse, rebuilding, and renewed conviction. I was not watching from the sidelines. In 2016, I joined ConsenSys as one of its early employees, when Ethereum was still experimental infrastructure rather than an established asset class. From that vantage point, I witnessed the early formation of key blockchain primitives and decentralized finance.

Today, I invest across digital assets and public markets, evaluating token design, protocol economics, governance structures, and market behavior with the discipline of traditional finance and the pattern recognition of a venture investor. I also serve on the board of the Enterprise Ethereum Alliance, where public blockchains intersect with corporate adoption, institutional capital, and regulatory reality.

I am writing this book because I have seen how easily intelligent investors can misprice risk in this space—not because they lack knowledge, but because they lack a framework. I have seen capital invested in narratives rather than structure, and decisions made in volatility without context.

I have also spent years trying to explain this opportunity to traditional investors—friends, family, colleagues—only to find that the conversation was almost always long, difficult, and incomplete. The subject would either become too technical, too abstract, or too emotional. The signal would get lost in the noise. This book is my attempt to solve that problem. It is the conversation, organized. It is a way to present the full picture in plain English, without dilution and without unnecessary complexity, so that you can do your own work and reach your own conclusions.

This book exists to provide that model and to help you understand what digital assets actually are, how they function as an asset class, and how they can interact with the rest of your financial life.

WHAT THIS BOOK IS—AND WHAT IT IS NOT

This book is written for investors making a first allocation decision, as well as those looking to clarify their stance, whether that allocation ultimately becomes meaningful, minimal, or zero.

It is a guide to:

- The digital asset investment landscape
- The main categories of digital assets and exposure
- The risks, uncertainties, and structural differences compared to traditional investments
- The ways digital assets can fit into a diversified portfolio

It is not:

- A recommendation to buy specific cryptocurrencies, tokens, or stocks
- A trading manual or shortcut to fast returns
- A manifesto about decentralization, politics, or the future of money
- An argument that everyone should own digital assets

Digital assets do not require belief. They require understanding. That is where this book focuses.

DIGITAL ASSETS ARE AN ASSET CLASS, NOT A WORLDVIEW

For most investors, digital assets are neither a replacement for traditional securities nor a passing curiosity.

It is something in between: a new, volatile, evolving asset class that blends elements of technology, venture capital, commodities, and monetary systems.

The right question is not, "Are digital assets good or bad?" but rather:

- What kind of exposure do they offer?
- How do they correlate, if at all, with other asset classes?
- How do they behave under stress?

This book approaches digital assets the same way a serious investor approaches any asset class: by examining its structure, incentives, risks, failure modes, and role in portfolio construction.

A BOOK ABOUT CHOICES, NOT PREDICTIONS

Markets are full of confident forecasts. Digital assets have more of these than most.

You will notice that commentary in this space tends to swing between extremes, with bulls urging investors to ignore volatility in the belief that prices will inevitably rise, and bears dismissing the asset class outright.

This book does not attempt to predict where prices will go, which networks will win, or how regulation will ultimately unfold. Those answers change—and often abruptly.

Instead, this book is about choices:

- Choosing between different types of digital asset exposure
- Choosing appropriate risk levels
- Choosing time horizons
- Choosing whether participation makes sense at all

These decisions matter far more than any single market cycle.

WHO THIS BOOK IS FOR

This book is for:

- Investors approaching digital assets for the first time
- Existing investors who want to have a deeper understanding of investment opportunities
- Traditional investors seeking context rather than conviction

- Professionals who want clarity without hype
- Readers who value risk management as much as upside

You do not need technical expertise or even enthusiasm. You only need curiosity, an openness to think carefully about uncertainty, and willingness to put some work into studying it.

HOW TO USE THIS BOOK

By the end, you should be able to:

- Understand the digital asset landscape in plain terms
- Identify the major categories of risk and opportunity
- Decide whether digital assets belong in your portfolio and under what conditions

Allocating cautiously is a valid outcome. Going all in is a valid outcome. Deciding digital assets are not appropriate for you is also a valid outcome.

The only mistake this book is trying to prevent is investing before you understand what you are investing in.

That is where we begin.

CHAPTER ONE

THE RISE OF DIGITAL ASSETS

ORIGINS, GROWTH, AND LEGITIMACY

Every great investor starts with curiosity—a desire to understand what others dismiss, to see opportunity where others see chaos. Crypto began as a fringe experiment, but for those willing to ask questions and explore, it became the catalyst for one of the greatest technological and financial revolutions of our time.

By the end of this chapter, you will gain a clear understanding of:

- The historical perspective and evolution of digital assets
- How the evolution of digital assets mirrors other asset classes in traditional finance
- Why digital assets have become a legitimate investment opportunity

A BRIEF HISTORY OF DIGITAL ASSETS

The history of digital assets follows a familiar pattern seen in major technological shifts: early skepticism, regulatory uncertainty, resistance from incumbents, and gradual adoption once the technology proves useful.

The internet followed the same path in the 1990s. It was initially dismissed as a niche tool for academics and hobbyists, viewed as insecure and commercially impractical. Governments struggled to regulate it, established industries pushed back, and many early internet companies failed. Today, it underpins global communication, commerce, and finance.

That same pattern began to play out in finance during the global financial crisis. In 2008, the world was shaken by a devastating financial crisis that exposed the fragility of traditional systems. At that very moment, an anonymous figure (or group) named Satoshi Nakamoto published a white paper titled *Bitcoin: A Peer-to-Peer Electronic Cash System*. This document offered a bold vision: a digital currency powered by blockchain technology, allowing people to transact directly without relying on banks or intermediaries.

Bitcoin wasn't born in boardrooms or regulatory offices—it emerged from online communities, forums, and the work of dreamers and engineers who questioned the status quo.

At first, Bitcoin was a curiosity, embraced by cryptographers, tech enthusiasts, and libertarians. It wasn't until 2010, when someone famously paid 10,000 Bitcoin for two pizzas, that the world started paying attention. Those 10,000 Bitcoins, worth almost a billion today, symbolize not just the potential of this new asset but the power of early curiosity and vision.

My First Encounter with Bitcoin

I first encountered Bitcoin in 2013 at the Bitcoin Center in New York City, founded by Nick Spanos. His pitch at an NYU technology meetup caught my attention in part because of the location of the center itself, just steps from the New York Stock Exchange on Wall Street where I used to work.

Walking into the Bitcoin Center felt like crossing into a parallel financial universe. It bore little resemblance to the structured, institutional environment I knew from the NYSE. Instead, it was an eclectic mix of builders, idealists, skeptics, and speculators, all drawn together by the sense that something new was taking shape.

Ideas were being pitched constantly. One person urged me to invest in PotCoin, a cryptocurrency designed for the cannabis industry. Another enthusiast described a token related to space, confidently predicting it would one day be used for commerce beyond Earth. In the center of the room, traders were exchanging cryptocurrency for cash in an improvised pit, a scene that felt less like modern finance and more like the early days of derivatives trading.

Yet amid the noise, there were flashes of brilliance. Companies like Coinbase, which had just launched in 2012, were starting to make Bitcoin accessible to everyday people. Bitcoin ATMs, exchanges, and startups were emerging at an accelerating pace.

It was chaotic, yes—but also alive with opportunity.

That experience taught me an important lesson: every great investment begins with curiosity. It's easy to dismiss something new as hype or being a fringe activity, but those who take the time to understand and explore often uncover opportunities others miss.

The Turning Point: Discovering Ethereum

By 2016, I had immersed myself in Bitcoin and the broader digital asset landscape when I met Joseph Lubin, one of Ethereum's co-founders, at the early stages of his journey with ConsenSys. At the time, ConsenSys was a scrappy operation of about 20 people, some of whom were working out of a small office in Bushwick, Brooklyn—a gritty, industrial neighborhood with little attempt at refinement.

At the time, I was fundraising for a robo-advisor project, and the plan was to pitch Joe for funding. But within two minutes of hearing him talk about Ethereum, I realized we weren't the ones with the big idea—he was.

Joe explained Ethereum's vision, and suddenly, it all clicked. While Bitcoin was designed as a form of digital cash, Ethereum was something entirely different: an open-source platform for developers to build decentralized applications (dApps). Joe called it programmable money, powered by smart contracts—self-executing agreements that required no intermediaries.

He described a future where Ethereum would power:

- *Digital finance: Financial tools like payments, trading and investing, accessible to anyone with an internet connection.*
- *Digital ownership: Digital property that would redefine art, gaming, and intellectual property.*
- *Decentralized governance: Communities and organizations running on blockchain, where decisions are made collectively and transparently.*

Joe and his team weren't just building technology—they were laying the foundation for a new internet where individuals could own their data, assets, and identities. By the end of that meeting, my co-founder and I scrapped our fundraising plans and joined ConsenSys, inspired by the immense possibilities Ethereum represented. A superior technology that could replace our entire financial system.

A Quick Map of the Terms

Words like crypto, cryptocurrency, tokens, digital assets, Web3, blockchains, and protocols are often used interchangeably as if they all mean the same thing. Digital assets is the most precise and neutral way to describe the broad category of blockchain-native assets.

Crypto (or "Crypto Assets")
Broad umbrella term for the entire blockchain ecosystem (cryptocurrencies, tokens, apps, and infrastructure).

Cryptocurrency
A digital currency designed as money, usually with its own blockchain, and used for payments and fees.

Altcoin
Any cryptocurrency other than Bitcoin, including Ethereum, Solana, or XRP. The term covers a wide range of assets with different purposes, including smart-contract platforms, payment networks, and application-specific tokens.

Tokens
Programmable digital assets built on an existing blockchain, representing things like access, value, or ownership.

Digital Assets

The neutral, institutional term covering cryptocurrencies, tokens, stablecoins, NFTs, and tokenized real-world assets.

Stablecoin

A digital asset designed to maintain a stable value, usually pegged to a traditional currency like the US dollar, and used for payments, trading, and moving money on blockchains.

Blockchain

A software technology that provides a decentralized, shared digital ledger that records transactions and data in a secure, transparent, and tamper-resistant way, without relying on a central authority.

Web3

A way of building internet applications on blockchains that emphasizes user ownership. It's not an asset, but an ecosystem and design approach.

Protocols

The underlying software rules that power blockchains and applications; tokens often capture their value.

Example: Ethereum

Ethereum is both a blockchain technology and a protocol. The Ethereum protocol issues a token called Ether (ETH), which is used to pay transaction fees and access applications across the Ethereum ecosystem. Ether is therefore a cryptocurrency for practical use and a digital asset that investors can buy, sell, and hold for exposure to the Ethereum network.

KEY MARKET CYCLES AND TRANSFORMATIVE EVENTS

The rise of digital assets is best understood as a series of market cycles, each marked by rapid growth, sharp corrections, and lasting progress beneath the surface. These cycles are not signs of fragility. They are how new technologies mature.

A useful comparison is the early growth of companies like Uber. When ride-sharing first emerged, it faced intense resistance from incumbents and regulators alike. That opposition was not evidence that the technology was flawed. It was a natural response to a more efficient system challenging established business models. Over time, regulation adapted, usage expanded, and ride-sharing became part of everyday life.

Digital assets follow a similar pattern. Periods of excitement are often followed by pullbacks, regulatory scrutiny, and skepticism. Yet with each cycle, the underlying infrastructure improves, participation broadens, and integration with the traditional financial system deepens. What may look like instability on the surface is often the friction that accompanies meaningful change (see Figure 1.1).

Early Foundations (2009–2012)

Bitcoin emerged from the aftermath of the 2008 global financial crisis, gaining traction among cryptographers, cypherpunks, and early technologists. Its use cases were experimental and largely confined to niche communities exploring decentralized money. The initial focus was on peer-to-peer payments within small online communities, with the idea of being able to send digital cash (Bitcoin) between individuals, bypassing banks and traditional intermediaries. The primary question during this

Figure 1.1 Bitcoin halving cycles.

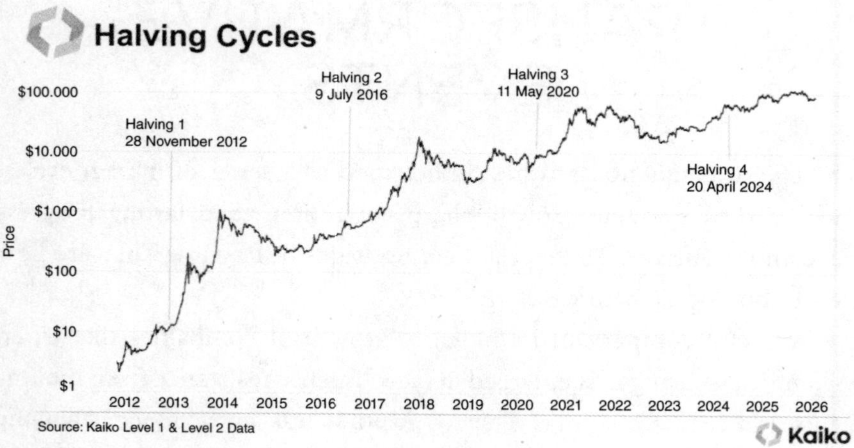

phase was not valuation, but viability: *Could decentralized networks reliably store and transfer value?*

As usage increased, foundational infrastructure began to form. Kraken launched in 2011 with a security-first approach,[1] while Coinbase followed in 2012,[2] focusing on regulatory compliance and ease of access for mainstream users.

A few early alternatives to Bitcoin also appeared. Litecoin tried to make transactions faster. Ripple focused on acting as a gateway for moving money between financial institutions. These projects showed that blockchains could be adapted for different purposes, not just one form of digital money.

Prices during these years moved sharply, not because of hype, but because the market was still deciding whether decentralized digital assets had any value at all.

Many projects were issuing liquid, tradable tokens while they were still early-stage startups, a dynamic more comparable to Google going public a year after its founding than to investing in a mature company. Bitcoin traded from essentially $0 in 2009 to single digits and low double digits by 2011, rose to around $30 in its first major surge, then fell sharply before settling into the $5–15 range through 2012.

Who Is Satoshi Nakamoto?

Satoshi Nakamoto is the pseudonym used by the person or group of people who created Bitcoin, the first cryptocurrency, and authored its original technical specification, software, and white paper.

The name first appeared in 2008 on the Bitcoin white paper, "Bitcoin: A Peer-to-Peer Electronic Cash System," which outlined a decentralized digital currency designed to operate without banks or governments.

Under this name, the Bitcoin protocol was developed, and the network was launched in early 2009. Satoshi contributed to Bitcoin's early development, communicated with early developers, and helped guide the project during its formative period.

In April 2011, Satoshi made their last known public communication on the Bitcoin Talk forum, writing that they had "moved on to other things." To this day, no one knows with certainty who Satoshi Nakamoto really is. Whether the creator was an individual or a group has never been publicly confirmed, making it one of the most enduring mysteries in modern technology and finance.

Over the years, many programmers and cryptographers have been suggested or claimed themselves to be possible candidates, but none has been definitively proven to be Satoshi.

It is widely believed that Satoshi controls the largest untouched holdings of Bitcoin held in a wallet that has been identified—possibly around one million BTC—that have never been moved.

Early Adoption and Growing Pains (2013–2014)

By 2013, Bitcoin had reached broader public awareness. Trading volumes increased, media attention intensified, and early digital asset exchanges became central points of liquidity. The first Grayscale Bitcoin Trust was created for investors to gain exposure to Bitcoin's price movements. At the same time, Bitcoin's use on platforms such as Silk Road[3] created persistent associations with illicit activity—an overhang that would shape regulatory perceptions for years.

A key moment in this cycle came in early 2014 with the collapse of Mt. Gox, then the largest Bitcoin exchange globally. Hundreds of thousands of Bitcoin were lost, exposing severe weaknesses in custody and operational controls. For investors, Mt. Gox functioned as the sector's first systemic failure, akin to an early brokerage collapse in traditional markets.

Importantly, this failure catalyzed improvement rather than extinction. In response to unreliable banking access and settlement risk, Tether (originally Realcoin) introduced USDT, a US dollar-denominated stablecoin[4] designed to function as a cash equivalent within digital asset markets. A stablecoin is a digital asset designed to maintain a stable value, typically one US dollar. It allows investors to move cash within digital asset markets without relying on traditional banks and is intended to remain firmly pegged at $1 rather than rise or fall in price. Around the same time, Circle began building regulated payment and settlement infrastructure that would later give rise to its own dollar-denominated stablecoin, USDC.

Exchanges such as Coinbase and Kraken expanded their compliance, security, and custody practices, learning directly from Mt. Gox's failures, while dedicated custody providers like BitGo emerged. Beyond infrastructure, early application-layer projects also emerged. BitPay enabled merchants to accept Bitcoin, Stellar focused on low-cost cross-border transfers, and Monero introduced enhanced transaction privacy in response to Bitcoin's transparent ledger.

Market prices reflected both optimism and fragility. Bitcoin rose from approximately $13 in early 2013 to over $1,000 by year-end, before declining sharply throughout 2014 into the $200–$400 range. This marked the sector's first full boom-and-bust cycle, reinforcing a lesson familiar to seasoned investors: innovation often precedes durable market structure, and volatility is the cost of early participation.

Infrastructure, Regulation, and Institutional Learning (2015–2016)

After Mt. Gox, the digital asset sector entered an important phase. The focus shifted from rapid growth to rebuilding trust and infrastructure. Exchanges improved security and internal controls. Custody became a serious discipline. Regulators began engaging more directly: the Commodity Futures Trading Commission formally recognized Bitcoin as a commodity,[5] the Internal Revenue Service classified digital assets as property for tax purposes, and the New York Department of Financial Services introduced the BitLicense, one of the first comprehensive regulatory frameworks for digital asset businesses.

This period also marked a major technical shift. Ethereum launched in 2015, introducing smart contracts and turning blockchains from simple payment networks into platforms for applications. Smart contracts are automated agreements on a blockchain that execute on their own. For example, they can transfer funds once conditions are met, such as releasing collateral when a loan is repaid or settling a trade immediately after payment. This change expanded the sector's potential well beyond digital money.

Other networks matured alongside Ethereum. Ripple gained traction with banks for cross-border settlement. Infrastructure quietly advanced. ConsenSys emerged as an early Ethereum venture studio, supporting wallets like MetaMask—software applications that allow users to securely store private keys, manage digital assets, and interact directly with blockchain networks—and essential developer tools. IPFS introduced decentralized storage, a concept that later became critical for nonfungible tokens (NFTs) and Web3 applications.

Privacy also became a focus with two protocols. Monero gained broader use, and Zcash launched with advanced cryptography designed to shield transaction details.

All of this occurred during a period of consolidation. Bitcoin recovered from below $300 in early 2015 to roughly $900 by the end of 2016. Ethereum traded under a dollar when it launched in mid-2015 and reached a high near $10 at the end of 2016.

Governance Under Stress: The DAO Hack of 2016

In 2016, the Ethereum ecosystem faced a defining test with the failure of The DAO.[6]

The DAO was designed as a decentralized investment fund built on Ethereum. Investors contributed Ether to a smart contract, received voting tokens, and collectively decided which projects to fund, without managers or intermediaries. The concept gained rapid traction and raised roughly $150 million worth of Ether.

The failure was caused by a flaw in the DAO's code, not in Ethereum itself. A vulnerability in the DAO's smart contract code allowed an attacker to repeatedly withdraw funds before balances were updated. About one-third of the DAO's Ether was drained. Because the funds were temporarily locked, the community had time to decide how to respond.

That decision centered on whether a blockchain should be changed to correct a mistake. In July 2016, the community chose to reverse the hack and return funds to investors by modifying the blockchain. Others disagreed, and the disagreement led to a permanent split. Ethereum continued on the modified chain, while Ethereum Classic preserved the original transaction history.

The episode highlighted an early reality of digital assets that code is not law and anyone abusing the system cannot argue that it was due to the initial code mistake. While blockchains reduce reliance on intermediaries, governance decisions still matter, especially in young systems.

Ethereum and the ICO Cycle (2017–2018)

A defining feature of Ethereum is that it made it possible to raise capital directly through the blockchain. This led to the rapid growth of Initial Coin Offerings, or ICOs, which allowed projects to sell tokens to a global investor base with few barriers while getting funding in Ether. An ICO is a method of raising capital in which projects sell digital assets directly to investors, often before a product is fully built. Investors would send Ether to the project and receive project tokens in return. As a result, many of these early ICO projects received a significant amount of Ether, which they maintained on their balance sheets. Capital flowed quickly, experimentation accelerated, and excess followed. The 2017–2018 period became known as the ICO mania.

Estimates suggest at least $12 billion was raised between 2017 and 2018, with EOS raising more than $4 billion on its own.[7] By 2019, ICOs had collectively raised more than $31 billion (see Figure 1.2).[8]

Figure 1.2 Capital flows into blockchain projects during the ICO boom.
Source: NFT Tech.

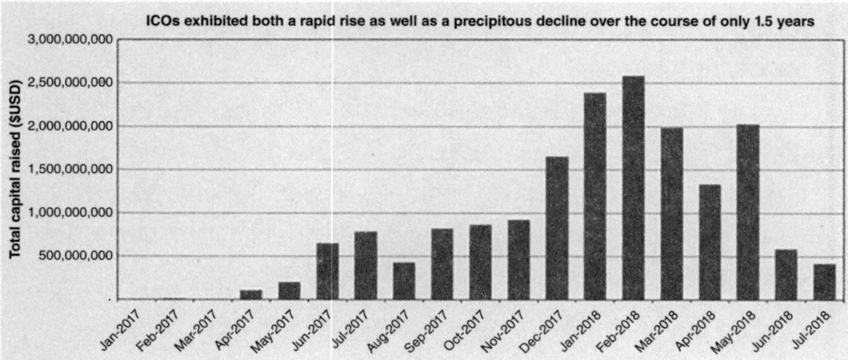

Many ICOs were poorly designed or outright fraudulent. After the market peaked in early 2018, prices collapsed and more than 80% of the market's value was erased. The correction was severe, but it did not erase what had been built.

The legacy of the ICO era was not the tokens that failed, but the infrastructure that remained.

Despite the losses, the ICO cycle funded lasting infrastructure. Aave used early funding to build on-chain lending. Chainlink solved the problem of bringing external data onto blockchains. MakerDAO showed that a crypto-backed stablecoin could function under stress. Uniswap later transformed on-chain trading through automated markets.[9] On-chain means activity that happens directly on the blockchain and is enforced by code. This contrasts with "off-chain" activity, which happens outside the blockchain and relies on people or institutions to operate correctly.

Access improved just as quickly during this period. Binance launched in 2017 and rapidly became one of the world's largest digital asset exchanges, providing the liquidity and global reach needed to support a growing ecosystem.

At the same time, more traditional institutions were quietly getting involved. In 2017, under the leadership of CFTC Chairman J. Christopher Giancarlo, US regulators "greenlit" Bitcoin futures to trade on CME and Cboe. The decision was less an endorsement of Bitcoin than a judgment that risk could be better managed inside the regulated futures system.[10] By imposing high margins, surveillance, and clearing safeguards, the CFTC enabled hedge funds and asset managers to gain exposure through familiar, regulated instruments, marking an important step in Bitcoin becoming a more institutional asset.[11]

Custody, long a practical barrier for institutional investors, also began to take shape. Coinbase launched its institutional custody solution, addressing security and compliance concerns. Anchorage, Fireblocks, and Copper were founded at that period.[12] Soon after, Fidelity introduced Fidelity Digital Assets, reinforcing the idea that established financial firms were preparing for client demand rather than dismissing it.[13]

Beyond markets and trading, large corporations were exploring blockchain technology for operational use. Groups such as the Enterprise Ethereum Alliance brought together banks, technology firms, and enterprises, including founding members JPMorgan, Chicago Mercantile Exchange, Santander, Microsoft, Accenture, and BNY, to develop standards on Ethereum.[14] At the same time, IBM and others advanced Hyperledger Fabric, while financial institutions collaborated through R3 to build private-market infrastructure.

Price moves reflected the extremes. Ethereum rose from under $10 to about $1,400. Bitcoin climbed from roughly $1,000 to nearly $20,000. Both fell sharply in the following year, with Ethereum dropping more than 90%.

New Layer-1s, NFTs, and DeFi Summer (2020–2021)

The 2020–2021 cycle marked a broad expansion of digital assets beyond payments and trading. New applications emerged across finance, culture, and digital ownership.

Decentralized finance, or DeFi, turned basic financial functions into on-chain software. DeFi refers to financial services built as software applications on blockchains, allowing users to trade, lend, or borrow directly without banks or brokers. Protocols such as Uniswap, Aave, Circle, and MakerDao enabled trading, lending, and borrowing without these intermediaries. This activity accelerated during "DeFi Summer" in 2020, when users began moving capital between protocols to earn yield and access liquidity. For the first time, lending, borrowing, and trading operated together on-chain at a meaningful scale, demonstrating that decentralized finance, or DeFi, was functional rather than theoretical (see Figure 1.3).

Figure 1.3 DeFi summer asset performance.

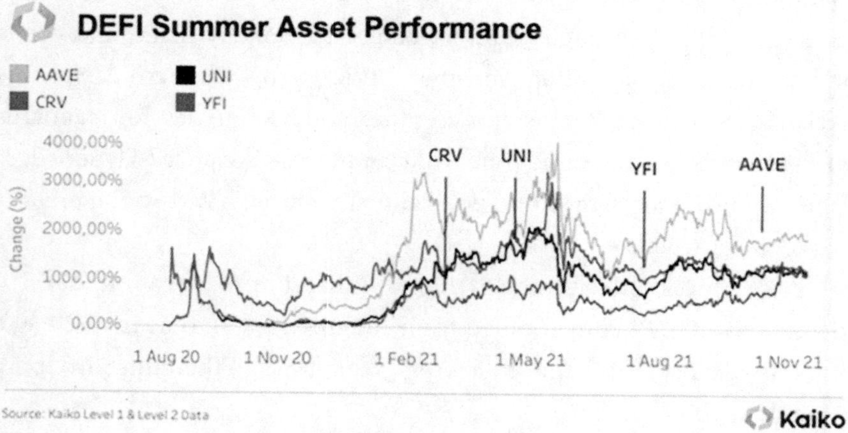

At the same time, NFTs—unique digital tokens recorded on a blockchain that represent ownership of a specific digital item, such as art, collectibles, or in-game assets—brought digital assets into mainstream culture. Platforms like OpenSea, Axie Infinity, and NBA Top Shot introduced digital ownership tied to art, gaming, and entertainment. NFTs demonstrated that blockchains could support creator economies and consumer-facing applications.

New layer-1 blockchains also gained traction. Networks such as Solana, Avalanche, or Polkadot offered faster performance or alternative designs, attracting developers and capital.[15]

Prices reflected the surge in activity and attention. Bitcoin rose from roughly $7,000 in early 2020 to about $69,000 in late 2021. Ethereum climbed from under $150 to over $4,800. Both later declined sharply, ending the cycle.

Early NFTs: Cryptokitties, Cryptopunks, and BAYC

NFTs introduced a new concept to digital assets: unique digital ownership. Unlike cryptocurrencies, where each unit is interchangeable, each NFT represents something distinct.

Before NFTs became a market, they were experiments. What made the earliest projects important was not speculation, but what people were willing to value purely on the blockchain.

CryptoKitties (2017)

The first NFT project to reach mainstream attention. Users bought, bred, and traded unique digital cats, with some selling for over $100,000.[16] CryptoKitties demonstrated that NFTs could attract non-technical users, create demand through digital scarcity, and even congest a blockchain on their own.

CryptoPunks (2017)

A fixed collection of 10,000 NFTs on Ethereum originally given away for free. Over time, CryptoPunks became cultural and historical artifacts. At peak, floor prices exceeded $400,000, with individual sales reaching $10–$23 million. They proved that scarcity and provenance alone could sustain high valuations.

Bored Ape Yacht Club (2021)

BAYC reframed NFTs as identity, access, and brand. Ownership conveyed membership, social signaling, and future benefits. At peak, floor prices exceeded $400,000, and the collection reached multi-billion-dollar valuations. BAYC showed NFTs could function like digital luxury brands or private clubs.

Why These Early Valuations Matter

Early NFT prices were not driven by cash flows or traditional fundamentals. They reflected cultural significance, scarcity, provenance, community, and historical "firsts." Like early art markets or luxury brands, value emerged from social consensus. At the height of the NFT boom in 2021, some digital artworks sold for staggering sums at major auctions. *The Merge* by Pak fetched $91.8 million, while *Everydays: The First 5000 Days* by Beeple sold for $69.3 million.[17]

Many prices later collapsed—but the underlying idea endured. Unique digital ownership can carry real economic value, permanently expanding what digital assets can represent. Today, a smaller number of NFT collections continue to sustain active communities, either through strong social followings and real-world brand extensions, such as toys, licensing, and events, or through a closer association with digital art and creative culture.

Systemic Stress and "Crypto Winter" (2022–2023)

The 2022–2023 period marked the digital asset sector's most severe stress test. Weak governance, excess leverage, poor risk controls, and, in some cases, outright fraud that had built up during the prior cycle were exposed in rapid succession.

One of the most consequential failures was the collapse of Terra, whose algorithmic stablecoin attempted to maintain a one-dollar value without holding sufficient dollar-like reserves. An algorithmic stablecoin is designed to maintain a stable price, typically $1, using software rules and market incentives rather than holding cash or other hard assets as backing. Its stability depends on continued confidence and demand rather than reserves. Terra relied on those incentives and confidence to sustain its peg. When confidence broke, there were no assets to absorb selling pressure, and the system collapsed rapidly and permanently. Losses then spread to centralized lenders such as Celsius Network and BlockFi, which had marketed themselves as low-risk while taking concentrated counterparty exposure and operating with limited liquidity.

The crisis culminated in the collapse of FTX in late 2022 (see Figure 1.4). Unlike earlier failures driven by poor risk management, FTX involved the misuse of customer funds and deliberate misrepresentation. Trust in centralized digital asset intermediaries was severely damaged.

These failures shared a common theme. The risks were not technological. Blockchains continued to operate as designed. The failures were institutional, driven by hidden leverage, opaque balance sheets, and reliance on trust rather than transparency. The result was a push toward clearer regulation, proof of reserves, stronger custody standards, and greater separation between customer assets and proprietary activity.

Figure 1.4 A timeline of the 2022 "Crypto Winter," an intense bear market period for the sector.

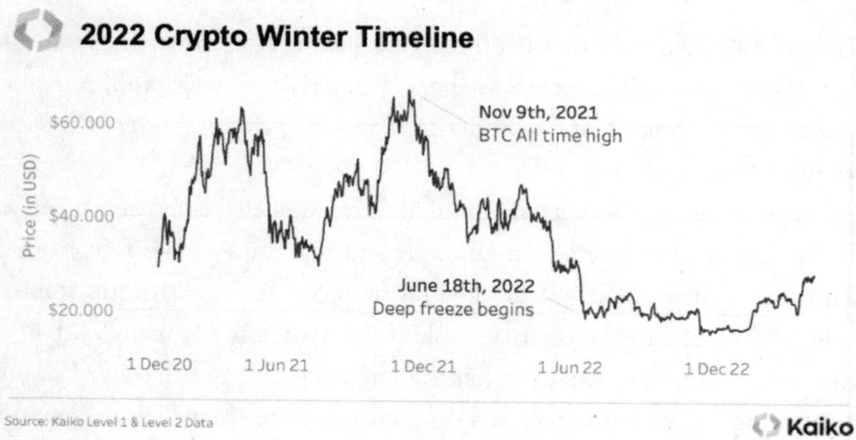

Despite the challenging environment, builders continued to work toward the long-term vision. Major layer-2 networks such as Arbitrum and zkSync launched to improve scalability, while new layer-1 blockchains like Aptos and Sui emerged with a focus on performance. At the same time, activity within established ecosystems continued to grow, including new decentralized finance protocols such as Kamino and Drift in the Solana ecosystem and Etherfi in the Ethereum Virtual Machine (EVM) ecosystem.[18]

Prices reflected the severity of the reset. Bitcoin fell from around $69,000 in late 2021 to near $15,000 in 2022. Ethereum dropped from above $4,800 to near $1,000. Total digital asset market capitalization declined by roughly 75–80%, marking a prolonged market downturn focused on consolidation and rebuilding.

FTX and the Failure of Trust

If one failure shook the foundations of the digital asset sector, it was FTX. During its rapid rise to prominence, driven by aggressive marketing, political donations, and high-profile institutional endorsements, FTX became one of the largest digital asset exchanges in the world and was widely viewed as institutional-grade. In late 2022, it collapsed after it was revealed that customer funds had been secretly transferred to an affiliated trading firm and used for leveraged trading and investments.

When customers attempted to withdraw funds, FTX could not meet the surge in requests. The exchange no longer held enough accessible assets to satisfy withdrawals in full. Customer funds that were expected to be available had been diverted to risky trading activities or locked into illiquid investments. As withdrawal demands continued to rise, FTX halted withdrawals, suspended trading, and disclosed a substantial shortfall between customer liabilities and remaining assets.

The exchange filed for bankruptcy, and its co-founder and CEO, Sam Bankman-Fried, was later convicted of fraud and sentenced to 25 years in prison.

Customer claims have since been managed through a court-supervised bankruptcy estate, with repayments proceeding gradually under legal oversight.

Lesson: Centralized intermediaries require strong governance and transparency. When customer assets are misused, failures are swift and recovery is slow.

Stablecoins, Tokenization, Derivatives, AI, and Institutional Adoption (2024–2026)

The current phase of digital assets is defined by maturation. Market structure has improved, regulation has become clearer in key jurisdictions, and institutional participation has increased.

A major turning point came with the approval and launch of US Bitcoin and Ethereum exchange-traded funds by asset managers such as BlackRock and Fidelity. These products provided regulated access for a broad investor base and integrated digital assets more directly into traditional portfolios. Spot Bitcoin ETFs have since attracted tens of billions of dollars in net inflows, with Ethereum ETFs also seeing meaningful demand (see Figure 1.5).

Figure 1.5 The growth of the largest stablecoins by market capitalization.

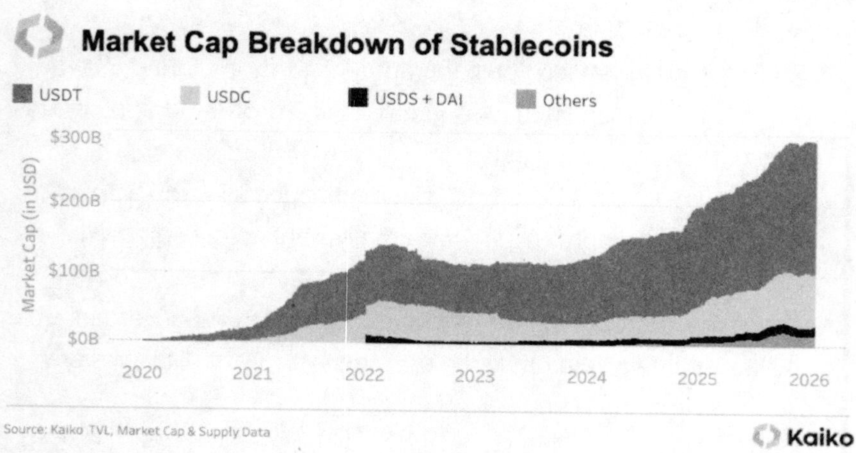

At the same time, stablecoins have expanded beyond trading into payments and settlement. Circle's IPO marked a notable moment in this shift. Circle issues USDC, one of the most widely used stablecoins, and its public listing reflects growing recognition of stablecoins as practical financial infrastructure rather than niche crypto products. Asset tokenization has advanced as institutions test tokenized funds and tokenized stocks and securities. Derivatives markets have deepened, supporting hedging and risk management, while crypto-native innovations such as perpetual futures and prediction markets are also moving into the mainstream through platforms like Hyperliquid and Polymarket. Early applications combining artificial intelligence with blockchain infrastructure have begun to emerge. The introduction of Bitcoin Volatility Futures on CME allows investors to trade and hedge expected volatility directly, much as the VIX transformed volatility into a distinct asset class for equity markets. The development is significant not because it predicts Bitcoin's direction, but because it expands the institutional toolkit available to manage risk independently of price exposure.

Why the BlackRock Bitcoin ETF Mattered

In January 2024, BlackRock's iShares Bitcoin Trust (IBIT) became one of the first US-approved spot Bitcoin ETFs, meaning it holds actual Bitcoin rather than futures contracts. That structure allowed investors to gain direct Bitcoin price exposure through a familiar, regulated ETF, using standard brokerage and retirement accounts.

IBIT's market impact was immediate. It became one of the fastest-accumulating ETFs in history, reaching tens of billions of dollars in assets in record time and approaching $100 billion in assets under management as adoption accelerated alongside Bitcoin's price appreciation.

This performance mattered for more than headline numbers. It signaled that regulated digital asset exposure had moved from niche to mainstream, supported by:

- Large-scale institutional participation
- Growing acceptance of Bitcoin as an investable asset
- Easy integration of digital assets into traditional portfolios

Artificial Intelligence and Blockchain Infrastructure

During this period, artificial intelligence became the market's dominant investment theme. Venture funding, public market capital, and investor attention increasingly flowed toward AI, reducing speculative liquidity across digital assets. Rather than slowing innovation, the shift accelerated the industry's focus on infrastructure, tokenization, stablecoins, and institutional adoption over retail-driven speculation. Artificial intelligence has also begun to intersect with this infrastructure in practical ways, offering potential alternatives to centralized platforms and hyperscalers. At the protocol level, networks such as Bittensor[19] demonstrate how digital tokens can be used to coordinate AI development, run models, and reward contributors in a decentralized system.

Major developments are also enabling decentralized AI agents to operate more independently online. New technical standards and payment protocols are emerging to support this.

Technical standards now define how software agents can establish an on-chain identity, build reputation, transact, and verify counterparties. Payment standards like x402 are designed to allow AI agents to automatically pay small amounts for digital services, such as data, software access, and computing power, using digital dollars, without relying on banks or traditional payment processors.

Regulation, Institutional Participation, and Price Discovery

After years of education, industry engagement, and sustained lobbying met by hostile regulators, a change under the leadership of President Donald Trump enabled the United States to pass major legislation alongside a clear shift in regulatory posture. Agencies such as the Securities and Exchange Commission (SEC), the Commodity Futures Trading Commission (CFTC), and the Office of the Comptroller of the Currency (OCC) moved from restraint and regulation-by-enforcement[20] toward structured engagement, creating a framework that allowed large financial institutions to participate fully in digital assets. This marked a clear turning point in the adoption of digital assets by financial institutions and enterprises.

Recent legislative efforts in the United States are translating clearer regulatory intent into concrete proposals. In 2025, the GENIUS Act established a federal framework for stablecoins, requiring them to be backed with safe assets and subject to oversight. The CLARITY Act aims to define how different types of digital assets and trading venues are regulated, separating the roles of key agencies and creating clearer rules for marketplaces. Parallel market structure discussions in Congress focus on protecting investors and defining infrastructure for trading, custody, and compliance. Taken together, these efforts signal a shift from uncertainty to a more defined regulatory foundation.

Yet an important barrier to institutional adoption remains. Under the Basel banking framework, Bitcoin, Ether, and most other digital assets carry a 1,250% risk weight, requiring banks to hold capital equal to the full value of their exposure. The result is that activities such as holding digital assets on the balance sheet, lending against them, or making markets become far less attractive from a capital perspective. As regulators revisit these rules, the debate is shifting toward a simpler principle: capital requirements should reflect the actual risk of an asset, not the technology used to record ownership. If that happens, regulated banks could play a much larger role in digital asset markets.

The digital asset market also experienced extreme price events during this period that shaped sentiment. On October 10, 2025, a massive liquidation wave wiped out nearly $19 billion in leveraged positions across digital asset markets, triggering a sharp drop in prices and shaking confidence across the ecosystem. The episode is widely seen as a turning point in how risk and liquidity are understood in digital asset markets.

Then on February 5, 2026, BlackRock's iShares Bitcoin ETF (IBIT) experienced extraordinary volatility, with more than $10 billion in shares trading hands in a single day. The fund declined more than 13%, as traders, including large institutional participants, adjusted positions in response to broader market pressures and weakness in Bitcoin's price.

These regulatory shifts and periods of volatility were reflected in broader price trends. After the 2022–2023 downturn, Bitcoin reached new highs above roughly $126,000 in October 2025 before entering a significant drawdown. Ethereum similarly rallied toward multi-year highs near $5,000 before retracing. In early 2026, both assets declined notably: Bitcoin slid below $70,000 and Ethereum fell below $2,000 amid broader risk-off sentiment and reduced ETF inflows. Together, these developments suggest a market increasingly influenced by institutional capital—one that may be deeper and more structured than prior cycles, yet still subject to volatility and macroeconomic repricing.

Memecoins and Retail Market Cycles

While institutions focused on infrastructure, regulation, and access, a parallel part of the market continued to evolve on the retail side. Memecoins, often dismissed as jokes, have followed a consistent pattern tied to investor psychology, platform design, and how easily tokens can be distributed.

The first phase was cultural. Dogecoin, launched in 2013, began as a satire of Bitcoin and developed a tipping culture across online communities. It has no supply limits, no road map, and no pretense of seriousness. Yet it sponsored a NASCAR car and funded the Jamaican bobsled team. The lesson was simple: attention tends to arrive before capital.

The second phase emerged during the 2017–2018 boom. Ethereum made token creation easy, exchanges made it easy to trade them, and retail speculation surged. Meme-style tokens multiplied, many with little substance beyond community enthusiasm. When the cycle turned in 2018, most collapsed alongside the broader market. Memes alone were not enough.

That changed in 2020 and 2021. Decentralized exchanges such as Uniswap enabled tokens to launch without intermediaries, while social platforms amplified narratives at unprecedented speed. Projects like Shiba Inu and SafeMoon showed that rapid distribution, and coordinated communities, could generate real wealth without traditional funding or formal development plans. Memecoins became a vehicle for retail participation rather than a novelty.

By 2022 and 2023, memecoins evolved again. They became less about humor and more about attention itself. Tokens like PEP, BONK, and later dogwifhat offered no promise of utility.

Their value came from speed, low transaction costs, and rapid circulation. On networks like Solana, they even helped revive activity by pulling users and liquidity back on-chain.

The latest iteration adds politics to the mix. Trump-themed coins surged during election headlines, driven less by ideology than by visibility. The pattern was familiar: a recognizable symbol, nonstop social chatter, fast distribution—and a rush of retail money looking for momentum and community.

The takeaway isn't that memes replaced fundamentals. It's that retail behavior keeps adapting. Memecoins have become a kind of market weathervane—showing where attention is flowing, how fast capital can move, and how retail investors express risk appetite when traditional narratives stop resonating.

THE BIGGER PICTURE: DIGITAL ASSETS AS AN EMERGING ASSET CLASS

"Crypto has delivered the best risk-adjusted returns of any asset class over the past decade—yet institutional capital has barely arrived. That's about to change. As the infrastructure matures—regulated custody, institutional-grade derivatives, clearer regulatory frameworks—the question for endowments, pensions, and sovereign wealth funds is no longer whether to allocate, but how. They need what they've always needed: disciplined risk management, documented processes, and compoundable returns over a series of years. The opportunity for managers who can deliver institutional-quality exposure to this asset class is generational."

—Sam Gaer, CIO of Directional Strategy at Monarq Asset Management; former CIO of NYMEX and FINRA

Today, digital assets are a legitimate investment opportunity that are following a path seen in other transformative financial innovations.

What began as a fringe movement led by cryptographers and enthusiasts has caught the attention of institutional investors, Fortune 500 companies, and even governments. Major players, such as JPMorgan, Visa, BlackRock, and Fidelity are actively betting on crypto's future. This trajectory mirrors the mainstream adoption of financial innovations like derivatives, hedge funds, and Gold ETFs, and provides insight into how digital assets are evolving as part of this broader financial movement.

Drawing Parallels: Gold ETFs and Bitcoin ETFs

The rise of Gold ETFs in the early 2000s provides a clear precedent for how a niche asset can evolve into a mainstream investment product. Before the launch of Standard & Poor's SPDR Gold Shares (GLD) in 2004, gold was primarily held by central banks, institutions, and private investors who were willing to manage physical bullion. GLD revolutionized gold investment by offering a convenient, liquid, and regulated way for everyday investors to gain exposure to the commodity without dealing with storage or security.

The introduction of Gold ETFs played a pivotal role in legitimizing gold as an asset class for portfolios, driving its institutional adoption and price stability over time. Similarly, Bitcoin ETFs were hailed as one of the most successful ETF launches in history, drawing $36 billion in net inflows in their first year—and they are now poised to play a transformative role in the Digital Asset sector's trajectory. With products like the iShares Bitcoin Trust ETF (IBIT) ProShares Bitcoin Strategy ETF (BITO) in the United States and similar ETFs in Canada and Europe, Bitcoin is becoming increasingly accessible to traditional investors.

It is important to understand the distinction between "spot" and futures-based products. "Spot" refers to the price of an asset today and to direct ownership of the underlying asset itself. A spot Bitcoin ETF holds actual Bitcoin in custody, rather than derivatives contracts that speculate on its future price. The approval of spot Bitcoin ETFs, as pursued by BlackRock, would further cement its position as a mainstream asset, just as GLD did for gold (see Figure 1.6).

Building on this momentum, the approval of spot Ethereum ETFs represents the next critical step in the maturation of digital assets. Backed by leading issuers such as BlackRock, Fidelity Investments, and Grayscale Investments, these products extend the ETF playbook beyond Bitcoin, validating Ethereum's role as core digital infrastructure rather than a niche asset. The approval of staking-enabled Ethereum ETFs could further differentiate the asset class by pairing price exposure with native yield—a development with no real analogue in traditional commodities. This is likely only the beginning: the SEC has also approved exchange-traded funds tied to assets such as Solana and XRP, signaling that a broader range of digital assets may increasingly access regulated investment wrappers over time.

Figure 1.6 US spot Bitcoin ETFs' assets under management.

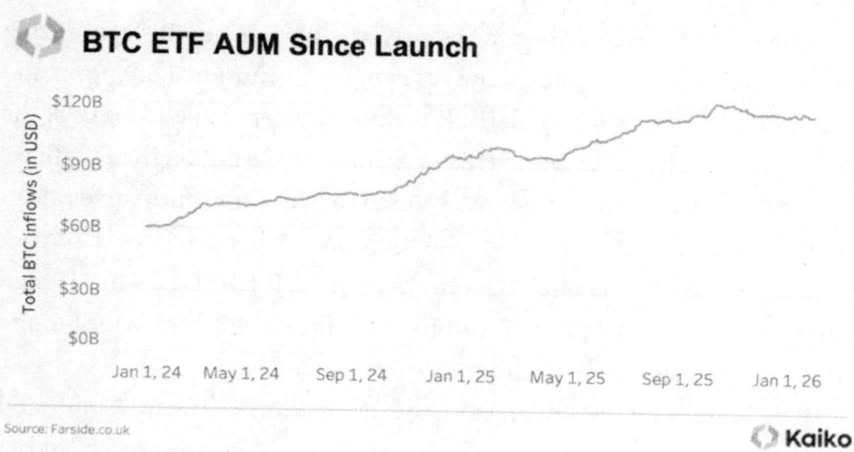

Derivatives and Hedge Funds: A Road Map for Institutionalization

The development of derivatives and hedge funds provides another important parallel. In the 1980s, derivatives were considered complex and speculative tools used primarily by financial insiders. Over time, however, regulatory frameworks and standardized products like futures contracts and options brought transparency and accessibility to the market.

Similarly, hedge funds were once viewed as secretive, high-risk investment vehicles for the ultra-wealthy. Over the decades, they became integral to institutional portfolios as they matured and demonstrated their ability to generate alpha and hedge risk.

Digital assets are following a similar path. Once regarded as speculative and opaque, their integration into traditional finance began in 2017, when the CFTC approved Bitcoin futures trading on the CME. The central question for regulators was not enthusiasm for Bitcoin, but whether markets linked to it were sufficiently mature and resilient to operate within the US regulated derivatives system.

Regulators focused on three concerns. First was market integrity. Most Bitcoin trading occurred on unregulated, offshore spot exchanges, yet futures prices would inevitably reference those markets. There were concerns that manipulation, thin liquidity, or operational failures in spot markets could distort futures pricing. Second was risk management. Bitcoin's volatility far exceeded that of traditional commodities, requiring higher margins and robust clearing controls to ensure large price moves would not threaten clearinghouses or the broader financial system. Third was investor protection and systemic risk. Futures opened the door for hedge funds, asset managers, and eventually pension-linked capital, making it essential that losses be contained within margin and clearing mechanisms.

Under CFTC Chairman Chris Giancarlo, the solution was to rely on the existing futures framework. CME and Cboe self-certified their contracts, implemented elevated margin requirements, enhanced surveillance, and coordinated with major spot exchanges. The CFTC did not endorse Bitcoin itself, but allowed regulated futures as a way to bring risk into a transparent, supervised market rather than leaving it entirely offshore. This marked a turning point in the institutionalization of digital assets, providing familiar tools for exposure, hedging, and price discovery.

Institutional Adoption: A Catalyst for Growth

Just as ETFs and derivatives brought credibility and scale to gold and hedge funds, institutional interest is driving digital assets toward mainstream adoption. BlackRock's push for a Bitcoin spot ETF and Fidelity's digital assets products are just the beginning. Increasingly, Bitcoin is being recognized not only as an investment asset but also as a strategic reserve. For example:

- Corporate Treasuries: Companies like Tesla and Strategy (formerly MicroStrategy) have added Bitcoin to their balance sheets.
- Federal and State Reserves: Governments and states are exploring Bitcoin reserves as a hedge against inflation and currency instability, mirroring historical practices of holding gold reserves. US states like Texas and Wyoming[21] have led the way, with proposals for Bitcoin reserves gaining traction in policy discussions.
- Pension Funds: Some large public pension funds, including those in California[22] and Wisconsin,[23] have gained exposure to Bitcoin, typically through indirect investments such as private funds, ETFs, or publicly traded companies tied to the digital asset ecosystem. These positions reflect a cautious approach to diversification and long-term optionality rather than a broad reallocation of capital.

- Banks and Payment Providers: Visa, Mastercard, and PayPal have incorporated digital assets into their payment networks, while Fidelity is launching its own stablecoin,[24] reducing the gap between traditional finance and blockchain.[25]
- Tokenized Assets: Financial institutions are moving real-world assets onto blockchains. Apollo, Goldman Sachs, and JPMorgan have issued and settled tokenized bonds and funds, while platforms such as Robinhood, Coinbase, and Kraken expanded access to tokenized securities for retail investors.

By including Bitcoin as a reserve asset, federal and state entities, as well as pension funds, signal growing confidence in its role as a hedge and store of value. This shift not only legitimizes Bitcoin further but also highlights its emerging importance in global economic planning.

Just as Gold ETFs opened the door for gold's rise as an investment, the success of ETFs and tokenized assets could redefine the boundaries of finance in the decades to come.

"Blockchain, Not Crypto": A False Distinction

In the early days, many institutions claimed to support *blockchain technology* while rejecting *Bitcoin* and *digital assets* more broadly. Blockchain was seen as serious and enterprise-ready, digital assets as speculative and risky.

This distinction misses a critical point: public blockchains exist because of tokens, not despite them.

Bitcoin and Ethereum were not built by corporations or consortia. They were launched into open markets and sustained by token economics. These are the rules that incentivize participation, secure the network, fund development, and align strangers around a shared system. Tokens provided the coordination and security budget that made public blockchains possible.

What's often dismissed as early "speculation" was, in fact, the growth engine. Speculation attracted capital, developers, and real-world stress-testing that made public blockchains stronger long before enterprises arrived.

You cannot separate public blockchain technology from token incentives without misunderstanding how it evolved. Tokens were not a flaw—they were the price of decentralization, and the reason blockchain infrastructure is robust enough to matter today.

DIGITAL ASSETS ARE HERE TO STAY

"Crypto is real, if you mean blockchains, stablecoins. . . I mean you can move stuff. Smart contracts are real. All that stuff is real. It will be used by all of us to facilitate better transactions and customer service."

—Jamie Dimon, CEO of JPMorgan[26]

Today, digital assets have achieved recognition as a legitimate asset. Unlike the early days, when their value hinged solely on speculative trading, digital assets now plays a crucial role in:

- Institutional Portfolios: Hedge funds, pension funds, and asset managers invest in digital assets. Traditional asset managers like Fidelity and BlackRock offer digital asset investment products. Institutional interest legitimizes Digital Assets and stabilizes markets by introducing larger, long-term investors.

- Cross-Border Transactions: Stablecoins are increasingly used for global remittances, reducing fees and processing times compared to traditional banking.
- Financial Innovation: DeFi protocols offer services like lending, borrowing, and yield farming, challenging the traditional financial system by providing faster, permissionless alternatives.
- Tokenized Assets: From money market funds to stocks, blockchain is enabling the tokenization of financial instruments creating more efficient ways to trade assets.
- Macroeconomic Hedge: In times of economic uncertainty, digital assets, particularly Bitcoin, has been perceived as a hedge against inflation and currency devaluation.

INVESTOR TAKEAWAY

Digital assets have evolved from a niche experiment into an emerging asset class embraced by institutional investors, public companies, and governments. That transition has produced some of the strongest investment returns of the past decade—but also suggests the story is still being written.

For investors, the lessons are practical:

- Stay curious. Many of the biggest opportunities were easy to dismiss early on.
- Focus on vision. Strong long-term investments were tied to clear, transformative ideas.
- Accept risk. Volatility and uncertainty were the price of early participation.
- Think long-term. Staying invested through full market cycles mattered more than perfect timing.

Investing in digital assets does not require a technical background or large amounts of capital. It does require effort, discipline, and a long-term perspective. The goal is not to chase trends but to understand what you own and why you own it.

Returns alone do not explain why digital assets matter. Their significance lies in how they challenge long-standing assumptions about money, ownership, and financial infrastructure. They raise fundamental questions about how value moves, how trust is established, and how markets settle in a digital world. To evaluate this opportunity properly, investors need to understand the technology underneath the assets. The next chapter focuses on how public blockchains work, the real-world use cases that have already gained traction, and how traditional financial institutions are integrating this infrastructure into existing systems.

CHAPTER TWO

DIGITAL ASSET TECHNOLOGY AND USE CASES

HOW DIGITAL ASSETS WORK

"Disruptive technologies bring to market a very different value proposition than had been available previously. Products based on disruptive technologies are typically cheaper, simpler, smaller, and more convenient to use."

—Clayton Christensen, Professor at Harvard Business School and author of The Innovators Dilemma

History shows that when a better technology meets clear user demand, it eventually replaces older systems. Uber reshaped transportation by making rides cheaper, faster, and easier, even in the face of early resistance. DoorDash did the same for food delivery by meeting consumers where they already were, on their phones, with speed and choice.

In the early years, blockchain technology and smart contract platforms were often dismissed as solutions in search of problems. Critics questioned whether decentralized systems offered any real advantage over existing financial infrastructure. Economist Nouriel Roubini famously called blockchain "the most over-hyped technology ever," arguing it was no better than a spreadsheet.

At the time, that skepticism was understandable. Adoption was limited, use cases were narrow, and much of the activity appeared speculative rather than practical.

That view has changed. Blockchain systems are now being used in real financial activity, including payments, settlement, and tokenized assets. What was once theoretical is moving into production. This shift marks the early stages of a longer transformation in how financial infrastructure is built and used.

What makes digital assets different is not just potential returns, but access. For the first time, core financial infrastructure is available to anyone with an internet connection. There are no account minimums, no geographic barriers, and no intermediaries required to approve participation. An individual in Nairobi, Buenos Aires, or New York can hold assets, move value globally, and interact with financial applications on the same open networks. Ownership is direct, transactions settle without banks, and participation is not limited by income, credit history, or institutional relationships.

By the end of this chapter, you will gain a clear understanding of:

- How public blockchains work and the core differences between public and private blockchains

- The most widely adopted real-world use cases, including stablecoins, tokenized assets, and blockchain-based clearing and settlement
- How traditional financial institutions are integrating blockchain infrastructure into payments, markets, and operations

WHAT IS THE KEY INNOVATION?

"Bitcoin invented digital private property"
—Pascal Gauthier, CEO of Ledger

Before Bitcoin, digital things could not truly be owned.

A digital file could be copied endlessly. If you "owned" something online, that ownership depended on someone else keeping records and enforcing rules. A bank tracked your balance. PayPal tracked your account. Apple decided whether you still had access to what you purchased.

In every case, you did not hold the asset itself. You held permission.

Those systems worked, but they relied on platforms, administrators, and legal enforcement. Access could be changed, reversed, or revoked. You had access rights, not property rights.

Bitcoin changed that.

Bitcoin introduced a way for digital ownership to exist without relying on a central institution. It did this by making ownership public, verifiable, and difficult to alter. Instead of trusting a company or a database, ownership was recorded on a network maintained by thousands of independent participants.

This is what "digital scarcity" actually means.

Not that something cannot be copied as data, but that ownership of the original can be clearly identified and transferred. Only one party can control a given unit at a time, and the network agrees on who that is. When ownership changes, it changes everywhere at once.

That breakthrough laid the foundation for everything that followed.

At a deeper level, Bitcoin introduced a new kind of ledger—a shared ledger. Capital markets already run on ledgers. Banks, brokers, custodians, and clearinghouses all keep records of who owns what. The problem is that they each keep their own version, as it was not technically feasible to have a universal ledger before blockchain technology.

Because ownership is recorded in many places at once, those records must be constantly reconciled. Trades take time to settle. Errors occur. Disputes require manual intervention. Each layer adds cost, delay, and risk.

Modern finance is not built on one ledger. It is built on many.

Blockchain technology changes that structure. Instead of separate records that need constant coordination, a blockchain provides a single shared ledger that all participants can reference. Ownership is updated once, directly on that ledger, and everyone sees the same result.

There is no need to reconcile competing versions of the truth. Finality comes from shared agreement, not from intermediaries comparing notes after the fact.

That shift—from fragmented records to a shared source of ownership—is the core innovation behind digital assets.

Over time, this concept expanded beyond digital money. Blockchain networks became programmable, enabling software to manage assets, execute transactions, and enforce rules automatically. This led to the emergence of stablecoins for payments and settlement, smart contracts for financial applications, and tokenized representations of real-world assets such as stocks, bonds, and funds. Together, these systems form a new financial layer where ownership, transfer, and settlement are handled by code, not intermediaries, reshaping how value moves through the global economy.

UNDERSTANDING HOW DIGITAL ASSETS WORK

After more than a decade of development, it helps to step back and understand the systems that make digital assets function. At its core, cryptocurrency is not a new type of money. It is a new way of recording ownership and transferring value.

Blockchain technology allows people to send value directly to one another without relying on a bank, payment processor, or centralized platform to approve or execute the transaction. Instead of a single company maintaining records, blockchains rely on a distributed network of computers, known as nodes, that independently verify transactions and maintain a shared ledger.

This structure solves a fundamental problem in digital finance known as double spending. Digital files can be copied endlessly. Money cannot. Capital markets rely on ledgers that must be constantly updated and reconciled by intermediaries to prevent the same asset from being spent twice. Blockchains address this by requiring each transaction to be verified, recorded, and agreed upon by the network before it becomes final.

Once a transaction is confirmed and added to the blockchain, ownership is updated across the entire network. At any given moment, there is only one recognized owner of an asset. Reversing or altering that record is extremely difficult, which gives digital assets properties similar to physical cash or bearer instruments.

Because verification and settlement are built directly into the network, there is no need for a central authority to confirm ownership or process transactions. The system enforces its rules through cryptography and code rather than through trust in an intermediary.

Core Characteristics of Public Blockchains

To understand digital assets, it helps to focus on what public blockchains actually do. At their core, they are shared systems for recording ownership and transferring value.

Characteristic	What It Means
Open source	The software is publicly available. No single company owns or controls it. Anyone can review the code, use it, or build on top of it, allowing the system to improve without relying on a central authority.
Permissionless access	Anyone with an internet connection can use the network. There are no account minimums, approvals, or intermediaries required to send transactions or interact with applications.
Transparency	All transactions are recorded on a public ledger that anyone can view and verify. Users are identified by wallet addresses rather than names, making activity visible without revealing personal identities.
Censorship Resistance	No single authority can block transactions or shut down the network. As long as the network is running, transactions can be submitted and processed.
Immutability	Once transactions are confirmed, they cannot be changed or reversed. Altering past records would require controlling most of the network, making manipulation impractical.
Consensus-driven security	The network stays secure because participants must agree on which transactions are valid using predefined rules rather than trusting a central operator. In Proof of Work systems, participants contribute computing power to secure the network. In Proof of Stake systems, participants lock up their own assets as collateral.
Proof of Work (PoW)	Used by Bitcoin. Participants contribute computing power to validate transactions and secure the network. It is energy-intensive but has proven highly secure.
Proof of Stake (PoS)	Used by networks such as Ethereum and Solana. Participants lock up tokens to help validate transactions

Characteristic	What It Means
Smart contracts	Programs that run on blockchains and execute automatically when conditions are met. They enable applications like payments, lending, marketplaces, and other financial services without intermediaries.
Decentralized security	Thousands of independent computers maintain and verify the network. No single participant controls the system, reducing failures and limiting manipulation.
Wallet-based access	Users interact through digital wallets, not traditional accounts. Wallets hold cryptographic keys that prove ownership and authorize transactions. Control of the keys means control of the assets.

Adoption by Financial Services

> *"The core problem blockchains solve is trust. In the traditional world, establishing trust is expensive and often prohibitive; blockchains reduce the marginal cost of trust to nearly zero."*
>
> —Ruud Smets, Managing Partner,
> Theta Capital Management

Financial institutions recognized early that blockchain was not simply a new asset class, but a new way to move money, record ownership, and settle transactions. As early as 2017, major firms including JPMorgan, BNY Mellon, Microsoft, Accenture, and ConsenSys created the Enterprise Ethereum Alliance to explore these possibilities.[1] *Full disclosure*: I still serve on the Alliance's board today, and its work continues to focus on fostering dialog that bridges digital-asset–native protocols with the needs of the enterprise world.

But in those early days, public blockchains were still nascent technology. The technology was untested at scale, and the regulatory landscape was unchartered territory. To experiment safely, banks and corporations turned to private or "permissioned" blockchains—closed networks where only approved participants could join. These networks offered a controlled environment for exploring the technology without running afoul of compliance rules, unlike public blockchains such as Ethereum, where anyone in the world can participate without traditional onboarding.

Fast forward to today, and the picture looks entirely different. Public blockchains have matured into reliable, globally accessible infrastructure capable of supporting billions of dollars in transactions daily. Regulatory clarity followed.[2]

Taken together, these developments removed the largest barrier to adoption: uncertainty. With clear rules in place, banks, asset managers, insurers, and pension funds gained the confidence to move from experimentation to deployment.

One clear example of this deeper integration came in March 2026 when Kraken became the first digital asset company to gain access to the Federal Reserve's core payments system through a Federal Reserve master account.[3] This account allows financial institutions to settle US dollar transactions directly through the same payment rails used by banks. By connecting directly to this infrastructure, digital asset companies can reduce reliance on intermediary banks and move funds more efficiently between cryptocurrency markets and the traditional financial system.

Developments like this are significant because digital asset markets initially operated largely outside the traditional banking system. Direct connections to core financial infrastructure signal that the gap between the two worlds is beginning to narrow.

Difference Between Public and Private Blockchains

Public and private blockchains use similar technology, but they are designed for very different purposes. The key difference is who is allowed to participate and where trust resides.

Public blockchains are open networks. Anyone can run software, send transactions, or build applications without permission. Networks such as Bitcoin, Ethereum, Solana, and Avalanche are secured by thousands of independent participants who collectively verify transactions and agree on the state of the ledger.

Private blockchains are restricted systems. Only approved participants can run nodes, validate transactions, or access the ledger. They are typically operated by a single organization or a consortium of known entities. Common examples include Hyperledger Fabric, R3 Corda, and bank-led systems such as JPM Coin. Because participants are known and trusted, private blockchains can be faster and easier to control, but they sacrifice openness and decentralization. In practice, many function more like shared databases.

The distinction ultimately comes down to trust. Public blockchains minimize trust in institutions by relying on open participation and cryptography, making them suitable for global, permissionless applications. Private blockchains assume trust in the operator and are better suited for internal processes where control, privacy, and compliance matter more than openness.

CORE BLOCKCHAIN USE CASES TAKING SHAPE

> *"Blockchain does three things incredibly well: it automates data reconciliation, executes business logic, and enables straight-through settlement—fundamentally reducing frictions and costs in asset management."*
>
> —Jenny Johnson, CEO of Franklin Templeton[4]

As blockchain infrastructure matured, a small number of use cases moved from experimentation to real-world adoption. These applications share a common theme: they replace slow, fragmented financial processes with software that settles instantly, runs continuously, and operates on a shared ledger.

The most important of these today are payments via stablecoins, tokenization of financial assets, and blockchain-based clearing and settlement. Together, they form the foundation of how digital assets are being integrated into the global financial system.

Payments and Stablecoins

> *"I see stablecoins as just the next evolution of payments. . . a great opportunity. . ."*
>
> —Alex Chriss, Former CEO of PayPal[5]

Stablecoins are digital tokens designed to track the value of a national currency, most commonly the US dollar. They combine the price stability of traditional money with the speed and programmability of blockchains.

In traditional cross-border payments, funds move through multiple correspondent banks, reconciliation layers, and time-zone delays. Settlement often takes days. Stablecoins move value globally in minutes, at any time of day, with fees that are often a fraction of legacy systems.

Stablecoins emerged early as a practical solution to a specific problem: how to move dollars on blockchains when banks were unwilling or unable to participate. Tether's USDT, launched in 2014, introduced dollar liquidity to digital asset markets and evolved into a global payment rail. Circle's USDC emphasized transparency and regulatory alignment, while MakerDAO's DAI demonstrated that decentralized, crypto-backed "digital dollars" could scale without a central issuer.

Over the past decade, stablecoin issuers have repeatedly run into the same obstacle: access to the traditional banking system. Both USDT and USDC faced difficulties securing and maintaining bank relationships, while regulators questioned how digital dollars should be treated under existing financial rules. As this book is being written, lawmakers are debating the Digital Asset Market Clarity (CLARITY) Act, which would establish a clearer regulatory framework for digital assets by defining agency responsibilities and market rules. At the same time, banks are lobbying Congress to limit whether stablecoin issuers can pay interest, arguing that they should not compete directly with traditional deposits. The debate reflects a broader tension between protecting incumbent banking models and allowing new forms of digital money to compete.

This resistance is not new. Early online payments raised similar concerns around fraud, trust, and oversight. Banks were slow to support non-bank payment companies, and many doubted digital payments could work at scale. Over time, those doubts faded. PayPal became a standard checkout option. Stripe became a payments platform used by millions of businesses worldwide. What once felt risky became routine.

What Is the Difference Between Stablecoins and Tokenized Deposits?

Stablecoins and tokenized deposits are often discussed together because both move money on blockchains. In practice, they serve different roles and operate in different parts of the financial system.

Stablecoins are digital assets designed to maintain a stable value, typically pegged to the US dollar. Assets such as USD Coin (USDC), Tether (USDT), and DAI can be held by anyone with a digital wallet and transferred globally, often in real time. They circulate outside the traditional banking system and are backed either by reserves such as cash and government securities or by on-chain collateral. For users, they function as internet-native dollars: fast, programmable, and accessible without a bank account.

Tokenized deposits, by contrast, are traditional bank deposits represented as tokens on a blockchain. The funds remain inside the regulated banking system, and access is limited to approved participants. A common example is JPM Coin, issued by JPMorgan Chase, which is used to settle transactions between institutional clients. Other institutions exploring or piloting tokenized deposits include Citigroup, HSBC, and UBS. Existing rules around compliance, identity, and settlement continue to apply.

In practice, the two are likely to coexist: one extends money onto open networks, while the other modernizes how traditional money moves behind the scenes.

Stablecoins appear to be following the same path: challenged early, shaped by regulation, and gradually integrated as their usefulness becomes harder to ignore.

In just five years, stablecoins in circulation expanded from under $5 billion to more than $300 billion, with annual settlement volumes measured in the trillions. Forecasts suggest stablecoins could reach trillions of dollars in circulation by the end of the decade.[6]

Large institutions are already using stablecoins. JPMorgan settles cross-border transactions on blockchain networks using digital dollars, reducing settlement times from days to seconds. Payment networks such as Visa and legacy remittance providers like Western Union are testing stablecoin-based settlement to reduce costs and improve speed (see Figure 2.1).

Today, stablecoins are the gateway drug to digital assets for large institutions.

Figure 2.1 Citigroup report on stablecoins 2030—September 2025.
Source: Citigroup.

Investor confidence has followed adoption. Circle's IPO in 2025 marked a turning point, signaling that stablecoin issuers are increasingly viewed as payments infrastructure rather than speculative technology. Supported by clearer US regulation under the GENIUS Act, stablecoins are quietly becoming a foundational layer of global finance.

Tokenization of Assets and Securities

"We are at the beginning of the tokenization of all assets, from real estate to equities to bonds, across the board."

—Larry Fink, CEO of BlackRock[7]

Tokenization is a new way of recording ownership of assets.

Instead of tracking who owns an asset in bank ledgers, tokenization represents that ownership as a digital token on a blockchain. Each token corresponds to a real financial asset, such as a Treasury bill, an equity fund, a credit strategy, or a commodity, and carries the same economic rights as traditional ownership.

The chart below shows one possible path for how much real-world value could move onto blockchains as assets like stocks, bonds, and funds are tokenized (see Figure 2.2).

What changes is not the asset itself, but how it moves.

Once an asset is tokenized, it can be transferred, settled, and tracked using blockchain technology. Transactions that once took days can settle in minutes. Markets can operate continuously rather than during fixed trading hours. Ownership records are updated automatically, reducing the need for intermediaries and manual reconciliation.

Regulatory clarity around tokenized securities is also beginning to emerge. In March 2026, the Federal Reserve, Federal Deposit Insurance Corporation, and Office of the Comptroller of the Currency jointly clarified

Figure 2.2 The market for tokenized assets could top $16 trillion by 2030.

Source: BCG.

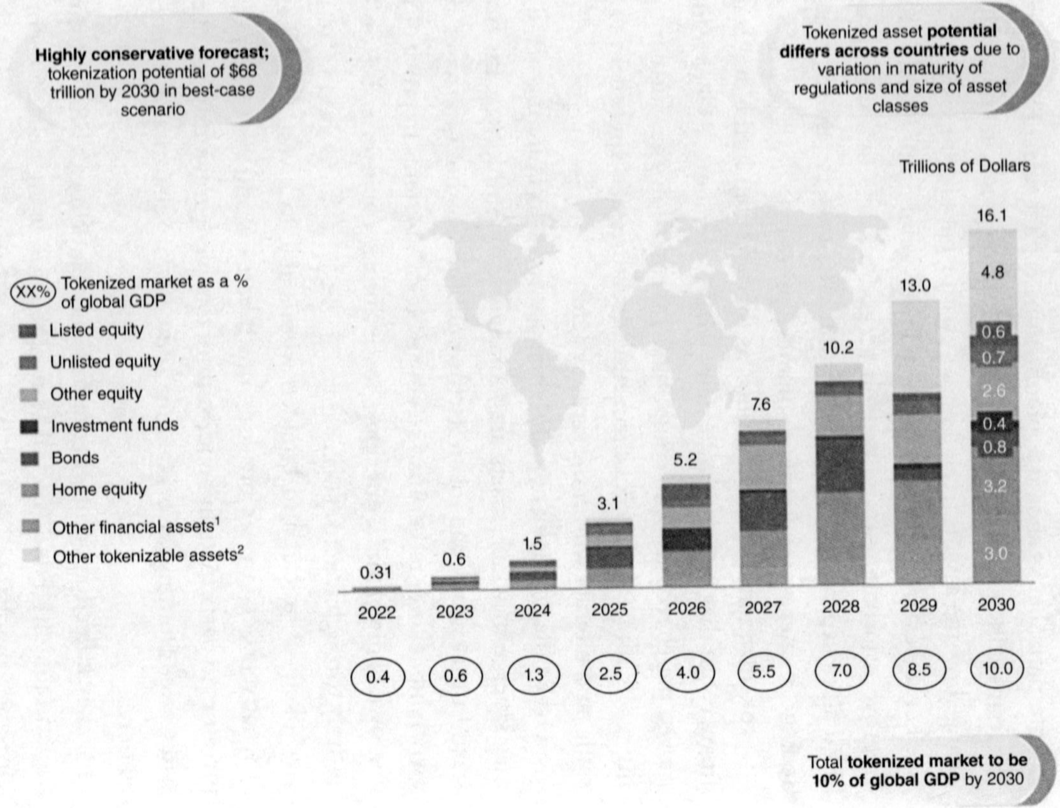

that tokenized securities should generally receive the same capital treatment as traditional assets.[8] If a Treasury bond, stock, or fund share is represented on a blockchain but conferred the same legal rights as their traditional counterparts, banks should apply the same capital rules. The agencies said the framework is "technology neutral," meaning blockchain usage does not change how the asset is treated under existing banking regulations.

For investors, tokenization can lower minimum investment sizes, improve transparency, and expand access to assets that were previously difficult or expensive to own. For institutions, it offers a more efficient way to issue, manage, and distribute financial products.

Tokenization is often described as the next step in the digitization of finance, but that framing understates what is changing. Earlier transitions moved paper records onto computers. Tokenization goes further by placing assets directly on blockchain infrastructure, allowing them to move, settle, and interact within the same system.

Over time, as regulation and financial infrastructure mature, a future may emerge in which assets are issued directly on blockchains from the start. In that world, the token itself would serve as both the asset and the ownership record, rather than relying on legacy systems to prove or reconcile ownership. Public offerings, for example, could one day be issued entirely through tokens.

Tokenization can also broaden who is able to invest. "By tokenizing alternative assets, we are breaking down barriers and allowing individual investors to participate in opportunities that were previously out of reach," said Carlos Domingo, Co-Founder and CEO of Securitize, a tokenization platform.[9]

A key inflection point was the launch of BlackRock's USD Institutional Digital Liquidity Fund (BUIDL) on Ethereum, using Securitize for issuance and compliance. BUIDL demonstrated that US Treasury exposure could be held, transferred, and settled on-chain within existing regulatory frameworks. "On-chain" means that actions such as sending assets, transferring ownership, or executing a transaction are recorded and settled directly on a blockchain. BUIDL's early adoption by firms such as Brevan Howard, Hamilton Lane, and Coinbase signaled institutional comfort with tokenized fund structures.

That success helped accelerate a broader market for tokenized Treasuries and funds. Ondo Finance expanded access to short-duration Treasury exposure through products like OUSG, while Apollo began tokenizing portions of private credit strategies for institutional clients.

At the same time, traditional firms stepped in. Franklin Templeton launched its BENJI tokenized money market fund, and JPMorgan introduced a tokenized money market product on Ethereum.[10] Together, these efforts showed that blockchain settlement was no longer limited to crypto-native assets but was being applied to familiar, regulated investment products.

As Figure 2.3 illustrates, assets held in tokenized US Treasury products have grown rapidly, with multiple issuers attracting billions of dollars as

Figure 2.3 Assets under management for tokenized US Treasuries.

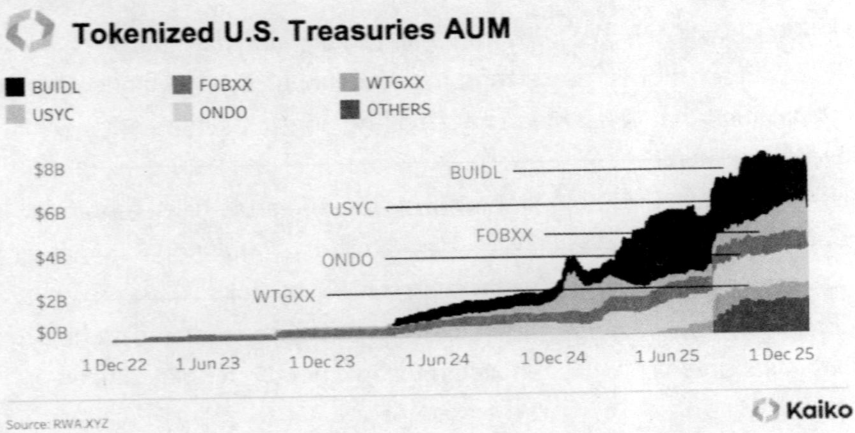

investors increasingly use blockchain-based funds to gain exposure to government securities.

Rather than displacing traditional finance, tokenized funds are quietly reshaping its mechanics. The underlying assets and investment strategies remain largely unchanged. What is evolving is the infrastructure: how ownership is recorded, how settlement is executed, and how capital flows across markets.

What began with Treasuries and money-market funds is now extending into private markets. Leading alternative asset managers, including Hamilton Lane, KKR, and Apollo, are actively tokenizing private-market strategies, with Apollo among those advancing tokenized credit fund initiatives.

At the same time, private credit, such as direct lending strategies and CLOs, is proving especially well-suited to tokenization. These investments have traditionally been complex, hard to trade, and accessible only to large investors. Tokenization offers a way to widen distribution, streamline settlement, and open access to a broader set of participants, without changing the fundamental economics of the assets themselves.

BlackRock's BUIDL Fund

The BlackRock USD Institutional Digital Liquidity Fund is a tokenized money market fund. It is a traditional cash-management product that uses blockchain technology for settlement and record keeping.

Launched in 2024, BUIDL invests in US Treasury bills, cash, and short-term government securities, similar to a traditional money market fund. Ownership is represented by tokens issued on Ethereum, allowing institutional investors to move cash-like assets on-chain while remaining fully within the regulated financial system.

BUIDL is not a stablecoin. Investors hold shares in a regulated BlackRock fund, not digital dollars. Its use cases include managing cash directly on blockchain networks, settling transactions almost instantly between approved institutions, posting collateral for tokenized securities, and running treasury operations continuously rather than only during banking hours.

BUIDL's significance lies less in yield and more in infrastructure. It demonstrates that tokenization can support real institutional capital on public blockchains. By late 2025, the fund exceeded $2.5 billion in assets, making it the largest tokenized money market fund issued on public blockchain networks.

Tokenized Equities

"I think tokenization is like a freight train. It can't be stopped, and eventually it's going to eat the entire financial system."

—Vlad Tenev, CEO of Robinhood Markets[11]

Equities are also beginning to move on-chain. Tokenized stocks represent digital claims on traditional shares, including fractional ownership, while trading on blockchain rails.

Platforms such as Backed Finance issue tokenized representations of major public companies like Apple and Tesla, allowing qualified investors to trade these assets across networks such as Ethereum, Solana, and Avalanche. Securitize provides regulated infrastructure for tokenized equities, funds, and private placements used by asset managers and institutions.

How Securitize Tokenizes Stocks

Securitize tokenizes stocks by representing traditional, regulated securities as digital tokens on a blockchain. As of late 2025, Securitize had tokenized more than $4 billion in real-world assets, working with institutional clients including BlackRock, Apollo, Hamilton Lane, KKR, and VanEck.

The underlying share remains a real security, issued and held under existing securities laws. Securitize creates a corresponding blockchain token that represents a legal ownership claim on that security, typically recorded on Ethereum or another public blockchain.

Compliance is built into the token itself. Only approved investors can hold or transfer it, and standard identity, eligibility, and regulatory requirements still apply. Tokens can be held in digital wallets and transferred between eligible parties, with settlement occurring faster than in traditional markets.

Key point: Securitize modernizes how securities are issued, held, and settled. It does not create synthetic assets or bypass regulation.

Tokenized equities are also reaching retail investors, with Robinhood playing a leading role. In Europe, Robinhood has launched tokenized equity products that give users exposure to US stocks with fractional ownership, extended trading hours, and faster settlement. The framing is deliberate: tokenization as an upgrade to market plumbing, not a speculative add-on.

That same logic is now showing up at the institutional level. The New York Stock Exchange is developing a digital trading venue designed to support tokenized assets, a sign that blockchain-based settlement is no longer viewed as experimental.[12] Citigroup also launched a blockchain-based platform that allows institutional clients to trade tokenized shares of private companies, while working with some of the world's largest private firms to expand participation. The initiative extends tokenization beyond funds and into traditionally illiquid private markets. When incumbents start rethinking how shares are issued, traded, and settled, the shift is less about disruption and more about modernization.

Not all tokenized equities are the same. Some products provide full economic and shareholder rights, while others only track the price of a stock without granting voting rights or dividends. Many of these offerings are currently available in Europe and other jurisdictions, with more limited access in the United States (see Figure 2.4).

Early providers include Kraken, through its xStocks initiative, which allows customers to trade blockchain-based representations of public

Figure 2.4 This chart compares different ways investors can hold assets using tokenized securities. On the left, investors directly own the asset in their own name, with full rights and strong legal protection. As you move to the right, ownership becomes more indirect—investors hold claims or contracts instead of the asset itself, which can be easier to trade but carries more risk if something goes wrong.

Source: Arche Capital.

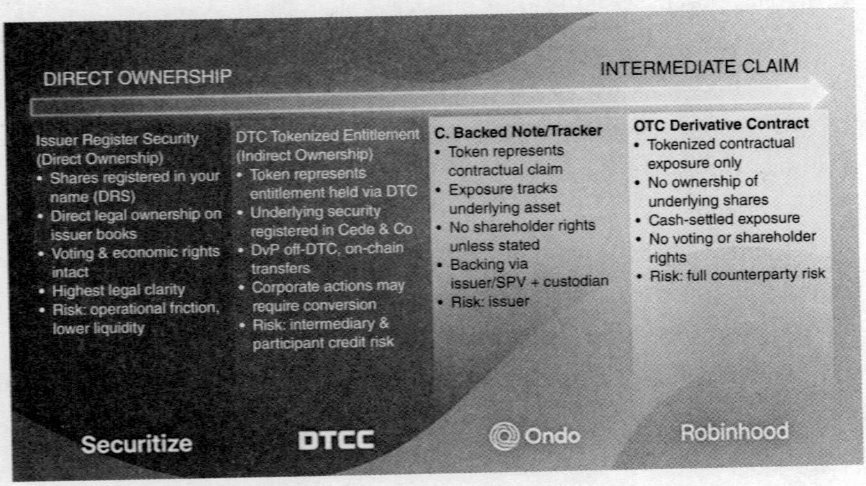

equities such as Apple, Tesla, and Nvidia. These products are backed by shares held in custody and are designed to support extended trading hours.

Robinhood has also launched tokenized stock and ETF products in Europe. In most cases, these function as on-chain price-linked instruments rather than direct ownership, meaning holders do not receive full shareholder rights.

Specialized platforms are also entering the market. Ondo Finance has rolled out a broad set of tokenized US stocks and ETFs across networks such as Ethereum and Solana, as part of a wider effort to bring regulated assets on-chain. Other companies, including Gemini, eToro, and Coinbase, have announced plans or are seeking regulatory approval to expand tokenized equity offerings.

Other Tokenized Assets

Some real-world assets have seen early traction. Tokenized gold products such as Pax Gold (PAXG) and Tether Gold (XAUT) represent physical gold bars held in secure vaults as digital tokens that move on blockchains.

When a token is issued, the provider, such as Paxos for PAXG or Tether for XAUT, purchases and stores physical gold in professional vaults. Each token represents a defined amount of gold, typically one troy ounce. The token itself is recorded on a blockchain, allowing it to be transferred, traded, or used as collateral, while the underlying gold remains in storage. Holdings can be verified through audits and serial numbers, and larger holders may redeem tokens for physical gold or cash.

Other categories, including real estate, fine art, music royalties, sports memorabilia, and carbon credits, are still in early adoption.

Many projects have struggled due to illiquidity, valuation challenges, and limited demand. These assets may gain traction over time, but broad adoption is likely to follow once financial markets become integrated with the blockchain.

Clearing and Settlement

"Tokenizing the U.S. securities market has the potential to yield transformational benefits such as collateral mobility, new trading modalities, 24/7 access and programmable assets, but this will only be achievable if market infrastructure provides a robust foundation to usher in this new digital era."

—Frank La Salla, President & CEO, Depository Trust & Clearing Corporation[13]

In traditional markets, executing a trade does not mean immediate ownership. Clearing and settlement require coordination among brokers, custodians, clearinghouses, and depositories. In the United States, this process typically takes two business days and introduces counterparty risk.

Blockchain replaces this fragmented structure with a shared, synchronized ledger. Once a transaction is confirmed, ownership updates almost instantly. This reduces operational risk, lowers costs, and improves transparency.

Institutions are already testing this model. The DTCC's Project Ion uses a permissioned blockchain to record US equity trades alongside existing systems, processing over 100,000 transactions per day, signaling how traditional market infrastructure is being adapted with distributed ledger technology. JPMorgan's Onyx network and Citi's tokenized deposits demonstrate how core financial plumbing is being rebuilt using blockchain infrastructure.[14]

On December 17, 2025, DTCC unveiled a partnership with Digital Asset and Canton Network to enable the tokenization of US Treasury securities held at the Depository Trust Company. For the first time, Treasurys will be issued directly on a blockchain, with a minimum viable product planned in a controlled production environment in 2026.

Trade Finance and Supply Chains

Global trade still relies heavily on paper documents and manual processes. Items like letters of credit, shipping documents, and invoices often move slowly between buyers, sellers, banks, and logistics companies, sometimes taking days or even weeks to complete. This slows down payments and increases the chance of mistakes or disputes.

Blockchain helps modernize this process by turning paper documents into shared digital records that all parties can access. When combined with smart contracts, payments and document transfers can happen automatically once agreed conditions are met, reducing delays and back-and-forth communication.[15]

Digitizing trade documentation can dramatically shorten processing times, free up capital tied up in slow settlements, and make supply chains faster and more reliable. For banks and large companies, blockchain-based documentation is increasingly viewed as a practical upgrade to existing trade finance systems rather than an experimental technology.

REWIRING OF THE FINANCIAL MARKETS

"As stablecoins and tokenized deposits move into traditional banking. . . we will see a complete rewiring of the banking system."

—Bill Winters, CEO of Standard Chartered

What's happening in financial markets is not a sudden replacement of the existing system. It's a gradual shift in how the system works underneath. Blockchain technology is changing how ownership is recorded, how value moves, and how transactions settle, often without changing the assets themselves.

This kind of change has happened before.

In the mid-1980s, a long-distance phone call in the United States could cost more than $3 per minute and required special calling cards issued by AT&T. Today, voice and video calls move instantly over the internet, often at no cost, using Wi-Fi and smartphones. The service didn't disappear, but the infrastructure did. Business models adapted because the old technology could no longer compete with a faster, cheaper alternative.

Media followed the same path. Early streaming services were dismissed as inferior and resisted by incumbents. Companies like Netflix and Spotify faced licensing hurdles, skepticism, and regulatory pressure. Over time, they proved that on-demand, internet-based delivery was more convenient and more scalable. Streaming is now the dominant model for video and music, and the industry has reorganized around it.

Finance is entering a similar phase. Many financial systems were built decades ago around batch processing and manual reconciliation, reflecting the constraints of the technology available at the time. Blockchain-based systems settle transactions in near real time, operate continuously, and reduce the need for intermediaries. These advantages do not eliminate existing institutions, but they do force change.

The key question is no longer whether the technology works. It is where it clearly improves outcomes, where it does not, and how to tell the difference. Some experiments will fail. Others will quietly become part of everyday financial infrastructure.

INVESTOR TAKEAWAY

When technology replaces infrastructure, incumbents rarely disappear overnight. They resist at first, then adapt. AT&T didn't fight the internet forever; it moved away from per-minute pricing, adopted flat-rate data, and learned to monetize the network rather than each call. Netflix and

Spotify shifted entertainment from ownership to access. Content became on-demand, subscription-based, and far cheaper to distribute.

Digital assets represent a similar shift in finance. They are replacing slow, expensive back-end systems with faster, cheaper ones. This does not happen all at once, and it does not require new brands to win immediately. It happens quietly, as costs fall and processes improve.

We are in the middle of a multi-decade transformation of the financial system.

For investors, the opportunity is to identify which digital asset technologies are becoming core financial infrastructure. The question is not whether change will happen, but which systems will remain essential once it does.

Understanding that path matters as much as understanding the technology itself. Infrastructure changes create opportunity, but markets move in cycles, adoption accelerates at different speeds, and regulation plays a decisive role in shaping outcomes.

The next chapter focuses on those forces—how digital asset adoption is growing, how these markets behave compared to traditional assets, and how policy is influencing the pace and direction of change.

CHAPTER THREE

THE INVESTMENT OPPORTUNITY

ADOPTION, GROWTH, AND MARKET CYCLES

"Fortune favors the bold." Or, in the original Latin often attributed to Virgil, Audentes fortuna iuvat.

The phrase dates back to ancient Rome. It was never an endorsement of recklessness, but a recognition that progress often requires acting under uncertainty, before outcomes are obvious and consensus has formed.

That dynamic has appeared repeatedly in financial history, and few areas illustrate it more clearly than digital assets.

In the early 2010s, long before digital assets were widely understood or institutionally accessible, a small number of investors encountered Bitcoin not as a short-term trade, but as a long-term opportunity.

Among the most visible examples are Cameron and Tyler Winklevoss. Known at the time for their involvement in the founding of Facebook, the twins later resolved a high-profile legal dispute and received a settlement that included both cash and Facebook shares. Rather than following a conventional diversification path, they invested $11 million in Bitcoin in 2013, when it was trading around $120, reportedly accumulating as many as 70,000 Bitcoin—an amount that would be worth roughly $7 billion when Bitcoin first reached $100,000 in 2024.[1]

The decision required conviction and patience. Over the years that followed, Bitcoin experienced multiple boom-and-bust cycles and repeated declarations of its demise. The Winklevoss twins remained long-term holders throughout those periods.

Their early investment ultimately made them among the first widely recognized Bitcoin billionaires. They later built Gemini, a regulated digital asset exchange designed to meet institutional and compliance standards, translating early conviction into lasting infrastructure.

In hindsight, the outcome appears obvious. It was not.

A more recent and frequently cited example comes from Binance founder Changpeng Zhao, known as CZ. In 2014, Zhao sold his apartment to buy Bitcoin—much to his family's dismay—purchasing roughly 1,500 BTC at about $600 each.

In hindsight, the decision looks extraordinary.[2]

It is also not a recommendation.

No sound investment framework suggests selling one's home to buy a volatile asset. But the story captures something essential about investing in this space: meaningful participation has typically required either very high conviction, or a willingness to experiment with capital one could afford to lose, combined with a disciplined approach to managing risk.

Over the past decade, most investors who benefited from digital assets followed one of these paths. Some developed conviction early and endured volatility across multiple cycles. Others started small, learned through experience, and increased exposure as the ecosystem matured. Both required patience, humility, and comfort operating outside the consensus.

For many investors, participation did not begin with a single decisive bet, but with a process. Rather than attempting to time entry points or predict short-term price movements, they allocated capital gradually over time—a method known as dollar-cost averaging. This approach spreads investment across multiple periods, reducing the impact of volatility and the risk of committing capital at an inopportune moment. In markets as volatile as digital assets, dollar-cost averaging has often served as a practical middle ground: allowing investors to build exposure, learn through experience, and remain invested through cycles without requiring perfect timing or extraordinary conviction.

From the beginning, digital asset investing has been a non-consensus bet. Every meaningful investment in digital assets began this way: early, uncertain, and widely doubted.

That does not mean boldness alone is enough. Most non-consensus ideas fail. The opportunity in digital assets has never been about blind optimism, but about balancing conviction with risk management, and understanding that innovation rarely arrives with universal agreement.

> "I've spent 35 years trading every asset class. I've seen every major market paradigm shift and crisis of the last three decades from the inside. What I've learned is that the best opportunities emerge when serious capital meets a maturing market that still scares people. That's exactly where we are in digital assets today.

Crypto is a $3 trillion market—still a fraction of gold, a rounding error compared to U.S. equities. The institutional capital is there; it's waiting for the right partners. Not gunslingers chasing 10x returns, but managers who deliver disciplined risk-adjusted returns, sound portfolio construction, and access to crypto's fat right tails—while protecting downside risk in a mature and understandable way. Institutions want documented, best-in-class processes and strategies that can scale. The infrastructure finally exists. The regulatory clarity is coming. The allocators who move now—thoughtfully, with the right partners—will look very smart in five years."

—Sam Gaer, CIO of Directional Strategy at Monarq Asset Management; former CIO of NYMEX and FINRA

By the end of this chapter, you will gain a clear understanding of:

- Why digital asset adoption is accelerating
- How digital assets trade compared to traditional assets
- How regulation and policy are reshaping the asset class

GROWTH IN DIGITAL ASSET USERS

By 2025, the number of people worldwide who owned digital assets had surpassed 700 million, a 16% rise in just one year.[3] Between July 2024 and June 2025 alone, investors purchased more than $1.2 trillion worth of Bitcoin, $724 billion in Ethereum, and $497 billion in stablecoins.[4] These figures reflect not speculative curiosity, but sustained global participation on a large scale.

In the United States, adoption has become increasingly mainstream. What was once the domain of tech enthusiasts has become an integral part of everyday financial life, with an increasing number of people buying, holding, and experimenting with digital assets.[5]

Globally, adoption is shaped by very different economic realities. In countries such as Colombia, India, and Nigeria, where access to traditional banking is limited, cryptocurrency provides a practical alternative for saving, making payments, and facilitating cross-border transfers. In high-inflation economies like Argentina, Turkey, and Venezuela, stablecoins help preserve purchasing power while Bitcoin serves as protection against currency instability. In contrast, in North America and Europe, digital assets are primarily used as investment vehicles and portfolio diversifiers.

DIGITAL ASSETS AND THE NEXT GENERATION OF INVESTORS

Younger investors are digital-first. Having grown up with smartphones and online payments, digital assets feel intuitive to them. They expect speed, transparency, and control, and prefer managing investments themselves through apps rather than traditional brokers.

Digital assets have become a natural entry point into investing. According to Coinbase's State of Crypto Q4 2025 report, 45% of younger US investors already own cryptocurrency, compared with only 18% of older investors, illustrating a clear generational shift in ownership.[6] Research from the OECD similarly shows that digital assets holders tend to be younger, with many making their first investment in digital assets.

Many Millennials are already more likely to put their first investment dollars into digital assets than into traditional stocks. In one widely cited survey by Galaxy, 38% of Millennials reported owning digital assets, compared with 37% who owned equities, with Gen Z showing even higher participation across asset types.[7] For younger investors, this isn't about speculation—it's about familiarity. Digital assets feel native in a world of apps, instant access, and online communities in a way traditional brokerage accounts often don't.

That said, ownership is not evenly distributed across the population. While about 14% of US adults overall report owning Bitcoin or another digital asset, participation is significantly higher among men under 50, where ownership reaches roughly 25%. Rates are notably lower among older adults and among women across age groups.[8] These gaps reflect differences in comfort with technology, access, and financial confidence rather than long-term demand.

The generational divide isn't limited to individual investors. Anthony Scaramucci, founder and managing partner of SkyBridge, has noted that similar patterns are emerging among professional asset allocators, policymakers, and regulators, with younger decision-makers generally more open to digital assets than their older counterparts.

This shift is unfolding alongside one of the largest wealth transfers in history. Over the next two decades, an estimated $124 trillion is expected to pass to Millennials and Gen Z, a transition that is likely to accelerate digital asset adoption as these generations gain income and inherit wealth.[9] Digital assets, which are accessible, global, and available around the clock, align naturally with how younger investors already manage money.

As these generations gain income and inherit wealth, their preferences are already reshaping markets. Institutions are responding with exchange-traded funds, custody solutions, and tokenized products. This is not a passing trend. Younger investors have long-time horizons and strong conviction, providing lasting momentum as digital assets move from the fringe into the financial mainstream.

THE ROLE OF WEALTH MANAGERS, BROKERS, AND RIAS IN DIGITAL ASSET INVESTMENTS

For much of their early history, digital assets remained outside the comfort zone of traditional wealth managers, broker-dealers, and registered investment advisors (RIAs), largely due to high volatility and regulatory uncertainty. Although clients could access digital assets directly through exchanges or via public-market products, many advisors viewed the asset class as complex and difficult to align with fiduciary standards.

That caution is now beginning to ease. Recent survey data shows that familiarity with digital assets among advisors has increased sharply, even if full adoption remains uneven. In the Bitwise/VettaFi 2025 Benchmark Survey, nearly half of US financial advisors reported personally owning digital assets—the highest level recorded since the survey began. Advisors closest to portfolio construction, particularly registered investment advisors, were the most likely to have firsthand experience, suggesting comfort is increasingly driven by direct exposure rather than abstract debate.[10]

Client demand has also become impossible to ignore. Nearly all advisors report receiving questions about digital assets from clients, and the share of advisors allocating digital assets in client portfolios has doubled over the past year. Once included, these allocations tend to remain in place, with most advisors planning to maintain or modestly increase exposure rather than reverse course.

The main constraint is no longer belief, but implementation. Only about one-third of advisors say they are currently able to access digital assets directly within client accounts. As a result, many clients invest independently. More than two-thirds of advisors report that clients hold digital assets outside the advisory relationship, limiting oversight and integration with broader financial planning.

When advisors do engage, they favor familiar structures. Regulated vehicles such as exchange-traded funds and diversified index products rank well ahead of direct token ownership. Cost, liquidity, and issuer credibility matter more than size alone, reflecting a cautious, fiduciary-first approach to a still-evolving asset class.[1]

Separate research from CoinShares shows that investors are moving faster than the advisory system built to support them. Among affluent investors who already hold digital assets, 89% said they planned to increase their exposure in 2025, and more than half monitor or trade digital assets daily, signaling that these investments are now part of ongoing wealth strategies rather than occasional speculation.[11] Many of these investors are not waiting for formal access through advisors or private banks, choosing instead to invest independently outside traditional advisory relationships. As Katharine Wooller of AssetPass notes, what began with early digital asset adopters has expanded well beyond "crypto natives" to a broader, wealthier investor base with no memory of a pre-internet financial system.[12]

Crucially, this is not a rejection of professional advice; 82% of investors say they would be more inclined to work with an advisor who offers credible digital asset guidance, and more than half say it is extremely important that their advisor understands digital assets. At the same time, 29% cite lack of advisor experience or poor risk communication as a red flag, explaining why many investors move ahead on their own when institutional support falls short.

Together, these findings show that advisors are no longer dismissing digital assets, and investors are no longer waiting for permission. What remains is a gap between intent and infrastructure—between growing comfort at the advisory level and the practical ability to offer digital assets within regulated, scalable frameworks. Closing that gap requires more than changing attitudes. It requires institutional follow-through.

That picture is now shifting. Major financial institutions have begun moving from observation to implementation, responding to sustained client demand and improving regulatory clarity. Citi announced plans to launch digital asset custody services in 2026. UBS, which oversees $6.6 trillion in assets under management, will allow select wealthy clients to trade Bitcoin and ether as part of a broader expansion into digital assets.[13] Similarly, European asset manager Amundi, with €2.3 trillion under management, has announced plans to launch a bitcoin investment product.[14] Bank of America has publicly discussed modest digital asset allocations within diversified portfolios. BlackRock has gone further, framing Bitcoin as a potential 1–2% portfolio allocation, while Fidelity and Morgan Stanley now support limited Bitcoin exposure for suitable clients.[15]

Even firms that were once firmly opposed are adjusting. Vanguard, long skeptical of digital assets, now allows clients to trade digital-asset ETFs on its platform. At the same time, companies that originated in the digital asset sector are stepping into more traditional wealth roles. Coinbase has expanded into wealth management services, offering support designed for high-net-worth investors and advisors seeking a more familiar framework.

For investors, these changes are increasingly visible through familiar platforms. Firms like Fidelity Investments allow advisors to hold and manage digital assets alongside traditional investments, using the same reporting and oversight. Morgan Stanley and Bank of America have widened access to crypto-related investment products, making them available to a broader set of clients, including through retirement accounts.

Even traditionally cautious institutions are exploring new approaches. JPMorgan has launched a blockchain-based money-market fund and plans to allow clients to borrow against their bitcoin holdings, signaling that digital infrastructure is beginning to support familiar investment products.[16] At the same time, firms such as BitGo and Anchorage Digital provide secure custody services behind the scenes, helping advisors offer digital assets within established wealth frameworks.

Together, these developments reflect a simple shift: investors no longer need to step outside traditional wealth channels to explore digital assets. Access is becoming more familiar, more structured, and easier to approach, especially for those at an early stage of understanding the asset class.

This shift is placing pressure on advisory firms to adapt. Spot Bitcoin and Ethereum ETFs, improved custody, and clearer regulatory signals are making digital assets easier to integrate into existing wealth management frameworks. Adoption will remain deliberate, moving through compliance and suitability reviews, but the direction is clear. Digital assets are increasingly becoming a supported, portfolio-level consideration rather than a fringe exposure, driven as much by client demand as by institutional endorsement.[17]

That principle helps explain why recent moves by traditional firms matter. Charles Schwab, long cautious on digital assets, plans to introduce direct Bitcoin and Ethereum trading within its core brokerage platforms. Until now, Schwab has offered only indirect investments through exchange-traded products and digital asset-focused stocks.[18] Moving toward direct ownership marks a meaningful shift by bringing digital assets closer to the same footing as stocks and bonds within mainstream wealth accounts.

TRADING AND TRANSACTION ACTIVITY NUMBERS

One of the clearest indicators that digital assets have entered the financial mainstream is the scale and structure of their trading activity. What began a decade ago on small, lightly regulated platforms has evolved into a globally integrated market measured in trillions of dollars (see Figure 3.1).

Figure 3.1 Total spot trading volume of centralized exchanges (CEXs) and decentralized exchanges (DEXs) since 2020.

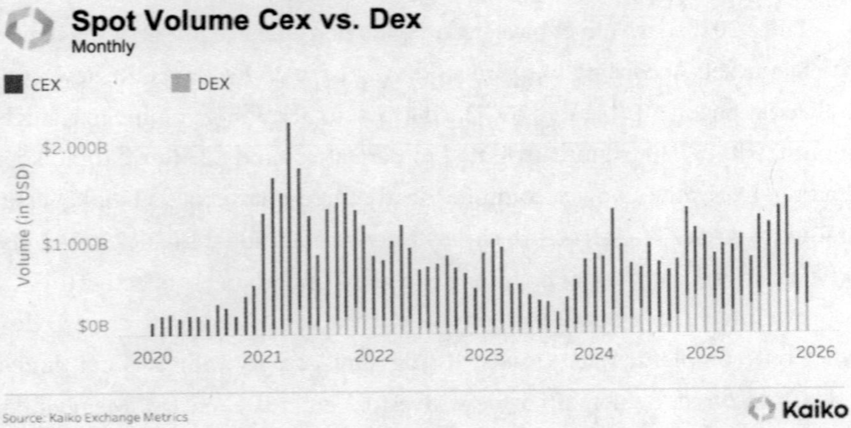

Today, that activity flows through two major channels: spot markets and derivatives markets. Spot trading is the most straightforward form of participation—it's the direct buying and selling of digital assets.[19] When you purchase Bitcoin or Ethereum on the spot market, you actually own it. It's the digital equivalent of buying gold and taking it home with you. For example, if you log in to Coinbase or Kraken and buy $100 worth of Bitcoin, that Bitcoin is now yours: you can hold it, transfer it to a wallet, or use it in a transaction. That's spot trading. It reflects real demand and real ownership, which is why spot markets serve as one of the clearest indicators of genuine adoption.

Derivatives trading operates differently. These markets consist of financial contracts—such as futures, perpetual swaps, and options—that provide exposure to price movements without requiring ownership of the underlying asset. This structure mirrors traditional commodities and equities markets, where investors routinely trade oil, gold, or equity index futures without taking physical delivery. In the digital asset space, derivatives are primarily used for hedging, leverage, liquidity provision, and advanced trading strategies, and they are increasingly dominated by professional trading firms and institutions (see Figure 3.2).

Since 2023, derivatives have become the dominant segment of the digital assets market. According to CoinDesk's August 2025 Exchange Review, centralized exchanges processed $9.72 trillion in total trading volume in a single month, with $7.36 trillion attributed to derivatives and $2.36 trillion to spot trading. Derivatives now account for nearly three-quarters of all digital asset trading volume. This structure closely mirrors traditional financial markets, where derivatives volumes have long exceeded underlying spot activity.

The divergence between spot and derivatives volume reflects two distinct but complementary trends. Rising spot activity indicates continued growth in direct ownership as new investors enter the market. Meanwhile, the dominance of derivatives signals increasing market sophistication, with institutional participants using futures and options to manage risk, provide liquidity, and express market views.

Figure 3.2 Total derivative trading volume of centralized exchanges (CEXs) and decentralized exchanges (DEXs) since 2020, including options, futures, and perps.

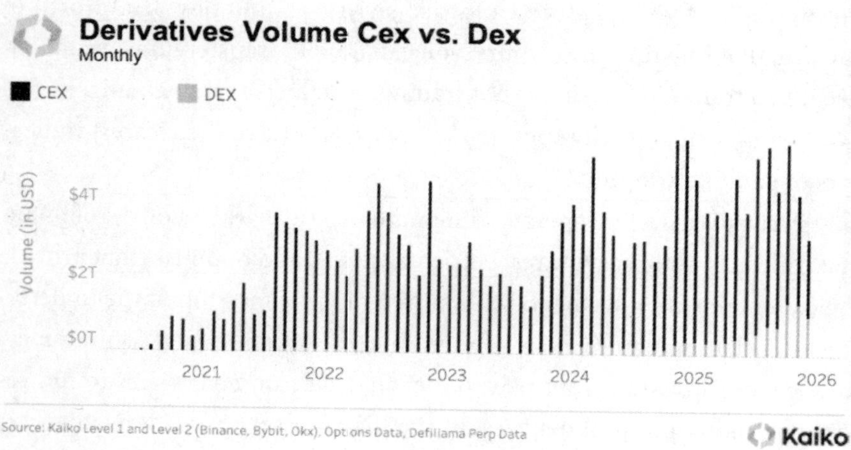

A RENEWED LEGAL AND REGULATORY FRAMEWORK

For much of their early history, digital assets operated in a regulatory gray zone, especially in the United States. Industry groups such as the Bitcoin Foundation, Coin Center, the Chamber of Digital Commerce, the Blockchain Association, and later the Crypto Council for Innovation spent years engaging regulators in an effort to explain the technology and establish basic legal clarity. Progress was slow. Skepticism was widespread, and constructive guidance was rare.

As a result, the US market spent much of the past decade constrained not by technology, but by uncertainty. That environment became even more restrictive under the leadership of Gary Gensler, who headed the Securities and Exchange Commission between 2021 and 2025. His four-year term was marked by an enforcement-first posture.

The SEC relied heavily on litigation rather than rulemaking, the Office of the Comptroller of the Currency issued restrictive guidance to banks, and informal pressure discouraged financial institutions from engaging with digital asset firms. Startups were forced to spend millions of dollars on legal defense instead of building products. Access narrowed. Participation slowed. Large institutions largely stayed on the sidelines.

The cumulative effect was not simply oversight, but effective exclusion. Banks were hesitant to offer custody or payment services, asset managers struggled to bring products to market, startups could not open a bank account, and retail investors faced a fragmented and often offshore ecosystem. For years, digital assets operated below their potential—not because demand was absent, but because the rules of the road were unclear and they operated in a hostile environment.

That stance has begun to change.

With the return of the Trump administration, US policy shifted toward engagement rather than obstruction. Paul Atkins was appointed Chair of the Securities and Exchange Commission, signaling a move away from enforcement-led regulation, while Michael S. Selig was named Chair of the Commodity Futures Trading Commission, reinforcing a more coordinated, market-structure-focused approach across agencies.

Since early 2025, Congress has moved decisively to establish a workable regulatory framework. In July 2025, lawmakers passed the GENIUS Act, the first comprehensive federal law governing stablecoins. The legislation requires one-to-one backing with dollars or other low-risk assets and sets clear standards for issuance, transparency, and oversight.

At the same time, the House advanced the Digital Asset Market CLARITY Act, a market-structure bill designed to clarify regulatory jurisdiction between the SEC and the Commodity Futures Trading Commission (CFTC) and define the roles of exchanges, brokers, and dealers. Earlier efforts, including the FIT21 Act and executive guidance under Executive Order 14178, laid much of the groundwork for this progress.

If enacted and effectively implemented, these measures could reduce regulatory uncertainty, encourage institutional participation, and support the continued maturation of U.S. digital asset markets. As with all major financial legislation, however, the scope and impact of the CLARITY Act and related reforms remain subject to ongoing rulemaking, judicial interpretation, and potential amendment as market conditions and political priorities evolve.

Viewed in hindsight, digital assets spent nearly a decade constrained by regulatory friction. For the first time, they are beginning to operate within a defined framework that allows innovation, institutional participation, and market access to coexist.

The United States is not acting alone. Jurisdictions such as Hong Kong, the European Union, and several countries in the Middle East have moved aggressively to establish clear digital asset regimes, giving banks and asset managers the confidence to build.

The result is a convergence. As regulatory clarity spreads and the United States reasserts leadership in global financial markets, digital assets are entering a new phase—no longer defined by uncertainty, but shaped by structure.

Operation Choke Point and Operation Choke Point 2.0

Operation Choke Point refers to a government strategy that restricts certain industries indirectly by limiting their access to banks, rather than banning them outright. Beginning in the 2020s, regulators set their sights on the digital asset industry.

The Original Program (2013–2017)

Led by the US Department of Justice, the FDIC, and other regulators, Operation Choke Point pressured banks to stop servicing legal but politically sensitive industries, including payday lenders, firearms dealers, gambling businesses, adult entertainment, and physical dealers of precious metals and collectibles.

There were no formal bans. Instead, regulators warned banks about "reputational risk" and subjected them to increased scrutiny. Many banks chose to exit these relationships rather than deal with the added oversight. The program officially ended in 2017 after criticism that it amounted to backdoor regulation.

"Choke Point 2.0" and Digital Asset (2022–2024)

"Operation Choke Point 2.0" is an informal term used in cryptocurrency and banking circles to describe a similar dynamic applied to digital assets.

Regulators repeatedly emphasized the risks of servicing crypto firms, including volatility, liquidity, compliance, and reputational concerns. Banks working with crypto faced more exams, higher capital expectations, and quiet pressure to de-risk, even in the absence of explicit anti-crypto laws.

Key Bank Failures

This pressure intensified after several high-profile collapses. Silvergate Bank shut down in 2023 after deposit outflows and regulatory strain. Signature Bank was seized in March 2023, with digital asset exposure cited as a risk factor. The failure of Silicon Valley Bank, while not digital asset-focused, accelerated de-risking across fintech and startup banking.

Why It Matters

For digital asset firms, the issue was access, not legality. For investors, the episode highlighted how regulation can shape markets indirectly, through banking relationships, rather than through clear rules.

CRYPTO IS MACRO

Digital assets do not exist in a vacuum. Their performance is increasingly shaped by the same broad forces that move global markets: how high interest rates are, how easy it is to borrow or invest money, concerns about inflation, and major political decisions. As the market has matured, digital assets have started to behave less like experimental technology and more

Figure 3.3 Bitcoin has outperformed major assets and indexes.

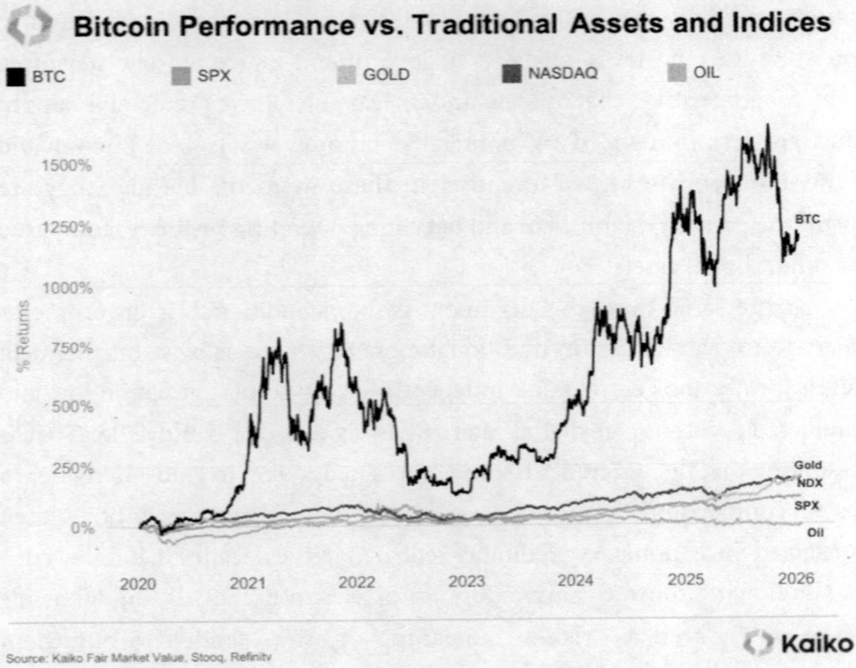

like other global investments, often moving alongside stocks and other growth-oriented assets (see Figure 3.3).

That connection becomes most visible during periods of market stress. When interest rates change, when central banks signal a shift in policy, or when geopolitical events rattle confidence, prices tend to react quickly. In early 2025, for example, new tariff announcements briefly unsettled global markets. Stocks, currencies, and digital assets all moved at the same time, driven by shared concerns about economic growth, inflation, and tighter financial conditions—not by events unique to the digital asset sector.

Demand for digital assets is likely to persist as long as rising public debt and heavy government involvement in monetary systems continue to weigh on confidence in traditional currencies. When investors begin to question the long-term reliability of government-issued money, they often look for alternatives that operate under clear rules, have predictable supply, and are less influenced by political decisions. Assets like Bitcoin and Ethereum tend to attract attention in these moments because they are widely used, well established, and have long operating histories, compared to other digital assets.[20]

At the same time, this argument isn't unconditional. If governments manage to rebuild trust in traditional monetary systems by stabilizing debt levels, protecting central bank independence, or keeping inflation low and predictable, interest in digital alternatives as a hedge could fade. That is assuming that Bitcoin trades effectively as a hedge akin to gold. Gold offers a useful comparison. It performed well during the inflation-heavy 1970s, then struggled once monetary credibility returned in the decades that followed.[21]

Following the very early adoption phases in the 2010s, digital assets were widely seen as "risk-on," meaning investors tended to buy them when they were more willing to take risks in pursuit of higher returns, and were treated as stand-alone, high-risk, high-reward assets. Meaningful conclusions about correlation with other assets, however, only became possible around 2020; prior to that, the market was too small and fragmented to allow reliable comparisons. Since then, a clearer pattern has emerged.

When central banks cut interest rates, liquidity expands, and investors grow more confident in economic growth. Digital assets tend to benefit under these conditions. When rates rise, monetary policy tightens, or markets turn defensive, capital typically pulls back. This pattern reflects not narrative enthusiasm, but the underlying cost and availability of capital.

For investors, the macro case isn't a promise of smooth returns. It's a way to understand why these assets may continue to matter over time, whether as a hedge against currency erosion, a potential diversifier, or a stake in a new kind of financial infrastructure.

Interest Rates and Risk Appetite

Interest rates play a central role. When policy rates rise, capital becomes more expensive, discount rates increase, and investors shift toward cash, short-duration bonds, and defensive assets. In these environments, higher-volatility assets, including technology stocks, venture investments, and digital assets, tend to underperform.

Conversely, when rates fall or are expected to fall, risk appetite returns. Lower real yields reduce the opportunity cost of holding non-yielding assets like Bitcoin, while easier financial conditions encourage leverage, speculation, and long-duration investments. Historically, major digital asset bull markets have aligned with periods of monetary easing or expectations of future easing, rather than sustained tightening cycles.

Liquidity Matters

Beyond headline interest rates, liquidity is now the dominant driver. Federal Reserve balance sheet expansion, bank reserves, repo facilities, and global dollar availability all influence how much capital is actively seeking risk. When liquidity increases, excess capital flows through equities and credit markets and eventually into riskier assets, including digital assets. When liquidity contracts, through balance sheet reduction or tighter financial conditions, those same assets face headwinds.

DIGITAL ASSET CORRELATION WITH TECH STOCKS, GOLD, AND OTHER ASSETS

In its early years, Bitcoin behaved like something entirely new (see Figure 3.4).

For much of the 2010s, its price movements appeared largely independent of traditional financial markets. Stocks could rise or fall, gold could rally or stall, and Bitcoin often moved to its own rhythm. That independence was one of the reasons early adopters viewed it as a powerful portfolio diversifier. Early research supported this view.

A 2017 white paper from Cathie Woods' ARK Invest, described Bitcoin's returns as largely uncorrelated with traditional asset classes, arguing that price independence was a defining feature of a new asset class.[22] At the time, Bitcoin's investor base was small, its market structure was fragmented, and macroeconomic forces played a limited role in its day-to-day trading.

Figure 3.4 Asset Class Correlation Matrix for Bitcoin and other major asset classes.

	BTC	NDX	SPX	GOLD	SILVER	REIT
BTC		0.17	0.15	0.04	0.13	0.07
NDX	0.17		0.97	–0.01	0.21	0.52
SPX	0.15	0.97		–0.01	0.21	0.64
GOLD	0.04	–0.01	–0.01		0.64	0.09
SILVER	0.13	0.21	0.21	0.64		0.17
REIT	0.07	0.52	0.64	0.09	0.17	

Source: Kaiko Fair Market Value, Stooq

But markets evolve—and Bitcoin evolved faster than most.

As digital assets attracted institutional capital, a broader retail audience, and growing integration with traditional financial infrastructure, Bitcoin's behavior began to change.

As Figure 3.5 illustrates, Bitcoin has consistently exhibited higher volatility than traditional asset classes such as equities, gold, oil, and silver. In its early years, Bitcoin's annualized volatility frequently exceeded 100%, reflecting its small market size, limited liquidity, and retail-dominated trading environment.

Over time, volatility has declined as the market matured. Deeper liquidity, institutional participation, and regulated derivatives markets have

Figure 3.5 While correlation explains how Bitcoin moves relative to other assets, volatility explains how much it moves.

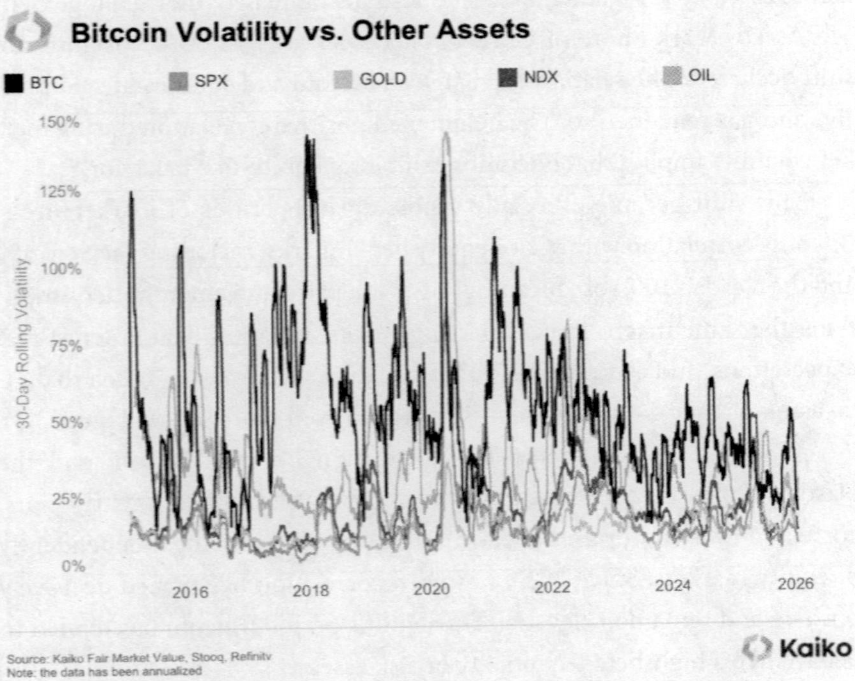

helped reduce the frequency of extreme swings. Even so, Bitcoin remains structurally more volatile than traditional assets. During periods of market stress, its price movements tend to amplify broader risk dynamics rather than dampen them.

For new investors, this is a critical distinction. Bitcoin may increasingly trade alongside traditional risk assets, but it still behaves like a high-volatility investment, requiring thoughtful position sizing and a long-term perspective.

By the late 2010s and early 2020s, it was no longer trading in isolation. Instead, it increasingly moved alongside risk assets, particularly technology stocks.

The turning point came around the pandemic. Extraordinary monetary stimulus, near-zero interest rates, and a surge in speculative activity tied asset prices together across markets. When liquidity expanded, prices across assets rose together. When conditions tightened, they fell together.

As Dr. Mark Shore of CME Group observed: "In 2020, a significant shift occurred. The relationship between Bitcoin and equities turned positive and has remained so. The heightened positive correlation during market volatility implies that bitcoin is exhibiting equity-like behavior."[23]

This shift became especially visible during periods of market stress. Bitcoin's correlation with major equity benchmarks, including the S&P 500 and the Nasdaq 100, rose meaningfully, with price movements often amplifying the same macro forces affecting stocks. Inflation data, interest rate expectations, and central bank policy began to matter just as much to digital assets as they did to equities—sometimes even more so (see Figure 3.6).

As Figure 3.7 illustrates, the correlation between Bitcoin and the Nasdaq 100 varies over time and is not constant.[24] In Bitcoin's early years, correlation was low or unstable, with the asset often moving independently of equity markets. Since 2020, however, correlation has turned decisively positive and remained elevated. During this period, Bitcoin has tended to behave like a high-beta technology or risk asset.

Figure 3.6 This chart shows Bitcoin's correlation with the S&P 500. Since 2021, Bitcoin has at times shown a stronger correlation with the index, though the relationship has varied over time.

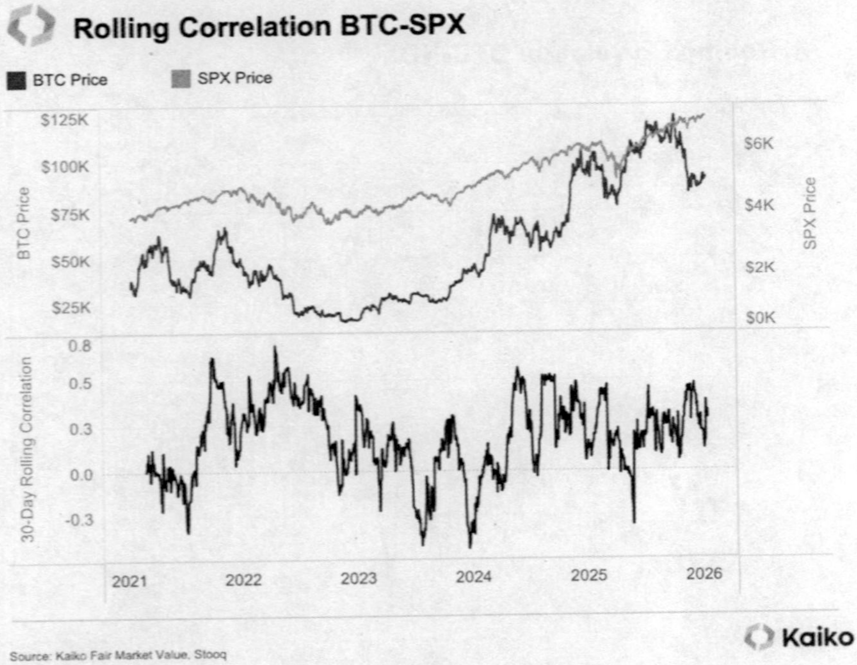

Higher correlations tended to cluster around moments of uncertainty. During the initial COVID-19 shock in early 2020, the tightening cycle of 2022, several volatility spikes in 2023, and renewed macro stress in early 2025, digital assets and equities frequently moved in the same direction. These periods reflected a shared "risk-off" mindset, where investors reduced exposure across speculative and growth-oriented assets at once.

This changing dynamic has not gone unnoticed on Wall Street.

Analysts at JPMorgan, including Nikolaos Panigirtzoglou, have pointed out that digital assets have become increasingly correlated not

Figure 3.7 Since 2020, Bitcoin's correlation with the Nasdaq has increased during certain periods, particularly during the pandemic, though the relationship has not been consistent over time.

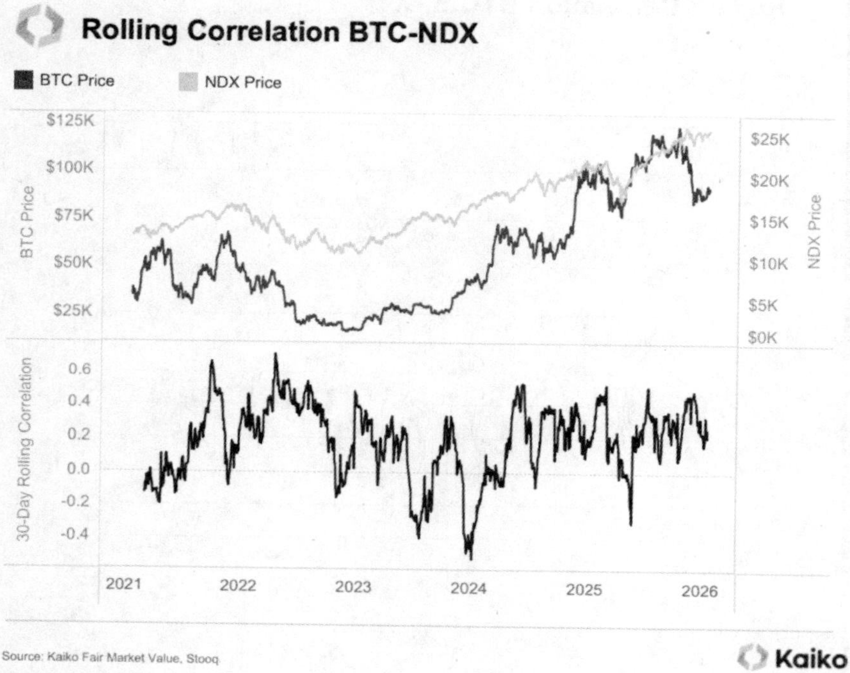

only with large-cap technology stocks, but also with smaller-cap equities such as those in the Russell 2000.[25] According to this view, two forces are driving the relationship.

First, retail participation. Many of the same investors who trade high-growth tech stocks also trade digital assets, often using leverage in both markets. Second, narrative overlap. Digital assets and tech are both tied to innovation, software, networks, and future growth. When optimism rises, capital flows into both. When sentiment breaks, it leaves both just as quickly.

As Bitcoin matures and becomes more deeply embedded in the global financial system, it naturally absorbs some of the behaviors of that system. Over time, its correlation profile may continue to evolve, just as gold, equities, and emerging markets did as they moved from the fringe to the mainstream.

Correlation With Nasdaq

As Bitcoin became institutionalized, many trading desks began grouping digital assets alongside other volatile, growth-oriented assets such as the Nasdaq. As a result, sharp declines in technology stocks often triggered meaningful pullbacks in Bitcoin and the broader digital asset market, as investors reduced risk and, in some cases, sold positions to meet margin requirements.

For investors, the key takeaway is that diversification is dynamic, not static. Assets behave differently as they grow, mature, and attract new participants. Understanding those shifts is essential for navigating the next chapter of digital asset markets with clarity and confidence.

Correlations are not permanent—they shift as market conditions change. At several points in 2025, for example, digital assets and equities briefly began to diverge again, with periods of negative correlation re-emerging.

These moments tended to coincide with digital assets-specific catalysts such as ETF-related inflows, network-level developments, regulatory progress, and the unwinding of excessive leverage that drove market behavior independent of broader equity markets.

Correlation With Gold

Bitcoin is often described as "digital gold," but its relationship with gold has been uneven and correlations have been historically low (see Figure 3.8).

At times, the two assets have moved together. At other times, they have behaved very differently. Looking at the data since 2020 helps explain why.

Figure 3.8 Bitcoin and gold don't consistently move together, with their short-term correlation shifting sharply over time.

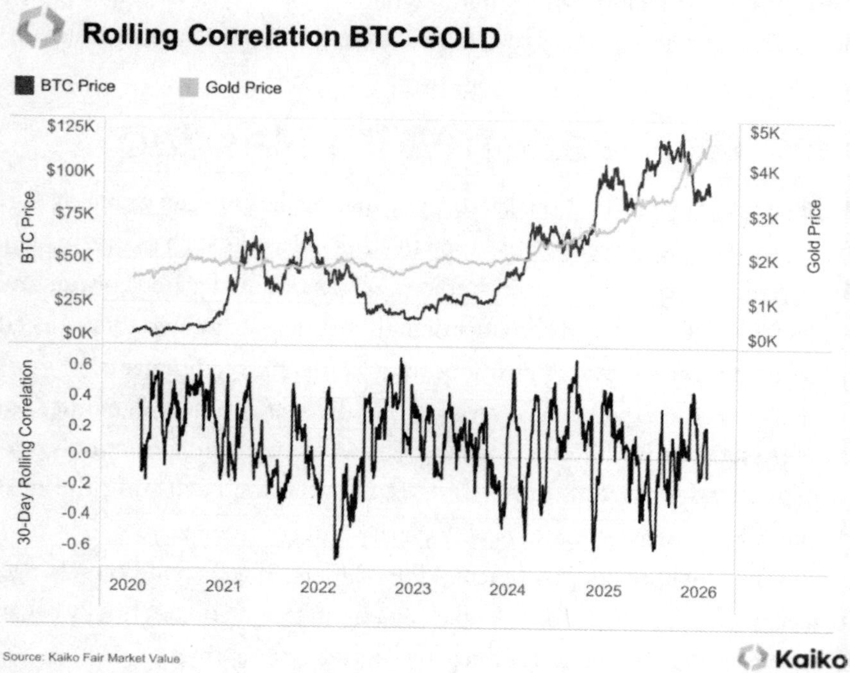

In early 2020, during the initial shock of the COVID crisis, both Bitcoin and gold briefly sold off as investors rushed to cash. Soon after, massive stimulus from central banks pushed both assets higher. During this period, Bitcoin and gold were treated similarly—as protection against money printing and falling real interest rates—and their prices moved more closely together.

That relationship broke down in 2022. As inflation surged and central banks raised interest rates aggressively, gold held up relatively well, behaving as a traditional defensive asset. Bitcoin, by contrast, fell sharply alongside stocks, trading more like a high-risk growth asset. The connection between the two weakened and, at times, disappeared altogether.

In 2023 and 2024, the gap remained. Gold responded mainly to interest rates, geopolitical risk, and central bank buying. Bitcoin's performance was driven by factors unique to the digital asset space, including liquidity cycles, ETF approvals, and adoption trends. Any correlation during this period was inconsistent and short-lived.

That divergence became even clearer in 2025 and into 2026. According to Grayscale Research, Bitcoin's short-term correlation with gold turned negative at times, meaning the two assets were moving in opposite directions.[26] While gold benefited from demand for traditional safe havens, Bitcoin increasingly traded in line with growth assets, responding to shifts in liquidity and broader risk appetite. Grayscale noted that Bitcoin's behavior during this period looked less like a defensive store of value and more like a technology-driven asset. This shift reinforced a broader pattern: despite the "digital gold" narrative, Bitcoin and gold do not maintain a stable or predictable relationship.

Looking across the full period, one pattern stands out: Bitcoin and gold are not reliably linked. Their prices tend to move together only during moments of broad financial stress or heavy monetary expansion. In more normal conditions, they follow different paths.

For investors, Bitcoin has not consistently behaved like gold in a portfolio. While it can show gold-like traits during periods of currency stress, it remains a distinct asset with its own drivers, risks, and opportunities—better understood on its own terms than as a simple substitute for gold.

This does not mean Bitcoin cannot evolve into a store of value over time, particularly as younger generations grow more comfortable with a digital analogue to gold. However, investors should be careful to distinguish long-term aspirations and narratives from what the data currently supports.

THE 4-YEAR CYCLE IN DIGITAL ASSETS: HOW IT WORKS—AND WHETHER IT STILL HOLDS

For years, investors used the "four-year cycle" as a simple way to think about Bitcoin's price. The idea was tied to the Bitcoin halving, an event that occurs about every four years when the number of new Bitcoin created as a reward for miners is cut in half, slowing the pace of new supply (see Figure 3.9).

In Bitcoin's early years, these halvings often lined up with major price cycles.[27] After the 2012, 2016, and 2020 halvings, Bitcoin rose sharply before eventually falling back. Over time, investors began to treat this

Figure 3.9 Bitcoin's price history has often clustered into roughly four-year cycles following each halving, with periods of sharp appreciation followed by extended pullbacks.

pattern as a rough roadmap: reduced supply, rising prices, growing speculation, and then a downturn.

That pattern still describes the past, but it no longer reliably explains the present.

In recent years, Bitcoin has broken several assumptions behind the four-year cycle. In 2022, its price fell below the previous cycle's peak for the first time. In 2024, Bitcoin reached a new all-time high before halving—something that had never happened before. These changes suggest that halving alone is no longer a dependable way to predict price.

A key reason is that the market has changed. Bitcoin is no longer driven primarily by its supply schedule. When Bitcoin was smaller, a reduction in new supply had a visible impact on price. However, following the 2024 halving, only 450 new Bitcoin are mined per day—an amount that is modest compared to the scale of capital now moving through the market. Even assuming a $100,000 Bitcoin price, that represents about $45 million in daily new supply. At times, spot Bitcoin ETFs have purchased between $500 million and $2 billion worth of Bitcoin in a *single day*. In that context, the supply shock created by the halving is small relative to overall capital flows.

Interest rates, liquidity, investor sentiment, and broader economic conditions now play a much larger role. As a result, Bitcoin often trades in step with other risk assets during tightening cycles, rather than moving independently.

This reflects a deeper structural shift. Many hedge funds and macro allocators no longer approach Bitcoin primarily as a "halving-cycle" asset. Instead, they increasingly view it as a high-beta liquidity asset—one that tends to respond quickly and sometimes sharply to changes in global liquidity conditions. When liquidity expands, Bitcoin can benefit. When liquidity tightens, it can face pressure, regardless of where it sits in the four-year halving calendar.

Access has changed as well. Spot Bitcoin ETFs, institutional investors, regulated custody, and corporate adoption have brought larger and steadier pools of capital into the market. Price movements are shaped less by retail speculation and more by global financial flows.

The halving still matters, but it no longer acts in isolation. The four-year cycle is useful history, not a reliable forecast.

For investors, this marks a shift. Bitcoin is increasingly behaving like a macro asset—one influenced by the same forces and investor flows that move markets more broadly. Understanding those forces may matter more than counting down to the next halving.

DIGITAL ASSETS SECTOR'S PERFORMANCE

One of the clearest reasons investors pay attention to digital assets is performance. Over the past decade, early adopters were rewarded with returns rarely seen in traditional markets. Bitcoin, for example, rose by roughly 26,900% over a 10-year period—turning a $100 investment in 2014 into nearly $27,000 by 2025.

By comparison, traditional assets delivered far more modest gains over the same period. The S&P 500 returned about 193%, gold roughly 126%, and 10-year US Treasury bonds under 90%. The gap is striking and helps explain why digital assets are often viewed as a high-growth category rather than a conventional investment (see Figure 3.10).

These outsized returns were largely a function of timing. Digital assets spent much of the past decade in the earliest phase of adoption, when new networks were forming, use cases were emerging, and relatively small

Figure 3.10 Long-term returns favor Bitcoin, while shorter-term performance varies across equities, gold, and oil.

As of 13th January 2026	BTC	S&P 500	Gold	Oil
YTD Returns	5.15%	1.53%	5.88%	7.77%
1-Year Returns	–0.01%	19.32%	72.21%	–19.18%
3-Year Returns	386.29%	74.13%	138.77%	–23.23%
5-Year Returns	166.72%	82.78%	148.55%	16.79%
10-Year Returns	21425.67%	268.40%	319.33%	116.00%

Source: Kaiko Fair Market Value, Stooq, Refinitiv

amounts of capital had an outsized impact. As with the early internet, growth was driven as much by expansion as by discovery.

Past performance is not a guide to what comes next. As regulation becomes clearer and more capital enters the market, digital assets are no longer defined by a lack of structure. That does not mean the opportunity has disappeared. It means it has changed.

In the early years, simply owning Bitcoin or Ethereum was often enough. Going forward, outcomes will depend more on what you own, how you size positions, and when you take risk. The opportunity remains substantial, but it increasingly rewards investors who understand the market and manage risk carefully, rather than those who rely solely on early timing.

Why 2025 Didn't Play Out As Expected

Many investors entered 2025 expecting a familiar post-halving rally for Bitcoin and digital assets. Instead, the year unfolded differently; for long-term holders, it proved to be a strong moment to take profits, particularly in Bitcoin after its move above $100,000.

Several forces shaped the outcome.

First, Bitcoin's place in markets has changed. It now trades alongside other major risk assets, rather than in isolation. In 2025, investor attention shifted toward US equities, especially the AI-driven "Magnificent Seven," as artificial intelligence became the dominant growth story. Capital that might once have flowed into digital assets was drawn instead to AI-related stocks.

Second, inflation reshaped investor behavior. Persistent price pressures increased demand for traditional inflation hedges like gold and silver, which absorbed capital that might otherwise have rotated into Bitcoin. At the same time, early Bitcoin holders used record prices as an opportunity to lock in gains, adding supply just as new demand softened.

Third, the digital asset market itself matured. Bitcoin continued to dominate market value, leaving little room for broad altcoin rallies. Speculation cooled, leverage was reduced, and investors became more selective. Stablecoins quietly stood out as one of the year's most successful use cases, gaining traction in payments and settlement while offering lower volatility.

The takeaway is that 2025 marked a transition. Bitcoin behaved less like a cyclical trade and more like a maturing asset—one competing for capital alongside stocks, commodities, and new technologies. For investors who understood that shift, 2025 and 2026 offered something valuable: a chance to rebalance, take profits, and reassess where digital assets fit in a changing market.

When one thinks about digital assets these are the key characteristics:

- **Diversification Potential:** Digital assets have historically moved differently from traditional assets, which means a small allocation can improve portfolio diversification. Allocations are typically kept modest, often around 5%, to capture upside without taking on excessive risk.
- **Inflation Hedge Narrative:** Bitcoin's fixed supply has led some investors to view it as a potential hedge against inflation, earning it the nickname "digital gold," especially during periods of economic uncertainty. However we see that recent data shows otherwise and that flows went in majority to gold and now silver as a hedge against inflation and market uncertainty.
- **High Liquidity and Easy Access:** Digital asset markets operate 24/7, allowing investors to buy or sell at any time. With global access and low barriers to entry, access is globally available.
- **High Volatility and Growth Potential:** While prices can swing sharply, digital assets have also delivered strong returns over relatively short periods, often outperforming traditional markets during expansion phases.

This combination of volatility, evolving correlations, and asymmetric return potential is what makes digital assets both challenging and compelling for investors willing to understand its dynamics rather than fear them.

KEY DIFFERENCES BETWEEN DIGITAL ASSETS AND TRADITIONAL ASSETS

Feature	Digital Assets	Traditional Assets (Stocks, Bonds)
Price Behavior	Characterized by sharp and frequent price movements, often within short time spans.	Generally experience lower volatility, particularly when held over longer investment horizons.
Regulatory Environment	Regulatory frameworks are still evolving, creating periods of uncertainty and uneven oversight.	Governed by long-standing legal and regulatory systems with clear investor protections.
Market Liquidity	Trade continuously, 24 hours a day, across global venues, allowing rapid entry and exit.	Liquidity depends on asset type and market hours; many markets operate on fixed schedules.
Investor Access	Open to a global user base with internet access, including participants outside traditional banking systems.	Typically require brokerage accounts or banking relationships, which may limit access for some investors.
Asset Custody	Can be held directly by investors using digital wallets, without reliance on custodial intermediaries.	Ownership is usually mediated through custodians, brokers, or financial institutions.
Income Potential	May offer yield through network participation, such as staking or on-chain lending mechanisms.	Income is commonly generated through dividends, coupon payments, or interest-bearing instruments.
Transparency	Transactions are recorded on public blockchains, allowing real-time verification and auditability.	Information flow depends on centralized reporting and disclosures, which may be periodic or delayed.

A NEW CLASS, A FAMILIAR DISCIPLINE

Digital assets are new, but the questions investors ask about them are not.

For much of their history, there were valid reasons to hesitate before treating digital assets as a true asset class. The market lacked long-term data, price swings were extreme, and rules around regulation and custody were still evolving.

These concerns became clearer when digital assets were compared to established asset classes. Commodities are physical and widely used. Real estate and infrastructure generate predictable income. Bonds provide steady yield. Digital assets did not fit neatly into any of these frameworks, leading many investors to view them as speculative and limit exposure to small, opportunistic positions.

The challenge was not just external skepticism. Within digital assets, there was no single definition of what the asset class represented. Bitcoin was framed as a store of value, other networks as software platforms, stablecoins as payment tools, and tokenized assets as digital versions of traditional securities. These differences made it difficult to apply one investment framework to the entire space.

Those critiques remain reasonable, but the market is changing. Regulation is becoming clearer, custody and market infrastructure have matured, and digital assets are separating into distinct segments with clearer economic roles. What once appeared as a single, volatile trade is starting to resemble a multi-part asset class.

As a result, the conversation is shifting. The question is no longer whether digital assets qualify as an asset class, but how different parts of the market should be evaluated, grouped, and allocated within a portfolio.

INVESTOR TAKEAWAY

Digital assets are no longer defined by whether they will be adopted, but by *how* investors choose to participate. Markets are larger, regulation is clearer, and access is easier than at any point in the past decade. At the same time, outcomes have become more uneven. Bitcoin, stablecoins, platform tokens, and tokenized assets behave differently and respond to different forces.

The experience of recent cycles shows that simply "owning crypto" is no longer a sufficient strategy. Performance now depends on what you own, how you size positions, and when you take risk. In a more mature market, discipline matters as much as conviction.

Importantly, investors now have more ways to gain exposure. Participation no longer requires direct ownership through wallets or exchanges. Public-market vehicles, such as ETFs, listed companies, and funds, allow investors to track prices, express views, or gain indirect exposure without holding the underlying asset.

Those choices come with trade-offs. Owning an asset directly offers control and full participation in its upside and use but requires operational involvement. Tracking price through public markets can be simpler and more familiar but may limit flexibility and introduce new risks.

The next chapter focuses on these decisions. It explains the main public-market paths to digital asset exposure, how they differ from direct ownership, and how investors can align each approach with their objectives, risk tolerance, and portfolio structure.

CHAPTER FOUR

INVESTING IN PUBLIC MARKETS

ETFs, SPOT, DERIVATIVES, AND EMERGING PRODUCTS

"ETFs don't change the nature of crypto assets—they change who can access them and how. By embedding digital assets into established market infrastructure, ETFs help bridge innovation

with the risk management, governance, and operational standards that institutional investors require."

—Joseph Chalom, CEO of Sharplink, former Head of Digital Assets Strategy at BlackRock

If Chapter 3 answers *why* digital assets belong in a portfolio, Chapter 4 answers *how* investors actually gain exposure in practice through familiar, regulated, public market instruments.

By the end of this chapter, you will gain a clear understanding of:

- How to gain digital asset exposure through familiar public-market vehicles
- The difference between owning assets and tracking their price
- How derivatives and digital asset-linked equities change risk and returns

FROM DIRECT OWNERSHIP TO PUBLIC MARKET ACCESS

For much of the early history of digital assets, gaining exposure meant purchasing and holding cryptocurrencies directly through crypto exchanges like Coinbase, Kraken, or Gemini. That approach required investors to engage with new technology, novel custody considerations, and unfamiliar operational complexity, such as wallet management, transaction mechanics, and platform risks.

Over time, this changed. As institutional participation increased, public-market structures emerged that allowed investors to gain exposure without operating directly on blockchain networks.

Today, public markets offer multiple paths to digital asset investing, each positioned differently along the spectrum between direct ownership and indirect participation. These structures exist not by accident, but by design. Investors differ in objectives, constraints, regulatory requirements, and tolerance for complexity.

This evolution introduces a critical distinction: asset exposure is not the same as asset ownership.

In traditional markets, this difference is often invisible. Owning a stock through a brokerage account feels straightforward. But in digital assets, the difference between owning the asset itself and owning exposure to its price is far more explicit. Public markets have emerged as a bridge allowing investors to gain exposure to digital assets using familiar structures, without necessarily engaging directly with blockchain infrastructure.

This chapter does not advocate a single approach. Instead, it outlines the landscape so investors can understand what they actually hold, and the trade-offs embedded in being invested in digital assets.

PATHWAYS TO DIGITAL ASSET EXPOSURE IN PUBLIC MARKETS

Once an investor decides to allocate to digital assets, the next question is not whether to invest, but how that exposure is expressed. Public markets now offer a range of access points, each reflecting different assumptions about control, responsibility, liquidity, and risk.

At one end of the spectrum is direct ownership of the asset itself. At the other is indirect exposure through financial instruments that reference digital asset prices without requiring ownership of the underlying asset.

DIRECT SPOT EXPOSURE (VIA CENTRALIZED PLATFORMS)

The most straightforward way to invest in a digital asset is to purchase it directly at the prevailing market price, usually on a centralized cryptocurrency exchange like Coinbase or Kraken. This involves opening an account with the exchange, completing identity verification, and funding the account using cash or bank transfers. Once funded, the investor can buy, sell, and hold cryptocurrencies in much the same way stocks are traded through a brokerage account. Figure 4.1 shows the largest centralized crypto exchanges by Bitcoin trading volume.

In this structure, the investor owns the cryptocurrency itself rather than a contract, security, or proxy tied to its value. For investors building

Figure 4.1 Binance dominated global Bitcoin spot trading volume in 2025, accounting for nearly half of all exchange activity.

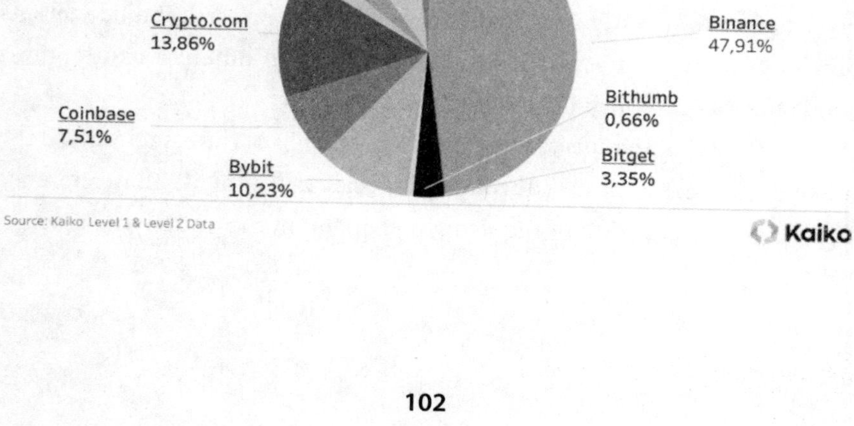

exposure gradually, direct spot purchases also pair naturally with a dollar-cost averaging approach. Rather than treating entry as a one-time decision, investors can allocate on a schedule and let the position build over time, reducing reliance on short-term timing. If you had invested $100 per month into Bitcoin starting in January 2020, you would have contributed roughly $7,200 over time. That investment would translate into approximately 0.14 BTC by the end of 2025, with a current value in the range of $12,000 to $14,500, depending on market prices.

What "ownership" means in practice, however, depends on how the asset is held. When an investor holds a digital asset directly, several characteristics apply:

- The asset's value moves directly with the market price.
- The asset may be transferable, withdrawable, or usable on-chain, depending on custody arrangements.
- The investor is exposed not only to price movements, but also to operational and custody risks.

How Digital Assets Are Held: Platform Custody, Self-Custody, and Price Exposure

When an investor buys a cryptocurrency on a centralized exchange, the asset is initially held on that platform. The exchange maintains custody on the investor's behalf, records balances internally, and facilitates trading and account management. For many investors, this feels similar to holding securities at a brokerage, with the exchange acting as custodian.

In practice, custody and transfer rights depend on the platform. Some allow assets to be withdrawn freely to personal wallets. Others provide price exposure but limit or delay transfers, meaning investors benefit from price movements without full control over where the asset is held. Ownership exists in both cases, but portability does not—and that distinction matters.

Some investors choose to move assets off platforms into self-custody by transferring them to a personal hardware or digital wallet they control directly. In this arrangement, no intermediary holds the asset. Control, security, and recovery rest entirely with the owner.

Both approaches represent direct ownership. The difference is not whether the asset is owned, but where it is held and who is responsible for safeguarding it.

Centralized exchanges are the primary gateway to spot cryptocurrencies, but they are not the only way investors gain exposure to digital assets. Some platforms provide direct ownership with the ability to transfer assets on-chain, while others offer economic exposure without full custody or portability.

Fintech platforms such as eToro, Robinhood, and Revolut typically follow a broker-style model. Investors gain exposure to price movements, but the underlying assets are held and managed by the platform rather than controlled through personal wallets. This structure mirrors traditional financial accounts, where ownership is reflected through account balances rather than direct control of the asset itself.

By contrast, decentralized exchanges enable spot trading through self-custody. Users connect personal wallets, retain control of their assets at all times, and transact directly on the blockchain without relying on a central intermediary.

These approaches represent different points along a spectrum—from full self-custody, to platform-held assets, to pure price exposure. The distinction is not whether an investor benefits from price changes, but how much control they have over the asset and whether it can be moved independently of the platform.

Understanding The Difference Between Centralized Exchanges (CEXs) and Decentralized Exchanges (DEXs)

Both enable buying, selling, and trading, but they differ meaningfully in structure, custody, and responsibility.

Centralized exchanges are companies that operate trading platforms and act as intermediaries. When an investor uses a CEX, such as Coinbase or Binance, the platform generally holds the digital assets on the investor's behalf, manages account balances internally, and facilitates transactions.

For new investors, this model feels familiar. The experience resembles a traditional brokerage account, with login credentials, customer support, and streamlined onboarding.

Decentralized exchanges operate without a central intermediary. Platforms like Uniswap are powered by blockchain-based software that allows anyone to trade directly from their own wallets. Figure 4.2 compares spot trading volumes across centralized and decentralized exchanges, while Figure 4.3 compares derivatives trading volumes between the two.

In this model, assets are never held by the platform. Investors retain full control at all times, and transactions are settled directly on the blockchain. This reduces dependence on third parties but increases personal responsibility—there is no intermediary to reverse errors or recover lost access.

While centralized exchanges have long dominated access to digital assets, decentralized exchanges are gaining ground. By 2025, DEX spot trading volume had grown to a meaningful share of centralized exchange spot volume (see chart below).

DEX to CEX Spot Trading Volume

Figure 4.2 Monthly spot trading volumes on centralized exchanges (CEXs) and decentralized exchanges (DEXs).

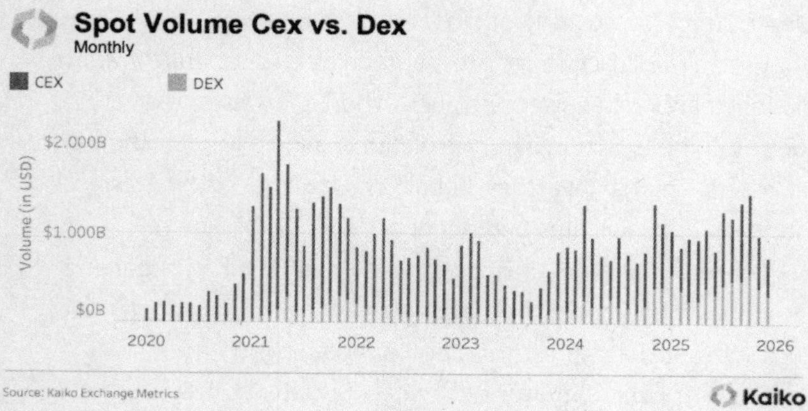

Derivatives Trading Volume: CEX vs. Perpetual DEXs

Figure 4.3 Monthly derivatives trading volumes on centralized exchanges (CEXs) and decentralized exchanges (DEXs).

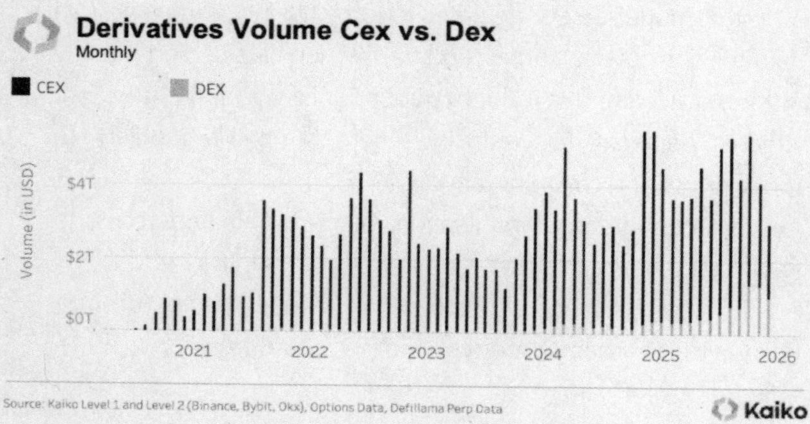

EXCHANGE-TRADED PRODUCTS (ETPs, ETFs, AND TRUSTS)

For many investors, particularly institutions and retirement savers, direct ownership of digital assets has historically been neither practical nor permissible. Exchange-traded products address this constraint by providing digital asset exposure through regulated, publicly traded instruments that can now be traded with any brokerage or retirement account.

These products allow investors to buy and sell exposure using traditional brokerage accounts, within established market and compliance frameworks.

For much of Bitcoin's history, spot Bitcoin ETFs were not permitted in the United States. In their absence, investors relied on publicly traded trusts, most notably the Grayscale Bitcoin Trust. Launched in 2013 by Grayscale, the trust held Bitcoin on behalf of investors and issued shares that traded on public markets. This structure provided early access within familiar investment accounts, but it also came with limitations, including reduced liquidity and periods where shares traded at significant premiums or discounts to the value of the underlying Bitcoin.[1] Before spot Bitcoin ETFs were approved, shares of the Grayscale Bitcoin Trust often traded far from their underlying value, at times at discounts exceeding 40%. Because investors could not redeem shares for Bitcoin, price gaps persisted. Those discounts only closed once markets began to anticipate ETF approval and the trust's conversion, highlighting the importance of structure, liquidity, and arbitrage in crypto investment vehicles.

ETFs have since become a significant catalyst for broader institutional participation in digital assets. This became especially evident in the United States following the approval of spot Bitcoin ETFs in January 2024, which marked one of the most successful ETF launches in history. Their rapid adoption reflected years of pent-up demand for regulated, scalable access to Bitcoin, rather than a sudden change in the underlying asset itself.

By January 2026, just two years after their introduction in the United States, digital asset ETFs had become a durable part of the investment landscape. Assets under management across US-listed products totaled roughly $146 billion, concentrated primarily in Bitcoin ETFs, with Ethereum products accounting for most of the remaining exposure. This growth positioned the United States as the center of the global digital asset ETF market, underscoring how regulatory clarity and established capital markets can accelerate institutional adoption.

When viewed in a global context, US-listed digital asset ETFs account for the majority of total assets, but they do not represent the entire market. As Figure 4.4 illustrates, global digital asset ETF assets are heavily concentrated in Bitcoin, with Ethereum comprising a growing but still secondary share, and smaller allocations across other assets such as Solana and XRP.

Figure 4.4 In the US digital asset ETFs held over $130 billion in assets under management as of end of 2025.

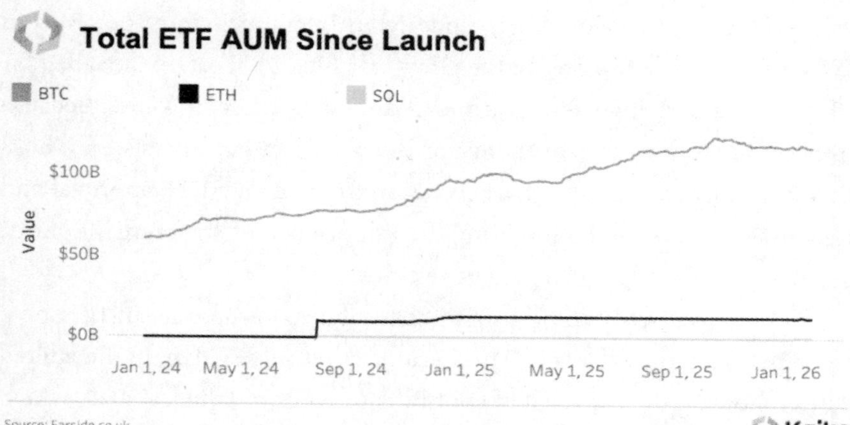

Today, investors can already gain digital asset exposure through familiar brokerage platforms such as Charles Schwab or Robinhood by purchasing spot ETFs tied to Bitcoin, Ethereum, Solana, or XRP. As regulation continues to develop, additional spot ETFs are expected to follow, potentially covering assets like Litecoin, Dogecoin, Chainlink, Cardano, Hedera, BNB, Polkadot, and Sui.

This shift allows investors to access digital assets without opening new accounts, managing wallets, or changing how they invest. Exposure can now be gained through regulated products, held alongside stocks and bonds, using the same tools and relationships investors already trust.

Spot-Based Products

Spot-based digital asset ETFs hold the underlying asset directly, with the goal of closely tracking its market price. They resemble commodity or Gold ETFs: they provide transparent price exposure without leverage, derivatives, or operating risk tied to a business. A spot Bitcoin ETF, for example, rises and falls with the price of Bitcoin itself. If Bitcoin declines by 30%, the ETF should move by a similar amount. These products do not generate income or participate in network activity; they are designed purely for price exposure. In the United States, spot Bitcoin ETFs are now offered by large, established asset managers including BlackRock through its iShares platform, Fidelity, Grayscale, Bitwise, ARK Invest in partnership with 21Shares, and VanEck.

Futures-Based Products

Futures-based ETFs gain exposure through regulated futures contracts rather than by holding the asset itself. In the United States, a common example is the ProShares Bitcoin Strategy ETF (BITO), which invests in Bitcoin futures traded on the Chicago Mercantile Exchange (CME). Futures contracts have expiration dates, meaning the fund cannot hold them indefinitely. As a contract approaches expiration, the ETF must sell it and replace it with a new contract dated further into the future—a process known as "rolling" futures. When newer contracts are priced higher than expiring ones, the fund effectively buys high and sells low, which can gradually reduce returns. Futures-based ETFs may lag Bitcoin's spot price over time, even if Bitcoin itself is rising. These products are often better suited for short-term or tactical traders than for long-term investors seeking straightforward price tracking.

Index and Basket Products: Diversifying Exposure to Digital Assets

As digital asset markets expanded, many investors looked for a way to participate without selecting individual cryptocurrencies or continually adjusting positions. Index and basket products address this need by grouping multiple digital assets into a single, rules-based investment.

Indexes define which assets are included, how they are weighted, and when changes occur. Asset managers use these benchmarks to create investable products such as ETFs, funds, or separately managed accounts. For example, the CoinDesk Indices CoinDesk Market Index is designed to track the broad digital asset market and serves as the foundation for diversified crypto funds. S&P Dow Jones Indices and MSCI also maintain digital asset indexes that asset managers use when constructing regulated products.

These index products allow investors to gain broad exposure to digital assets without choosing individual tokens or actively managing positions. A single purchase provides access to a diversified basket, much like a stock market index fund. For example, the Bitwise 10 Crypto Index Fund (BITW) holds a rules-based group of the largest digital assets, giving investors broad market coverage through one position. These products are typically available through standard brokerage accounts and are managed to stay aligned with their underlying index, adjusting holdings over time as the market changes.

Not all digital asset indexes are built the same. Market-cap weighted indices allocate exposure based on the size of each asset's market value. Bitcoin and Ethereum typically dominate these indices, often representing the majority of the allocation. This approach reflects the market's consensus on relative importance and liquidity. Rules-based or thematic indices, by contrast, follow predefined criteria unrelated to market capitalization alone. These may target specific sectors such as smart contract platforms, decentralized finance, infrastructure, or digital asset equities.

DIGITAL ASSET-RELATED EQUITIES: INVESTING IN THE OPERATING COMPANIES, NOT THE CRYPTOCURRENCY

Another pathway to digital asset exposure does not involve owning digital assets at all. Instead, investors can allocate to publicly traded companies whose business models are directly tied to digital assets.

These investments sit one step removed from the underlying networks.

Miners

Bitcoin mining companies earn revenue by validating transactions and securing the Bitcoin network. In exchange for this work, miners receive newly issued Bitcoin and transaction fees. Their financial performance is influenced by several variables: the price of Bitcoin, network difficulty, energy costs, access to capital, and the efficiency of their hardware.

In Bitcoin's early years, miners played a more visible role in market dynamics. Because the ecosystem was smaller and liquidity thinner, miner selling could at times exert meaningful pressure on price. As Bitcoin has matured, however, this influence has diminished.

There are now many publicly traded Bitcoin mining companies, including MARA Holdings (MARA) Riot Platforms (RIOT), CleanSpark (CLSK), Hut 8 (HUT8), TeraWulf (WULF) and Bitfarms (BITF).

More recently, the sector has attracted politically connected and brand-driven entrants, including American Bitcoin, a Bitcoin mining company associated with the Trump business ecosystem that went public through a reverse merger with Gryphon Digital Mining. While structurally similar to other large-scale miners, its emergence highlights how Bitcoin mining has evolved from a niche technical activity into an arena that increasingly intersects with capital markets, politics, and public narratives. In addition to mining operations, American Bitcoin holds a significant Bitcoin treasury, positioning it as both a miner and a balance-sheet holder of the asset.[2]

Investors who own mining equities receive exposure to Bitcoin, often with amplified price movements due to operating leverage. However, that leverage cuts both ways.

Investing in Bitcoin miners today no longer means exposure to mining alone. As mining economics have become more challenging—driven by rising energy costs, increasing network difficulty, and the most competitive post-halving environment in Bitcoin's history—many miners have been forced to adapt.

Exchanges and Infrastructure Providers

Beyond mining, other public companies play critical roles in the digital asset economy. Exchanges generate revenue by facilitating trading, custody, and settlement of digital assets. Their fortunes tend to rise with trading volume, volatility, and overall market participation rather than with the price of any single token.

Infrastructure companies provide wallets, custody solutions, payment rails, data services, and enterprise blockchain tools. These firms often resemble traditional fintech or software businesses, with revenue models based on fees, subscriptions, or enterprise contracts rather than token issuance.

As the digital asset market has matured and adoption has expanded, a growing number of exchanges and infrastructure providers have entered the public markets. The most prominent publicly traded crypto-native exchange is Coinbase (COIN), which serves as a primary access point for institutional and retail investors. Other platforms with significant digital asset exposure include Robinhood (HOOD), which integrates digital assets alongside equities and options.

Figure 4.5 illustrates the rolling correlation between Bitcoin and Coinbase's stock price.

Over time, Coinbase's equity has become increasingly correlated with Bitcoin, reflecting the company's direct exposure to digital asset market activity. While Coinbase does not hold Bitcoin as a core operating asset, its revenues are closely tied to trading volumes and investor participation, which tend to rise and fall alongside Bitcoin.

Figure 4.5 Bitcoin price movements and Coinbase's stock have remained strongly linked, especially during major market swings.

Digital Asset Treasury Companies and Ecosystem Focused Operating Companies

A newer category of public market exposure has emerged within digital assets: digital asset treasury (DAT) companies. These companies hold significant reserves of digital assets, most commonly Bitcoin and, increasingly, Ethereum, Solana, and other tokens as part of their balance-sheet strategy.

These companies are not digital asset service providers in the traditional sense. They do not primarily mine, custody, or facilitate transactions.

Instead, they use digital assets as a treasury strategy, positioning Bitcoin or Ethereum as a long-term store of value, a hedge against currency debasement, or a core component of corporate capital allocation.

Many of these firms are publicly traded, and for some, the accumulation of digital assets has become a central strategic objective. They pursue this model for several reasons: to differentiate themselves in public markets, to gain leveraged exposure to digital asset price appreciation, and to offer investors a regulated equity-based vehicle that reflects strong, long-term conviction in digital assets.

As a result, their stock prices tend to reflect a combination of factors:

- The market value of their digital asset holdings
- The company's use of leverage and overall capital structure
- Management's credibility and capital allocation discipline

This structure introduces an important distinction. Investors who invest in these stocks are not buying Bitcoin or Ethereum directly. They are buying a corporate wrapper around digital asset exposure, complete with the benefits of liquidity, regulation, and equity market access, but also the risks inherent in operating businesses, debt financing, and managerial decision-making.

The Strategy Model: From Experiment to Category

The treasury model gained prominence in 2020, when Michael Saylor transformed his business intelligence firm, MicroStrategy (MSTR)—later rebranded as Strategy—into a Bitcoin-focused treasury vehicle. The company began converting its cash reserves into Bitcoin, later issuing equity and debt to accelerate accumulation, while publicly committing to a long-term holding strategy.

That move ignited a broader trend. Since then, dozens of public companies have adopted similar approaches, collectively amassing a meaningful share of Bitcoin's circulating supply. What began as an unconventional treasury decision has evolved into a competitive dynamic—an arms race of sorts—among companies seeking to build scale, visibility, and leverage through digital asset accumulation.

Some large, established companies. including Tesla and Block, have also added Bitcoin to their corporate treasuries, though digital assets represent a smaller portion of their balance sheets and are not the core business strategy.

Alongside these firms, a more specialized group of companies has emerged whose primary business strategy is the accumulation of digital assets, making their equity performance closely tied to changes in digital asset prices.

How Investors Value Digital Asset Treasury Companies

DAT companies are often evaluated using a metric called mNAV, or *market net asset value*, alongside more familiar measures such as stock price and earnings.

What mNAV means

mNAV represents the current value of a company's digital asset holdings, minus its liabilities, expressed on a per-share basis. Put simply, it answers the following question: *Is the market paying a premium for the company, or valuing it below the digital assets on its balance sheet?*

mNAV is expressed as a ratio:

- mNAV = 1.0 means the market values the company roughly in line with its digital asset holdings.

- mNAV > 1.0 means the stock is trading at a premium and investors are paying more than the current asset value because they believe the company can grow assets per share.
- mNAV < 1.0 means the stock is trading at a discount because investors value the company for less than its current asset base, often reflecting concerns about leverage, dilution, or strategy.[3]

Key Investor Takeaway

DATs resemble financial vehicles rather than simple holding companies. mNAV helps anchor downside expectations, while any premium reflects confidence in the company's execution and long-term strategy. If those expectations are not met, valuations tend to move back toward mNAV = 1, as the market re-anchors the company's value to its underlying assets.

The key takeaway is that DATs sit between two worlds. They are neither direct ownership of digital assets nor traditional operating companies. Their valuation reflects both what they own today and what investors believe they can build over time.

Beyond Bitcoin: Ethereum, Solana, and Altcoin Treasury Companies

More recently, the treasury model has expanded beyond Bitcoin.

A growing number of publicly traded companies have adopted Ethereum- and Solana-focused treasury strategies, holding these assets on their balance sheets as long-term strategic positions rather than operating inputs.

Examples include:

- SharpLink (SBET) and BitMine Immersion Technologies (BMNR), both of which have built substantial Ethereum holdings, offering equity-market exposure to ETH rather than direct token ownership.

- Forward Industries (FWDI), which has pursued a Solana-focused treasury strategy, accumulating SOL and deploying it through staking and on-chain activities.

While smaller in scale than Bitcoin-focused treasury companies, these companies represent an important evolution of the model, signaling that digital asset treasury strategies are no longer limited to a single network.

TRADING DERIVATIVES: EXPOSURE WITHOUT OWNERSHIP

Many of the public market products discussed so far, particularly futures-based ETFs, are built on a deeper layer of financial infrastructure: derivatives.

In traditional financial markets, derivatives trading volumes routinely exceed activity in underlying spot markets, reflecting their role in hedging, price discovery, and risk management rather than direct ownership. Derivatives are also often the first instruments regulators approve when a new asset class begins to institutionalize.

Digital assets have followed the same path. Long before spot ETFs existed, regulated futures and options provided a way for professional investors to gain exposure, hedge risk, and manage volatility without holding the underlying asset. As shown in Figure 4.6, Bitcoin trading volumes are now dominated by derivatives markets. Among derivatives products, perpetual futures account for the largest share of activity (see Figure 4.7).

Figure 4.6 Bitcoin trading volume is dominated by derivatives, with perpetual futures consistently accounting for most daily activity.

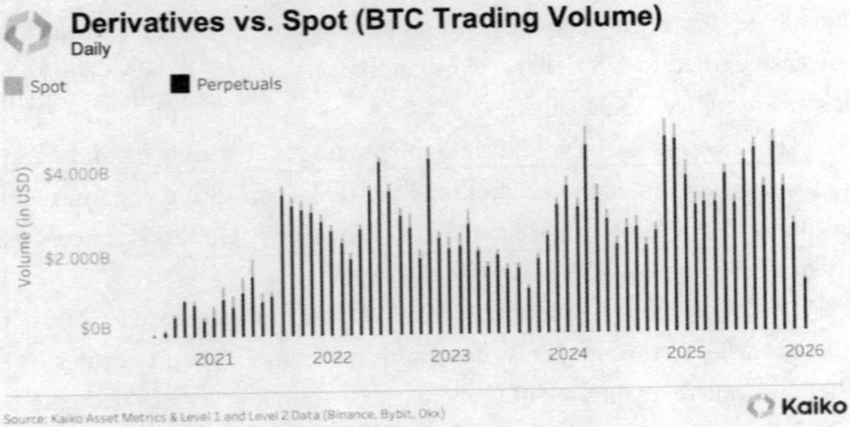

Figure 4.7 Bitcoin derivatives trading is overwhelmingly driven by perpetual futures, with options accounting for a small share of total volume.

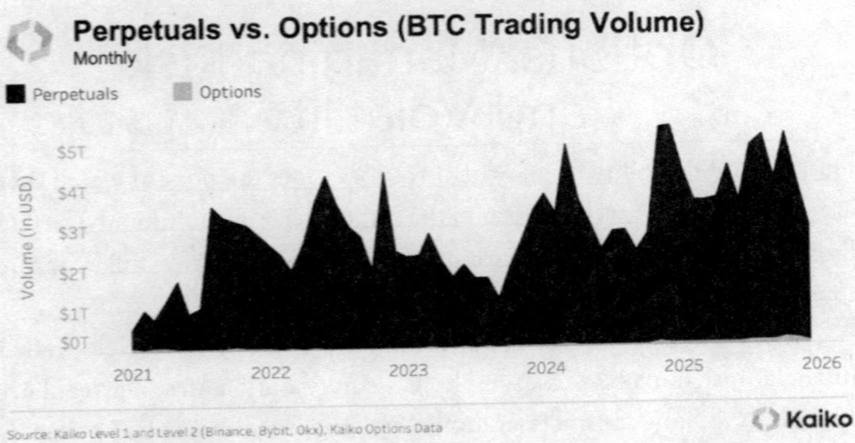

Futures: The Foundation Layer

The most established digital assets derivatives in traditional markets are futures contracts. On regulated venues such as the Chicago Mercantile Exchange (CME), investors can trade Bitcoin and Ethereum futures that are cash-settled in US dollars. No digital assets change hands. Gains and losses are settled financially.

These contracts serve multiple purposes. Asset managers and hedge funds use them to express directional views. Miners and companies with cryptocurrency exposure use them to hedge price risk. Market makers use them to provide liquidity and price discovery.

This same futures market underpins many futures-based ETFs discussed earlier in the chapter. When an investor buys a Bitcoin futures ETF, they are not accessing a different market—they are accessing the same CME futures contracts through a familiar wrapper.

This connection reinforces why futures-based products may behave differently from spot-based products over time. The divergence does not come from digital assets themselves, but from the mechanics of rolling futures contracts forward.

Options: Managing Risk and Volatility

Options add flexibility by allowing investors to set the price at which they are willing to buy or sell an asset in the future. They are commonly used to limit losses, lock in gains, or earn income, without requiring full exposure to price movements.

In traditional markets, options are among the most actively traded financial instruments. For example, US equity options trading regularly exceeds 10 billion contracts in annual volume, with major ETFs such as SPDR S&P 500 ETF Trust (SPY) and Invesco QQQ Trust (QQQ) routinely seeing millions of contracts traded on a typical day.[4]

By comparison, the cryptocurrency options market is smaller but growing rapidly. Combined Bitcoin and Ethereum options across major exchanges have averaged around $3 billion in daily notional trading volume in recent years—only a fraction of traditional equity options volumes but substantial for a nascent derivatives ecosystem.[5]

Open interest—the total value of outstanding contracts—on Bitcoin options alone has expanded toward $80 billion, rivaling the scale of crypto futures for the first time and underscoring increasing institutional engagement.[6]

More recently, the market has evolved again. With the approval of spot Bitcoin and Ethereum ETFs, investors can now trade options on those ETFs through mainstream brokerage platforms, including Robinhood. This marks an important shift. For the first time, cryptocurrency volatility is accessible through the same options infrastructure investors already use for stocks and equity ETFs.

A Deep Dive on Perps

Perpetual futures, commonly called perps, are digital-asset–native derivatives that allow traders to gain price exposure without an expiration date. Unlike traditional futures, which settle on fixed dates, perps can be held indefinitely as long as sufficient margin is maintained.

Perps were popularized by digital asset derivatives exchange BitMEX, which introduced a structure that replaces contract expiration with a funding rate. This funding rate periodically shifts payments between long and short traders, helping keep perp prices closely aligned with the spot market. Since their introduction, perpetual futures have grown into an enormous market by trading volume (see Figure 4.8).

Figure 4.8 Monthly perpetual futures volume on centralized exchanges.

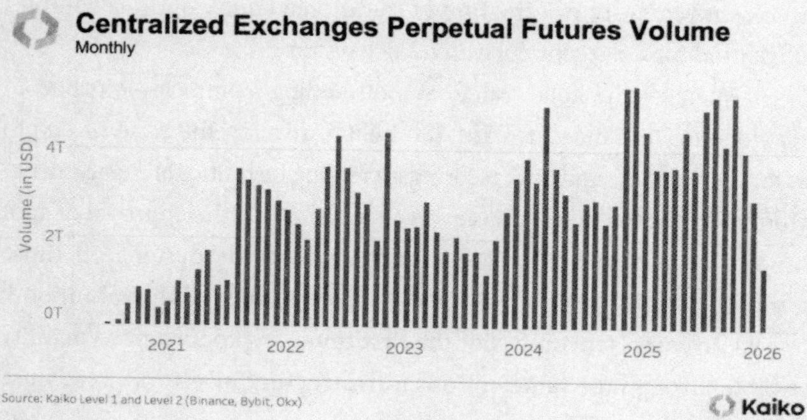

What makes perps distinct is their combination of features: 24/7 trading, easy long and short exposure, no contract rollovers, and significantly higher leverage than traditional regulated futures. These traits make perps highly capital-efficient and attractive to active traders, but also unforgiving, as small price moves can trigger rapid liquidations.

Because of these features, perps are overwhelmingly a digital asset-native phenomenon. Most trading volume occurs on centralized digital asset exchanges such as Binance, OKX, and Bybit, as well as decentralized platforms like Hyperliquid, Aster, and dYdX. A centralized exchange is operated by a company that acts as an intermediary, holding custody of user assets. A decentralized exchange allows users to trade directly from their own wallets using smart contracts, without a central custodian.

In the United States, retail access is generally restricted under current regulatory frameworks, while international markets permit broader participation.

What Exists—and What Doesn't

Despite this progress, traditional regulated markets remain conservative by design. Derivatives coverage is largely limited to Bitcoin and Ethereum on regulated exchanges. Products such as perpetual swaps, spot token options, and derivatives on smaller cryptocurrencies remain concentrated on crypto-native exchanges like Deribit, Binance, Coinbase, and Kraken rather than traditional venues alongside over-the-counter (OTC) solutions.

Outside the United States, the structure can differ. In Europe and other jurisdictions, cryptocurrency ETPs and notes often track Bitcoin or Ethereum using futures or structured derivatives, and in some cases options are available depending on the exchange. While these products may not always be labeled as derivatives to retail users, the exposure is still fundamentally derivative-based.

This reflects a familiar pattern. Public markets typically expand depth only after liquidity, regulatory clarity, and institutional demand are firmly established.

The Great Crash of October 10, 2025—What it Was And How Derivatives Played A Role

On October 10, 2025, digital asset markets saw their largest forced sell-off on record. In about one day, more than $19 billion of leveraged trades were automatically closed.

The trigger was a sudden global shock. News of possible 100% US tariffs on Chinese imports led investors to sell risky assets quickly.[7] That selling spilled into digital asset markets before public markets reopened the following Monday.

Bitcoin fell about 14%, dropping from roughly $122,000 to near $105,000 before stabilizing. Ethereum and many smaller tokens fell even more. In the weeks that followed, digital asset markets would erase more than $1 trillion in value, with Bitcoin briefly trading below $80,000.

This was not caused by a hack or an exchange failure. It was driven by leverage. Many traders had borrowed money to increase their positions. As prices fell, exchanges automatically closed those positions to limit losses. Each forced sale pushed prices lower, setting off more liquidations.

More than 1.6 million traders were affected. Long positions—bets that prices would rise—made up most of the losses.

In simple terms:

> A sudden shock caused prices to fall. Heavy borrowing turned that drop into a chain reaction of forced selling, making the decline much worse than it would have been otherwise.

How to Think About Derivatives in Digital Assets

Derivatives are not a separate path so much as the plumbing beneath many public market digital asset products.

They allow investors to:

- Gain exposure without custody
- Leverage or hedge existing positions
- Access digital asset volatility through familiar tools
- Receive additional yield via delta neutral or arbitrage

Understanding this layer helps investors see what they actually own, how risk is transferred, and why different public-market digital asset instruments behave the way they do.

Today, traditional markets let investors trade digital assets mainly through Bitcoin and Ethereum futures and options on regulated venues like the CME, as well as through ETFs and ETPs that may themselves have listed options, now including options on spot Bitcoin ETFs available via platforms like Robinhood. These products allow investors to trade price direction or volatility without holding digital assets, but they still represent a narrower and more cautious slice of the digital assets market compared to what exists on crypto-native exchanges.

THE NEXT TRADING FRONTIER: PREDICTION MARKETS

> *"Prediction markets will become an important part of market infrastructure and decision-making in the next four-to-five years."*
>
> —Dr. Nagendra Bharatula, Founder and CEO, G-20 Group

One of the more distinctive innovations to emerge from blockchain markets is the rise of decentralized prediction markets. These platforms allow participants to trade directly on the outcomes of real-world events, without relying on a centralized bookmaker or intermediary.

Among the most prominent examples is Polymarket, a prediction platform built on the Polygon protocol. Polymarket gained widespread attention during the lead-up to the 2024 US presidential election, when its markets consistently reflected a higher probability of a Donald Trump victory well before the outcome was settled.

That episode highlighted a broader insight. When participants commit capital rather than opinions, prices can become a powerful signal of collective belief. In that sense, prediction markets function less like traditional gambling venues and more like real-time forecasting tools, translating dispersed information into continuously updated probabilities.

Not all prediction markets behave the same way. Prediction market activity today is overwhelmingly concentrated in sports betting, which accounts for roughly 70% of total volume. The reason is structural: sporting events have clear outcomes, fixed end dates, and decades of historical data. That depth of data allows for systematic modeling, simulation, and repeatable trading strategies.

By contrast, macroeconomic and political events are much harder to trade. Each election, policy decision, or geopolitical shock is effectively a new data point, limiting the usefulness of historical analogs. This makes political and macro prediction markets more fragile and more vulnerable to narrative-driven trading rather than disciplined risk management.

Prediction markets are therefore most informative when traditional data is scarce or delayed, but they are also susceptible to coordinated positioning or uneven participation. This dual nature is why they are increasingly viewed as signals to be interpreted, not forecasts to be followed blindly.

Beyond politics and sports, these markets now span a wide range of use cases, including macroeconomic data releases, policy decisions, corporate actions, and even future prices of digital assets themselves which can be one leg of a trading strategy. Participation has expanded beyond retail users to include traders, researchers, and funds seeking faster signals than those provided by surveys or delayed market data.

Prediction markets are beginning to move beyond niche platforms and into the broader financial system. What started as small, experimental markets is now being woven into tools and channels that investors already use. Platforms such as Kalshi and Polymarket have partnered with Google to display market-implied probabilities directly within Google Finance. Instead of searching for specialized websites, users can now see how markets are pricing the likelihood of events alongside stocks, bonds, and economic data.

Access is also expanding through traditional investing platforms. Kalshi's integration with Robinhood allows retail investors to participate in regulated prediction markets within a familiar brokerage interface, lowering the barrier to entry and normalizing these products as part of everyday market activity.

Institutional interest is growing as well. Intercontinental Exchange, the owner of the New York Stock Exchange, has announced plans to invest up to $2 billion in Polymarket. This signals that prediction markets are no longer viewed solely as crypto-native experiments but as potential components of core market infrastructure.

Regulatory treatment, however, remains uneven. In the United States, access is limited and tightly controlled, with platforms like Kalshi operating under formal regulatory oversight. Many crypto-native prediction markets operate offshore and restrict participation by US users. As these markets grow, how they are regulated—and where—will play a central role in determining how widely they are adopted.

HOW THESE PATHWAYS FIT TOGETHER

Each public market pathway offers exposure to digital assets through a different lens:

- Spot ETFs provide direct price exposure without operational complexity
- Index and basket products offer diversification and rule-based discipline
- Crypto-related equities introduce leverage, and management decisions
- Derivatives to gain leverage or extra yield

None is inherently superior. Each reflects a different balance between simplicity, control, and risk. But they are all accessible via existing investment channels that most investors use, including brokers, retirement accounts, or fintechs like Robinhood and Revolut.

For many investors, these instruments are not substitutes, but complements. A single portfolio might hold a spot Bitcoin ETF for core price exposure, an index product for diversified participation across the broader market, and a small allocation to cryptocurrency-related equities that reflect business growth and operating leverage. Derivatives may be used sparingly by experienced traders to hedge risk, manage volatility, or adjust exposure without changing long-term holdings.

Taken together, these tools allow digital assets to sit alongside stocks, bonds, and commodities inside the same brokerage account. They are traded, reported, and governed under the same compliance, risk, and oversight frameworks that investors already use for traditional investments, without requiring new custody systems, operational workflows, or on-chain activity.

Bitcoin and Ethereum as Public Market Anchors

Although millions of cryptocurrencies exist, public market access to digital assets centers on just two: Bitcoin and Ethereum. This is not a judgment about innovation elsewhere in the ecosystem. It reflects how public markets operate.

Public markets favor assets that are large, liquid, and proven across multiple market cycles. Bitcoin and Ethereum are the only digital assets that consistently meet those standards. Bitcoin's market value exceeded $2 trillion in 2025, while Ethereum peaked above $500 billion. Both have remained dominant through repeated booms and downturns.

Just as important, both networks have endured stress. Bitcoin has fallen more than 70% several times and still recovered to new highs. Ethereum has weathered similar declines while completing major upgrades without disrupting the network. Many other digital assets that surged during individual cycles did not survive the next one.

Because of their size, liquidity, and track record, Bitcoin and Ethereum support regulated custody, derivatives, and exchange-traded products at scale. Their markets can absorb large flows, trade continuously, and meet regulatory standards for oversight and risk management. That is why futures contracts, ETFs, and options were built around them first.

They are also the only digital assets with consistent institutional research coverage, providing shared reference points for investors, regulators, and risk committees. Firms such as JPMorgan and Goldman Sachs regularly publish reports analyzing Bitcoin and Ethereum market structure, network activity, adoption trends, and valuation frameworks. This depth of coverage reinforces their role as benchmark assets, giving allocators, regulators, and risk committees a shared reference point that does not yet exist for most other digital assets.

What Is Bitcoin Dominance?

Bitcoin dominance measures Bitcoin's share of the total digital asset market. It is calculated as Bitcoin's market capitalization divided by the total market capitalization of all digital assets.

Historically, Bitcoin dominance has served as a useful signal of investor behavior within digital asset markets (see Figure 4.9). Since 2020, a clear pattern has emerged: dominance tends to rise during periods of uncertainty or risk aversion, when capital retreats into Bitcoin as the most liquid and established asset. Conversely, dominance often declines during speculative phases—commonly referred to as "altcoin seasons"—when investors take on more risk and rotate into smaller tokens.

Over time, however, the signal has become more nuanced. The growth of stablecoins, decentralized finance, NFTs, and multiple layer-1 networks has expanded the market well beyond Bitcoin

Figure 4.9 Bitcoin's share of the overall digital asset market—known as "Bitcoin dominance"—since 2011.

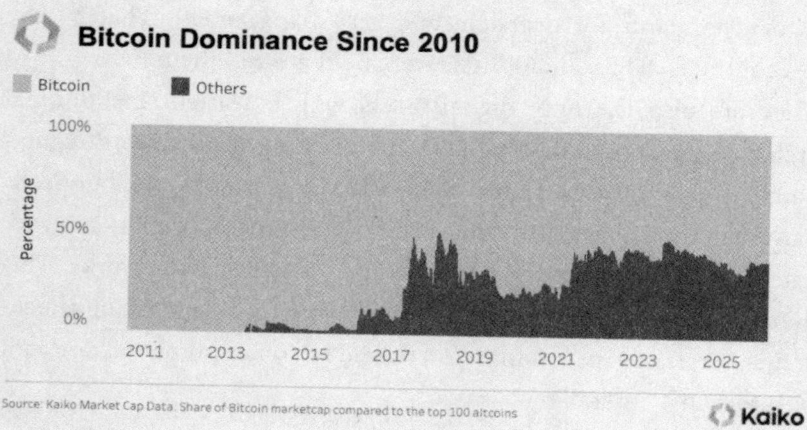

alone. As a result, Bitcoin dominance today is used less as a tool for predicting price direction and more as an indicator of capital rotation, showing where risk is being taken, reduced, or concentrated within the digital asset ecosystem.

Why Most ETFs and Indexes Start Here

ETF sponsors and index providers face constraints that do not exist in crypto-native markets. They must demonstrate sufficient liquidity, transparent pricing, reliable custody, and resistance to manipulation. They must also satisfy regulators that the underlying market can support large, long-term investment vehicles.

Bitcoin and Ethereum clear those hurdles. Most other assets do not—at least not yet.

As a result, broad "digital asset market" indices are often heavily weighted toward Bitcoin and Ethereum, even when they include many constituents. Similarly, the earliest and largest ETFs focus on these two assets, either directly or through derivatives.

In public markets, inclusion is not a judgment about technological merit. It is a judgment about readiness.

When (and Why) Investors Stop at Bitcoin and Ethereum

For many investors, Bitcoin and Ethereum are sufficient.

They offer exposure to the two most established use cases in digital assets: decentralized money and programmable infrastructure. Together, they capture the majority of network value, institutional interest, and long-term capital allocated to the space.

For investors seeking simplicity, clarity, liquidity, and long-term participation, stopping here is a rational choice. The incremental diversification gained by adding smaller assets may not justify the additional volatility, complexity, or tracking error introduced by more specialized products.

Public markets, by design, make it easy to stop early.

When Investors Go Beyond BTC and ETH

Many investors, however, choose to expand beyond these anchors.

This typically happens for one of two reasons. The first is diversification. As the ecosystem matures, investors may seek exposure to different technological approaches, geographic adoption patterns, or use cases not fully captured by Bitcoin and Ethereum alone.

The second is conviction. Investors with stronger views on specific networks, sectors, or adoption narratives may use index products or thematic ETFs to express those beliefs without selecting individual tokens directly.

Assets such as Solana or XRP may appear in these products not because they replace Bitcoin or Ethereum, but because they represent distinct segments of the digital asset landscape. In practice, exposure to these assets is often limited by liquidity, market depth, whether their tokens have been completely distributed, and regulatory considerations. They are more commonly included through diversified baskets rather than as standalone public market products.

Public markets expand access cautiously. In the United States, spot ETFs initially focused on Bitcoin and Ethereum because they met key regulatory criteria: deep liquidity, established futures markets, transparent pricing, and robust market surveillance. ETFs tied to other digital assets are now beginning to move through the approval process, but availability remains limited and incremental in the United States.

Public markets allow investors to go beyond Bitcoin and Ethereum, but they do so deliberately, prioritizing scale and regulatory clarity over speed. Investors seeking broader exposure must be prepared to do the work themselves.

WHAT PUBLIC MARKETS DO WELL—AND WHAT THEY DON'T

Public markets have played a critical role in making digital assets accessible to a broad range of investors. They translate a new asset class into familiar formats—ETFs, equities, and regulated instruments—lowering the barrier to entry and reducing operational friction.

At the same time, public markets are not neutral conduits. They shape what investors can access, how they participate, and which aspects of the digital asset ecosystem remain out of reach.

Understanding both sides of that trade-off is essential.

What Public Markets Do Well

- Simplicity and Accessibility: Public-market products make digital asset investing easy to initiate and easy to manage. Investors can buy, hold, and sell exposure using brokerage accounts they already have, without learning new interfaces, managing private keys, or navigating blockchain-specific processes.

- Regulatory Clarity: Public markets operate within established regulatory frameworks. Products are subject to disclosure requirements, custody standards, reporting rules, and oversight mechanisms designed to protect investors. While regulation does not eliminate risk, it clarifies where responsibility lies. Investors know who the custodian is, how assets are safeguarded, and which rules govern the product.
- Integration with Traditional Portfolios and Retirement Accounts: Public market cryptocurrency exposure integrates with traditional portfolio construction. ETFs, equities, and derivatives can be held alongside stocks, bonds, and commodities, reported on the same statements, and evaluated using the same risk and performance metrics. In many cases, these products are also eligible for retirement accounts (401ks and IRAs), allowing long-term investors to gain exposure within tax-advantaged structures that are otherwise inaccessible to direct digital asset ownership.

Can I Put Digital Assets Into a 401(K)?

Yes—but access is still limited.

Some retirement plans offer self-directed brokerage windows that allow participants to buy regulated digital-asset ETFs, including spot Bitcoin and Ethereum ETFs. Large providers such as Charles Schwab, Fidelity, and Vanguard support these brokerage windows. Whether an individual can use them depends on the employer and the plan sponsor.

Outside standard employer plans, self-directed IRAs and solo 401(k)s provide another option. These accounts can allow direct exposure to digital assets through specialized custodians such as Kingdom Trust, Bitcoin IRA, Broad Financial, iTrustCapital, and Bitcoin IRA. These structures permit digital-asset ownership, but they are not part of most employer-sponsored 401(k) offerings.[8]

Momentum toward broader inclusion is building. In August 2025, President Donald Trump signed an executive order aimed at expanding access to alternative assets, including digital assets, across retirement plans.[9]

What would need to change?

Expanding digital-asset access in retirement plans does not require new legislation, but it does require regulatory change. While the SEC oversees the investment products that could be offered, the Department of Labor regulates retirement plans under ERISA. Revising the Department of Labor's 2022 guidance, which urged plan sponsors to exercise "extreme care" with digital assets, is the key step. With clearer fiduciary standards and continued SEC oversight of regulated vehicles such as spot Bitcoin and Ethereum ETFs, plan sponsors could include digital assets in 401(k)s and pensions, most likely through professionally managed funds rather than direct token ownership.

What Public Markets Don't Do Well

The strengths of public markets are also their constraints.

- No Native Yield (Yet): Public market products typically provide price exposure only. They do not capture directly on-chain yield from staking, lending, or protocol participation. Any income generated by the underlying network is either excluded or absorbed within the product structure rather than passed through directly to investors. Over time, as regulatory frameworks evolve and more staking ETFs get approved in the United States, some of these limitations may narrow, but for now, direct yield remains largely an on-chain feature.

- Due to the volatility of digital assets and regulatory constraints, investors face restrictions on margin trading and borrowing in public markets. Regulators set maximum leverage, exchanges identify risk parameters, clearinghouses manage systemic safety, and brokers ultimately determine the margin actually available to investors. Today on certain trading platforms investors can buy IBIT on margin but not Bitcoin.
- No Protocol Participation: Investors in public market vehicles do not interact with the networks themselves. They cannot use decentralized applications, provide liquidity, or engage with smart contracts. Exposure is financial, not functional.

USING PUBLIC MARKETS AS A FIRST STEP, NOT A FINAL DESTINATION

For many investors, public markets represent an entry point into digital assets rather than an endpoint.

For some investors, public-market exposure will remain sufficient. For others, it becomes the foundation for more direct engagement. Both paths are valid, and both begin with clarity about what public markets do—and do not—provide.

Direct ownership, whether held in a personal wallet or through an exchange, gives investors the most control. Investors hold the asset itself, can move it freely, and can choose how to use it. That control comes with responsibility. Investors are responsible for security, access, and mistakes. Lost keys, failed transfers, or poor custody decisions can result in permanent losses.

Public market instruments shift that responsibility elsewhere. ETFs, equities, and derivatives remove the need to manage wallets, private keys, or on-chain transactions. Instead, investors rely on custodians, fund managers, clearinghouses, and brokers to hold assets, track prices, and manage risk. The experience is simpler, but investors trade direct control for trust in financial intermediaries and product structures.

Neither approach is risk-free. Direct ownership can fail due to user error or security breaches. Public market exposure can fall short due to counterparty risk, tracking differences, or structural limits built into the product. The key difference is not whether risk exists, but where it sits—and who bears the consequences when something goes wrong.

INVESTOR TAKEAWAY

By now, the public market menu should feel familiar: you can buy a spot ETF to track Bitcoin or Ethereum, use an index/basket product to spread risk across several assets, buy crypto-linked stocks to bet on companies in the ecosystem, or use futures/options if you understand how those contracts behave.

Before you buy anything, make one concrete decision first: *Are you trying to own the asset, or just track its price?*

Use this checklist:

- ☐ If you want simplicity: start with a spot Bitcoin ETF or a spot Ethereum ETF. You're tracking the price, inside a normal brokerage account, without wallets.
- ☐ If you want broader coverage without picking winners: use an index or basket product (and expect Bitcoin and Ethereum to be a big part of it).

- ☐ If you want a business bet, not a coin bet: use crypto-related equities (miners, exchanges, treasury companies). Just remember: company risks (debt, costs, management decisions) can matter as much as Bitcoin's price.
- ☐ If you're considering futures-based products or options: treat them as tools, not default holdings. They can behave differently than the underlying asset, especially over time.

The practical value of public markets is that they let you participate using familiar accounts and rules. The trade-off is that many of these vehicles track digital assets rather than letting you own and use them directly, and that difference shapes returns and risk.

Public markets are only one lane. The next chapter moves earlier in the lifecycle—private market investing, where returns come less from tracking prices and more from backing the companies building the ecosystem through venture and seed rounds, as well as private and liquid funds that actively trade and manage exposure.

CHAPTER FIVE

INVESTING IN PRIVATE MARKETS

FUNDS OF FUNDS, VENTURE FUNDS, AND LIQUID FUNDS

Most investors enter digital assets through public markets, buying them directly on exchanges. For those just starting out, there are other ways to gain exposure. Investors can allocate to fund-of-funds focused on digital assets, closed-end vehicles such as venture funds, or open-ended structures like liquid funds and hedge funds. Each approach offers a different mix of risk, liquidity, and time horizon.

Digital asset fund-of-funds are structured much like their traditional counterparts. Instead of investing directly in tokens or protocols, they allocate capital across a group of underlying managers. These may include venture funds, liquid hedge funds, or multi-strategy funds. The objective is diversification: spreading exposure across managers and approaches rather than relying on a single bet.

By investing in multiple funds, a digital asset fund-of-funds provides broad exposure to different parts of the ecosystem. Depending on its mandate, that exposure may include early-stage venture investments, actively traded token portfolios, decentralized finance strategies, or market-neutral approaches. For investors, this structure offers access to managers, strategies, and deal flow that can be difficult to reach directly, along with centralized oversight of risk, reporting, and allocation decisions.

Venture funds in the digital asset space invest in startups. They typically operate at the earliest stages, often before a token exists or before a company has proven its business model. This is where infrastructure is built, teams are formed, and ideas are tested long before markets assign a daily price.

Access to startups is rarely simple. Information is incomplete. Capital is typically locked up for years with uncertain outcomes. For most investors, participation happens indirectly, through funds of funds or directly in venture funds who source deals, conduct diligence, and structure investments on behalf of limited partners.[1]

Like traditional venture capital, private digital asset investing follows a power-law distribution. A small number of investments account for the majority of returns, while most deliver modest outcomes or fail entirely.

This dynamic is visible even in hindsight: an investor exposed to Solana at the pre-seed stage, before the network launched and adoption was uncertain, faced a high probability of loss but extraordinary upside, while a seed-stage investment came with a higher valuation, lower uncertainty, and a narrower range of outcomes. In both cases, the eventual result mattered far more than timing precision.

This shapes everything. Patience matters more than timing. Manager selection matters more than deal volume. Diversification across many early-stage bets is not optional—it is essential.

It also explains why direct angel investing is difficult for most individuals. Without access to consistent deal flow or the ability to build a sufficiently broad portfolio, investors are often making isolated bets in a market where the majority of outcomes go to zero. Success depends less on identifying a single promising asset and more on having enough exposure for a rare outlier to carry the portfolio.

Between public markets and venture capital sits a growing middle ground: liquid funds. These funds are often structured like hedge funds and focus primarily on digital assets that are already traded in the market, such as established tokens. Rather than backing startups years before they reach the public eye, liquid funds invest after a network has launched and a token has begun trading. This places them between the long-time horizons of venture investing and the daily price exposure of public markets.

Liquid funds are typically more active than venture funds even though venture funds end up with a lot of liquid tokens on their balance sheet. Managers may adjust positions as markets change, seek opportunities across different tokens, or focus on generating income through lending, staking, or other market-based strategies.

One of the defining features of liquid funds is flexibility. Unlike venture funds, which often require capital to be locked up for many years, liquid funds usually offer periodic opportunities to redeem capital. This liquidity allows investors to rebalance portfolios, respond to changing market conditions, or access capital when needed.

For many investors, liquid funds serve as a bridge. They provide more sophistication and active management than simply buying tokens outright, while avoiding the long lockups and high uncertainty of early-stage venture investing.

As the digital asset market has matured, many established digital asset-focused venture firms have expanded into liquid strategies alongside their venture businesses. Firms such as Pantera Capital and Polychain Capital now operate across both private and public markets. This reflects a simple reality of digital assets: networks move from idea to launch to active trading faster than in traditional markets. Managing across both stages allows firms to stay involved throughout that lifecycle, while offering investors different ways to balance return potential, liquidity, and risk.

By the end of this chapter, you will gain a clear understanding of:

- How digital asset funds of funds, venture funds, and liquid funds operate and how they differ from traditional venture capital and hedge funds
- The risk, return, and time horizons of investing in fund of funds, venture funds, and hedge funds
- How to think about due diligence specific to digital assets

INVESTING THROUGH A DIGITAL ASSET FUND OF FUNDS

"LPs in a fund-of-funds often seek asymmetric return profiles with low long-term correlation to traditional markets, akin to owning an out-of-the-money option."

—Ray Hindi, Managing Partner, L1D

By now, it should be clear that investing in digital assets isn't about making a single bet. The market includes early-stage companies, liquid assets that trade nonstop, trading strategies that behave very differently from one cycle to the next, and financial infrastructure that is still being built.

That mix creates opportunity—and often difficulty. Participating thoughtfully means deciding not just what to own, but how to manage custody, liquidity, regulation, and operational risk along the way. Doing all of that directly, across multiple strategies, is more work than most investors expect.

A fund of funds exists to solve that problem.

Instead of choosing individual assets or committing to one manager, a fund of funds spreads capital across several teams with different approaches. One may focus on early-stage investing, another on liquid markets, another on trading strategies. The goal isn't to guess which part of the market will outperform next, but to stay invested as the market changes.

Funds of funds offer a simple way to participate without selecting individual venture managers. Instead of choosing one or two funds, investors place capital with a firm that builds and manages a portfolio of funds on their behalf.

Firms such as Accolade Partners, L1D, Aspen Digital, and Theta Capital Management invest across a range of digital asset strategies. These may include early-stage venture funds focused on building new networks, as well as funds that trade more actively in liquid markets. Some also make selective direct investments, as SkyBridge Capital, led by Anthony Scaramucci, did when it became the first outside investor in BlackRock's Bitcoin ETF.

A fund of funds collects money from investors and uses it to invest in several underlying funds rather than in startups or tokens directly. The firm selects managers, reviews their approach, tracks results, and adjusts the mix over time as the market changes. Some funds of funds focus mainly on long-term venture investing, while others combine venture with more liquid strategies and hedge funds.

For investors, the benefit is delegation. Choosing strong digital asset venture managers requires time, technical knowledge, and access to closed networks. A fund of funds takes on that responsibility and spreads capital across multiple managers rather than relying on a small number of bets. While this structure adds an extra layer of fees, many investors accept the trade-off in exchange for simplicity, diversification, and access.

In practice, fund-of-funds managers spend less time picking individual assets and more time selecting managers, constructing portfolios, buying secondary LP stakes, and monitoring performance. Results depend on the quality of the underlying managers and how well exposure is balanced across strategies, liquidity profiles, and market cycles. The trade-off is straightforward: professional diversification and simplicity in exchange for an additional layer of fees and less direct control.

What a Fund of Funds Actually Does

- It avoids single-manager dependence: Backing one fund means living with that manager's decisions, timing, and blind spots. A fund of funds reduces that risk by spreading capital across multiple managers with different styles and time horizons.
- It pays attention to what's really owned: Reported returns don't show concentration, liquidity, or shared risks across funds. A fund of funds looks at positions underneath the surface to understand where exposure overlaps and where risks may build.
- It provides access that's hard to replicate alone: Some of the strongest teams in this space don't accept new capital freely. Relationships matter, and capacity is limited. A fund of funds builds and maintains that access over time.
- It focuses on the boring but essential details: Many losses in this market have come from weak controls, poor custody, or counterparties failing at the wrong moment. A fund of funds spends a disproportionate amount of time on these issues, so investors don't have to learn through loss.

Why Not Invest Directly?

Some investors should. And some do.

Direct investments offer more control and lower fees, but they also demand time, experience, and constant attention. Evaluating managers, monitoring risk, and handling operational details quickly becomes a job in itself.

For investors who want exposure without building that machinery from scratch, a fund of funds offers a more measured entry point. It allows participation, learning, and adjustment over time rather than forcing a large commitment upfront.

Existing fund-of-funds platforms provide curated, risk-adjusted access to venture capital and liquid strategies.

A digital asset fund of funds exists because this market is still uneven and fast-moving. Outcomes are lopsided, risks are not always visible, and direct access to strong managers is limited.

Custody Was a Major Barrier to Institutional Crypto Adoption

Custody became a major obstacle for digital assets because investment rules were written for traditional financial assets, not digital bearer assets controlled by cryptographic keys. Under frameworks such as the US Investment Advisers Act and the Employee Retirement Income Security Act (ERISA), funds and advisors are generally required to use a qualified custodian—typically a bank, trust company, or registered broker-dealer that holds assets in segregated accounts, undergoes audits, meets capital requirements, and provides legal accountability in the event of loss or fraud.

For years, digital assets made compliance with these rules difficult. Early exchanges and wallet providers were not regulated custodians, did not reliably segregate client assets, and could not offer the legal protections regulators expected. Funds also could not self-custody assets, even if technically secure, because custody rules require independent oversight. Compounding the issue, regulators had not clearly stated whether digital assets could be held by a qualified custodian at all. As a result, many funds were effectively unable to hold digital assets regardless of investor demand.

This began to change through regulatory interpretation rather than new legislation. Securities regulators gradually accepted that state-chartered trust companies and bank-affiliated custodians could satisfy custody requirements for digital assets. Banking regulators reinforced this shift when the Office of the Comptroller of the Currency clarified in 2020 and 2021 that digital asset custody is a permissible banking activity. Over time, this stabilized the regulatory footing for bank-based custodians.

Today, a limited but meaningful group of companies, such as Coinbase Custody, BitGo Trust, Anchorage Digital Bank, Fidelity Digital Assets, and BNY Mellon for select services, operate under bank or trust charters. The approval of spot Bitcoin ETFs in 2024 further validated these models, as ETFs depend on qualified custodians and robust controls.

Together, these developments finally allowed funds to participate at scale. However, because the number of recognized crypto custodians remains small, custody continues to function as a structural chokepoint rather than a fully solved problem—shaping how and how quickly institutions adopt digital assets.

INVESTING IN DIGITAL ASSET-FOCUSED VENTURE CAPITAL FUNDS

"This is an asset class where you actually can have something like early liquidity. That's not a bad thing—it's actually a good thing."

—Kyle Samani, Chairman, Forward Industries

Most long-term value creation in digital assets happens before tokens trade publicly. The earliest innovation—new blockchains, core protocols, infrastructure layers, developer tools, wallets, and middleware—typically begins as private projects. By the time a token lists on an exchange, much of the foundational risk has already been taken, and the range of possible outcomes is narrower.

Venture capital funds play a central role at this stage. They provide early capital that allows teams to build products, hire engineers, run security audits, and operate through long development periods with little or no revenue. In digital assets, this funding often supports open-source protocols and network infrastructure that do not resemble traditional companies yet become essential to the broader ecosystem.

Venture capital has been highly active in the blockchain and digital asset space. Some of the largest traditional venture firms remain deeply committed: in early 2026, Andreessen Horowitz announced it raised over $15 billion across multiple new funds, one of the largest fundraising hauls in the industry and a signal of sustained institutional interest in foundational technologies, including digital assets.[2]

This area of digital asset investing remains highly specialized and continues to benefit from domain-specific expertise and information advantages. At the same time, the investor base is expanding, with fintech-focused venture firms entering the space alongside corporate venture arms from large institutions such as Coinbase and Franklin Templeton.

More granular data from Galaxy's research shows this interest reflected in recent deal activity: in the third quarter of 2025, venture capitalists invested roughly $4.65 billion into crypto and blockchain startups across more than 400 deals, the second-highest quarterly total since the downturn. Figure 5.1 provides a more detailed breakdown of crypto venture capital funding since 2016.

While overall activity remains below the peaks seen in the 2021 bull market, these figures highlight that capital continues to flow into the space and that allocators are deploying funds across both early-stage and later-stage opportunities.[3] Between 2017 and 2025, an estimated $115 billion was invested in digital asset startups.[4]

Digital asset venture capital also differs from traditional software or technology venture capital in important ways. Returns are often driven by networks and tokens, not just equity.

Figure 5.1 Venture capital funding in blockchain and digital asset projects peaked in 2021.

Source: Galaxy.

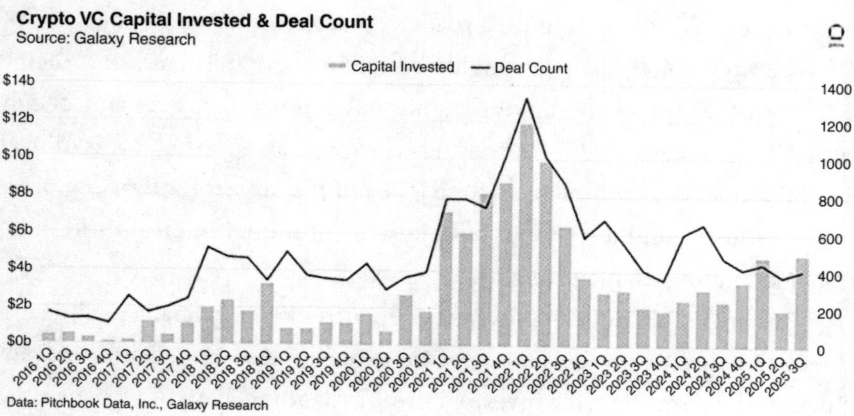

Liquidity events may also occur through token launches rather than acquisitions or IPOs, often much sooner, providing liquidity in the early years of a fund. This early liquidity is a distinctive trait of the crypto VC landscape. Imagine, instead of waiting 12 years for a startup to reach an IPO, seeing a liquidity event just three years after a pre-seed investment, sometimes at a multibillion-dollar market capitalization.

For most investors, accessing this early-stage innovation directly is impractical. Private digital asset deals require specialized legal structures, technical diligence, and deep founder networks. Minimum investment sizes are high, information is uneven, and failure rates are extreme. Venture funds address these challenges by pooling capital, diversifying across projects, and applying professional selection and oversight.

Data Point: Digital Asset VC Has Outperformed Traditional Venture Capital

A 2025 study by Cambridge Associates compared institutional-quality digital asset venture funds with traditional venture capital over the past decade.

What the data shows

- 5-year returns: ~19.7% net internal rate of return (IRR) for digital asset VC vs. 11.5% for traditional VC[5]
- 10-year returns: ~21.2% vs. 14.4%
- Top managers: Top-quartile digital asset VC funds delivered 24–25%+ net IRRs

Why this happened

- Early exposure to fast-growing digital asset networks and platforms

- Value creation at the ecosystem level, not just individual companies
- Strong asset price appreciation during early adoption cycles

Important context

- Results reflect a unique period of innovation and market growth
- Returns are highly uneven and driven by a small number of winners
- Performance depends heavily on timing and manager selection

Investor takeaway

Digital asset venture capital has delivered strong historical returns, but outcomes vary widely. Accessing this part of the market requires patience, tolerance for illiquidity, and careful manager selection—not broad exposure.

The Digital Asset Venture Capital Ecosystem

Venture capital in digital assets is not a single strategy. Funds differ in what they invest in, how early they invest, and how long money is committed. Those differences shape both risk and potential outcomes. For most investors, participation happens indirectly, either by investing in venture funds or by using funds of funds that invest across multiple managers.

Venture funds that started in the early days of crypto, such as Pantera Capital, Polychain Capital, a16z Crypto, Multicoin Capital, Paradigm, Blockchain capital, and Dragonfly, now run multibillion-dollar funds supporting innovation across various stages and verticals.

Pre-Seed and Seed Funds

Pre-seed and seed rounds are at the level of uncertainty. In many cases, there is no finished product, no revenue, and sometimes no issued token. These funds underwrite founders first—technical skill, credibility, and clarity of vision—because early design decisions around protocol architecture, token supply, and governance are difficult to reverse.

Early backers of Solana invested before the network was proven at scale and before its ecosystem existed. At the time, the bet was less about near-term adoption and more about whether the technology could support high-throughput applications and attract developers over time. As with most pre-seed and seed investments, outcomes were highly uneven: a small number of successes drove returns, while most projects failed to gain traction. Outcomes are highly skewed: a small number of successes drive returns, while most investments fail.

Later-stage funds tend to focus on more established parts of the digital asset ecosystem. Some concentrate on core infrastructure, others on user-facing applications, and several specialize even further by protocol, theme, or region. The common thread is that these funds invest once products are built, adoption is visible, and the path forward is clearer than at the earliest venture stage. We are seeing the emergence of PE type activity also developing although the sector remains constrained.

Infrastructure-Focused Funds

Infrastructure-focused funds invest in the foundations of the ecosystem: base blockchains, scaling solutions, developer tools, custody and security providers, data services, and middleware. These businesses often take longer to monetize, but they are less dependent on consumer trends and brand-driven adoption.

Early investments in companies like Alchemy or Chainlink paid off not because users recognized the brand, but because developers and applications quietly depended on them. Returns in this category are usually tied to overall network usage and ecosystem growth, with longer holding periods and steadier demand once adoption takes hold.

Application-Layer and Thematic Funds

Application-layer funds focus on products people actually use: trading platforms, games, marketplaces, payments, and social applications. These investments live closer to the end user, so adoption metrics—users, transactions, and retention—matter more than abstract network growth.

Examples include Uniswap in trading, OpenSea in collectibles, Axie Infinity in gaming, and Polymarket in on-chain forecasting. When these products work, growth can be fast. When sentiment shifts or competition intensifies, outcomes can reverse just as quickly.

Some funds narrow their focus further by betting on specific themes, such as gaming, payments, or decentralized finance, across multiple blockchains. Others concentrate on a single ecosystem. Colosseum, for example, focuses on early consumer and application projects built on Solana, giving investors concentrated exposure to that developer community.

There are also funds with a regional lens, investing where local knowledge matters most. Managers focused on India, Latin America, or Africa often look for adoption driven by real-world needs, such as limited banking access or cross-border payments, rather than speculative trends.

For investors, later-stage funds trade some upside for clarity. The risks are easier to see, the products are real, and the questions shift from "Will this exist?" to "How big can it get, and who wins?"

Why These Distinctions Matter

Fund structure determines:

- Where risk is concentrated (technical, market, or adoption risk)
- When liquidity may occur (token launch vs. acquisition or IPO)
- How returns are generated (network effects, token appreciation, or ecosystem growth)

Digital asset venture is not a single exposure—it is a collection of distinct strategies with very different risk and return profiles.

Case Study: When Governance, Not Markets, Breaks a Fund

In late 2025, Shima Capital, a digital asset venture firm known for early-stage investments, began winding down after regulators raised serious concerns about governance and disclosures.

According to the US Securities and Exchange Commission, the firm's founder allegedly misrepresented fund performance during fundraising and failed to disclose conflicts of interest related to personal trading activity.[6] The case did not involve a market crash or widespread portfolio failure, but rather alleged misconduct at the fund-management level.

Following the filing of the lawsuit, the founder stepped down and the firm announced an orderly wind-down, halting new investments and beginning the process of returning or liquidating remaining assets.

Key Investor Takeaway

This episode underscores a core risk in private digital asset investing. Beyond technology and market risk, investors are exposed to traditional governance and fiduciary risk. Even sophisticated LPs can suffer losses when transparency, controls, and ethical standards break down.

Fund Structures and Investment Instruments

Digital asset venture funds use a wider range of structures than traditional VC because value can accrue to both companies and tokens.

Some investments are straightforward equity—ownership in a company building infrastructure, custody, or enterprise software like Fireblocks or Kraken. Others are token-based, where the investment is in a network's native asset. Many deals are hybrid, combining equity in a development company with token rights tied to the protocol.

Early structures like SAFTs relied heavily on agreements tied only to future tokens. SAFT, or a Simple Agreement for Future Tokens, is a contract that gives investors the right to receive tokens at a later date, usually after a network launches. SAFTs do not provide ownership in a company or governance rights, which can limit investor protections if a project changes course or fails to launch.

Over time, investors learned that owning a right to tokens, without governance rights or legal protections, created real problems when projects stalled or changed direction. Today, most early-stage deals combine traditional equity ownership with rights to future tokens, aligning incentives while providing clearer accountability and long-term participation. One common structure combines a SAFE (Simple Agreement for Future Equity), which converts into equity ownership in a company, with token warrants, which grant the right to receive a set amount of tokens in the future. This approach allows investors to participate both as company owners and as holders of a network's token, balancing oversight with potential upside.

Liquidity works differently too. In traditional venture capital, exits usually come through an acquisition or IPO. In digital asset venture investing, liquidity can appear earlier when tokens launch, sometimes allowing earlier distributions. But trading doesn't equal access. Lockups, vesting schedules, and limited market depth often delay realizable returns, so investors shouldn't assume faster liquidity just because a token exists.

In practice, structure determines not just upside, but when, how, and whether returns can actually be realized.

Evaluating Digital Asset VC Managers

Manager selection matters more in digital asset ventures than in most asset classes.

Strong teams combine technical expertise and investing experience. Purely financial teams often struggle to assess technical innovation and protocol-level risk.

Track records must be evaluated carefully. Unrealized gains and token marks can exaggerate performance. Distributed returns and deal attribution matter more than headline multiples.

The best managers are disciplined, transparent, and selective. They communicate clearly during market stress and avoid chasing narratives. In an environment where losses can happen quickly, judgment and integrity matter as much as returns.

Risks Unique to Digital Asset VC

Digital asset venture capital carries traditional venture risk plus several additional layers.

In addition to the power law where 80% of investments go to zero, token mechanics create risks that do not exist in traditional venture capital. Token unlocks release previously restricted supply, which can pressure prices even in growing networks. Ongoing supply expansion through rewards and incentives can dilute value unless demand keeps pace. Regulatory changes can disrupt trading and custody, and decentralized governance decisions can materially alter outcomes.

Despite perceptions of fast liquidity, many positions remain illiquid for years. Capital is often tied up longer than expected, particularly when market cycles turn.

In plain terms, value in digital asset VC can be lost not just by backing the wrong project, but by how ownership, supply, and control are structured over time.

Most losses in digital asset venture investing have come from portfolio-level failures, such as protocol hacks (including Ronin, Wormhole, Nomad, and Poly Network) and custody or counterparty collapses like FTX, while far fewer losses have resulted from direct compromises of venture fund wallets.

Other operational risks and how investors assess them are covered later in the due diligence section.

Timing Mismatch: When Liquidity Exists but Returns Don't

A recurring challenge in digital asset venture investing is the gap between when tokens become tradable and when capital can actually be returned. Tokens may list on exchanges while funds remain constrained by lockups, vesting schedules, internal risk limits, or governance and reputational considerations. In other cases, tokens are technically liquid but trade in volumes too small to support meaningful sales without pushing prices down.

This mismatch is often compounded by accounting treatment. Depending on valuation methodology and GAAP reporting practices, funds may mark positions based on observable market prices even when selling at scale is not feasible or apply liquidity discounts to reflect practical constraints. Both approaches can be reasonable, but they can produce very different reported outcomes.

The result is a familiar source of investor frustration: portfolios that show strong paper gains while returning limited capital in the near term. Understanding this dynamic is essential when evaluating fund strategy, interpreting performance, and assessing how managers communicate progress to investors.

Returns, Liquidity, and Realization

If you invest in a venture capital fund, you should expect your capital to be locked up for a long period, typically 7–10 years. During that time, you will have limited ability to access or exit your investment. If that level of illiquidity is uncomfortable, venture capital may not be the right vehicle for you.

Measuring returns in digital asset venture capital can be misleading because value often appears before it can be realized.

Reported performance typically relies on three metrics. Multiple on Invested Capital (MOIC) shows how much an investment is worth relative to its original cost. More precisely, MOIC is the ratio of an investment's current value to the amount originally invested. It includes unrealized gains and does not indicate when, or if, those returns can actually be realized.

Internal Rate of Return (IRR) measures the annualized return over time and is highly sensitive to timing, which can exaggerate early paper gains.

Distributions to Paid-In Capital (DPI) is the most concrete measure. DPI represents the amount of capital actually returned to investors divided by the amount they contributed. It reflects realized returns and is often the most reliable measure of economic outcome. In digital asset venture capital, DPI often lags reported performance for long periods.

This gap reflects the difference between paper gains and realizable value. Token prices can move sharply on limited liquidity, making portfolios look highly profitable. But large venture positions may be locked, thinly traded, or constrained by legal or governance rules. Until value is converted into cash or freely tradable assets, gains remain theoretical.

Exit paths exist, but each has limits. Token liquidity is common but often constrained. Mergers and acquisitions occur, mainly in infrastructure or regulated businesses. Public listings are rare and typically apply to service providers rather than decentralized networks.

In plain terms, digital asset VC returns often show up early on paper but take much longer to turn into real money. Investors should focus less on headline multiples and more on how and when value can actually be realized.

In practice, digital asset venture returns often appear early on paper but take much longer to convert into cash. That makes realization discipline especially important. Some of the most consistent outcomes have come from managers who reduce exposure as liquidity emerges, rather than holding indefinitely. This approach is familiar in traditional venture capital, where firms often sell portions of a position at predefined milestones to manage risk and lock in gains. In digital assets, where tokens can become liquid well before a company reaches maturity, applying similar rules-based selling frameworks can help turn early paper gains into realized returns.

Portfolio Construction, the Power Law, and Fund Size

Venture returns are rarely evenly spread. A small number of investments usually do most of the work, while many others break even or fail. That reality shapes how funds are built.

Fund size is the starting point. A smaller fund can succeed with a handful of solid wins. A larger fund needs much bigger outcomes to move the needle. As funds grow, the list of investments capable of driving returns shrinks, which raises the bar for performance and puts more pressure on access to standout opportunities.

Position sizing follows the same logic. Early on, funds spread capital across many bets to keep options open. Over time, as teams execute and risks become clearer, more capital flows to the strongest performers. If early positions are too small, even big winners won't matter much. If they're too large, early losses can weigh down the entire portfolio.

Good portfolio construction isn't about equal bets. It's about staying flexible early, then leaning into the few investments that prove they deserve it.

One fund-of-funds manager observed that relatively few digital asset managers have shown consistent discipline in realizing gains when tokens become liquid and appreciate sharply. Knowing when and how to reduce exposure, rather than holding indefinitely, has proven to be a meaningful skill.

A useful comparison comes from traditional venture capital, where firms often sell portions of a position at defined stages. For example, Fred Wilson's long-standing approach at Union Square Ventures involved selling roughly one-third of a position before an IPO, another third at IPO, and holding the remainder long-term. In digital asset markets, where liquidity often arrives much earlier and volatility is higher, applying a similarly structured approach can help convert early gains into realized returns.

The Role of Market Makers, HFT Firms, and OTC Desks

Digital asset markets rely on specialized trading firms that provide liquidity, manage risk, and keep prices aligned across trading platforms.

Market makers are the most visible participants. They continuously quote buy and sell prices so assets can trade smoothly. In digital assets, firms such as Wintermute, Cumberland, Amber group, and GSR play a central role. Beyond day-to-day trading, they often help launch new tokens, seed early liquidity, support exchange listings, and stabilize markets during periods of volatility—activities that go beyond the traditional market-making role in equities.

Most market makers are proprietary trading firms, or "prop shops." They trade using their own capital rather than managing client funds. A small number have raised outside capital to scale their operations, and some may eventually pursue public listings, but their core business is trading, not asset management.

High-frequency trading (HFT) firms focus on speed, automation, and scale rather than issuer relationships. Firms such as Jump Trading, Jane Street, Citadel, and Tower Research operate across the digital asset spot, futures, and options markets, capturing small price differences across venues. While largely invisible to retail investors, their activity tightens spreads and improves price efficiency across the market.

Over-the-counter (OTC) desks serve institutions that need to move large positions. Firms such as Cumberland, Galaxy, B2C2, and FalconX help hedge funds, asset managers, and corporates execute large trades away from public order books, reducing market impact. Many OTC desks now operate more like digital-asset prime brokers, offering execution, financing, and treasury services alongside trading.

Together, these firms form the market infrastructure that allows digital assets to trade at scale; they work hand in hand with VC and liquid funds. Even when investors never interact with them directly, their activity shapes pricing, volatility, and execution quality across the entire market.

INVESTING IN LIQUID FUNDS AND HEDGE FUNDS

Not all professional digital asset investing is long-dated or illiquid. Alongside venture capital, a large and growing segment of the market operates through liquid strategies—approaches that can be entered, adjusted, and exited quickly, often on a daily to monthly basis, using tradable tokens, derivatives, or on-chain protocols.

Liquid funds differ from venture capital in both structure and intent. Capital is not committed for years, positions are actively managed, and risk is adjusted continuously rather than underwritten at inception, even though investors often remain committed to these strategies for several years. As a result, liquid strategies tend to resemble hedge funds more than traditional venture vehicles, even when they invest in the same underlying networks.

How Liquid Strategies Generate Returns

Most institutional liquid digital asset portfolios separate exposure into three functions: beta, carry, and alpha. These categories capture the primary sources of return but are not exhaustive, and many managers combine additional liquid strategies depending on market conditions and investment objectives.

In practice, professional managers often construct portfolios by allocating separately to each of these components. Directional exposure provides beta, staking and lending generate carry, and arbitrage, quantitative, or event-driven strategies seek alpha. This structure closely mirrors traditional hedge fund portfolio construction, but is implemented using tokens, derivatives, and on-chain markets rather than equities and bonds.

Market Exposure (Beta)

Market exposure strategies seek to benefit from price movements in major digital assets:

- Positions are typically held in highly traded assets such as Bitcoin, Ethereum, or Solana, either directly or through price-tracking contracts.
- These positions are liquid and easy to adjust, but returns move directly with the market.
- Risks include full exposure to market swings, concentration risk from holding a small number of assets, and counterparty risk when positions rely on exchanges or trading platforms.

Income Strategies (Carry)

Income strategies aim to earn yield rather than relying on price appreciation:

- Examples include earning rewards for supporting blockchain networks, lending assets to earn interest, or capturing price differences between related markets.
- These strategies can produce steadier returns than pure market exposure.
- However, they introduce platform risk, execution risk, and liquidity risk, particularly during periods of market stress.

Alpha Strategies (Independent Returns)

Alpha strategies aim to generate returns that are not dependent on whether digital asset prices rise or fall. Many are structured to reduce exposure to overall market movements, with profits driven by pricing differences, timing, or information advantages:

- Direct arbitrage: buying and selling the same asset on two different trading platforms when short-term price differences appear. These strategies rely on speed and execution to capture small gaps before they close.
- Funding rate arbitrage: holding equal but opposite positions in the same asset on different trading platforms when the ongoing cost of holding those positions differs. Returns come from earning the higher payment while paying the lower one.
- Rules-based and quantitative strategies: using systematic models to identify recurring price relationships, such as assets that tend to move together and temporarily diverge. Positions are adjusted as those relationships change.
- Data-driven and AI strategies: analyzing alternative information sources, including blockchain activity, news events, and shifts in market sentiment, to anticipate short-term market behavior.

Most arbitrage opportunities exist for specific reasons, including geographic separation, regulatory constraints, or structural differences between markets. As more participants identify the same opportunity, returns typically decline over time. Consistent performance therefore depends on execution quality, discipline, and risk management rather than long-term price direction.

Some managers operate between liquid markets and venture capital, trading early-stage tokens shortly after launch, buying tokens in discounted treasury deals, or holding ecosystem baskets following a token generation event. Liquidity exists, but volatility and information asymmetry remain high.

Market Conditions and Capacity Constraints

Liquid digital asset strategies are shaped as much by how markets function as by manager skill. Compared with traditional financial markets, where some strategies can absorb tens of billions of dollars, digital asset markets are smaller. For many market-neutral approaches, the amount of capital that can be put to work effectively is measured in hundreds of millions, not billions.

Liquidity and returns also change meaningfully across market cycles. Even strategies designed to reduce exposure to price direction tend to work best when markets are active and prices move sharply. Historically, these favorable conditions have not lasted long. In past cycles, periods of high trading activity and volatility typically lasted 6–12 months before fading. Liquidity and yields correlate strongly with bull/bear markets even for delta neutral strategies.

The post-2024 cycle looked different. During the 2021 bull market, Bitcoin and Ethereum experienced extremely large price swings. In 2024–2025, price movements were more subdued, even during the post-election rally. This reflects a larger overall market, greater institutional participation, and the introduction of exchange-traded funds, all of which make prices harder to move quickly. Outside of Bitcoin, Ethereum, and Solana, activity was more limited, and brief rallies in meme tokens and AI-related assets never reached the scale seen in earlier cycles.

Directional Strategies and Their Limits

Strategies that mainly bet on prices going up sound simple, but over full market cycles, they've been harder to justify. Many long-only funds have struggled to beat the returns of Bitcoin over four-year periods, which raises an obvious question for investors: Why pay active fees such as 2% management fees and 20% carry for returns you could get by holding the asset itself?

That gap was especially clear in 2025. While many hedge funds posted respectable gains, Bitcoin surged roughly 120% and crossed $100,000 for the first time. Few active strategies kept pace with that move. In many cases, managers limited their direct Bitcoin exposure in favor of more complex trades and missed a large part of the rally as a result.

Some managers have tried to adapt by softening pure directional bets. Instead of relying entirely on price appreciation, they pair long exposure with hedges or options and use income from staking or collateral to cushion drawdowns. The goal is smoother returns, not just upside.

Still, beating Bitcoin remains a tall order. Volatility cuts both ways, and hedge fund structures often force managers to reduce risk at the worst possible moments. Meanwhile, investors looking for straightforward exposure have increasingly turned to low-cost Bitcoin ETFs, which offer direct access without layers of fees.

As simpler options gain traction, hedge funds face a higher bar. To earn their place, they need to show they can do more than ride the market—they need to deliver results that justify the complexity.

Delta-Neutral Funds and Market-Neutral Funds

In digital asset investing, the terms delta-neutral and market-neutral are often used as if they mean the same thing. They are related, but they are not identical, and the distinction matters for understanding both returns and risk.

A delta-neutral strategy is designed so that returns are not driven by price movements in an asset like Bitcoin or Ether. Gains on one position are intended to offset losses on another. For example, a fund might buy Bitcoin in the spot market (*the direct purchase and ownership of the asset today*) while simultaneously shorting Bitcoin futures or perpetual contracts. When structured correctly, the portfolio is largely unaffected by whether prices rise or fall.

Removing the impact of price movements does not remove risk. Even when a strategy is designed so gains and losses cancel out if prices rise or fall, returns can still be affected by funding rates, changes in market conditions, limited liquidity, or problems at trading platforms or with counterparties.

Market-neutral describes a broader objective. A market-neutral strategy aims to reduce exposure not just to price direction, but to the overall market environment. In crypto, many strategies labeled market-neutral are best understood as delta-neutral approaches that still carry meaningful non-price risks.

For investors, the takeaway is simple. Delta-neutral refers to a hedging technique. Market-neutral refers to an investment goal. Understanding the difference helps clarify where returns come from and what risks remain.

Common approaches include:

- Market making and arbitrage: Earning small spreads by providing liquidity or capturing price differences across centralized and decentralized exchanges.
- Basis and funding trades: Buying assets in spot markets while shorting futures or perpetuals to collect funding payments or price gaps over time.
- Options strategies: Trading volatility rather than direction by buying options when price swings are cheap and selling when they are expensive.
- Quant and relative-value trades: Using models to go long on stronger assets and short related weaker ones, such as holding Solana while reducing exposure to its ecosystem tokens.
- DeFi strategies: Applying similar trades on decentralized platforms, including lending, liquidity provision, and incentive programs.

Market-Neutral Funds

Market-neutral funds aim to generate returns from how digital asset markets function. The goal is to earn steadier, more consistent returns that are uncorrelated to the market direction.

These funds focus on price differences, structural inefficiencies, and mechanical features of digital asset markets, many of which exist because digital assets trade 24/7 across fragmented venues, with different rules, participants, and risk constraints. Market-neutral funds try to get paid for how markets work, not where prices go.

How Market-Neutral Strategies Work

Most market-neutral crypto funds combine several repeatable strategies rather than relying on a single trade. Common examples include:

- Basis and cash-and-carry trades: Buying Bitcoin or Ethereum in the spot market while simultaneously shorting futures or perpetual contracts. When futures trade above spot prices, the fund earns the difference over time as prices converge.
- Funding-rate arbitrage: In perpetual futures markets, traders pay each other to keep prices aligned with spot markets. Market-neutral funds position themselves to receive these payments while remaining hedged.
- Cross-exchange arbitrage: Capturing price differences between exchanges by buying on one venue and selling on another.
- Term-structure trades: Exploiting differences between short-dated and longer-dated futures contracts.
- Volatility and curve trades: Trading differences in how volatility or pricing behaves across maturities rather than betting on direction.

Individually, these trades tend to produce modest returns. When combined and carefully scaled, they can generate attractive risk-adjusted outcomes with lower exposure to market swings.

Several established managers specialize primarily in market-neutral digital asset strategies, including but not limited to Monarch Asset Management, Abraxas Capital Management, Fasanara Capital, Edge Capital, and Nickel Digital.

Although these strategies may sound familiar, they are being executed within a hybrid of traditional finance and crypto infrastructure—a shift that is creating new market opportunities, according to Shiliang Tang, founder of Monarch Asset Management. Tang said:

> "*Venues like Hyperliquid have democratized market creation, allowing anyone to spin up a perpetual futures contract on virtually any asset class, from pre-market equities to niche commodities. Simultaneously, purpose-built order books like Lighter and Ostium are bringing high-fidelity feed data on-chain, allowing traders to seek alpha in FX and commodities markets that were previously gated by ISDA agreements and banking hours. This fragmented market structure—where an asset trades at one price on a traditional exchange and another on an isolated on-chain venue—creates a 'fragmentation premium.' These price discrepancies are not bugs; they are arbitrage opportunities for liquid funds who understand the latency between the real world and the block space.*"

Yield-Focused Bitcoin Funds

Investor interest has grown in strategies that generate income from Bitcoin itself and gives directional exposure to the asset.

Because Bitcoin does not produce yield on its own, these approaches use lending, arbitrage, or structured trades to earn incremental returns while maintaining Bitcoin exposure.

Return targets vary. Some investors seek low-teens returns, while others, such as miners or long-term holders, are comfortable with mid-single-digit yields in exchange for conservative structures and strong safeguards. Lower return goals reduce risk and allow more capital to be used effectively.

How Investors Can Earn Yield on Bitcoin

Bitcoin does not have native staking yield, but investors can still earn income in several ways:

- **Centralized lending platforms:** Investors can lend Bitcoin through regulated exchanges or institutional platforms. Yields vary over time and depend on market demand, collateral terms, and platform risk. Rates are typically lower for conservative, over-collateralized lending.
- **Bitcoin yield and lending funds:** Specialized funds pool Bitcoin and apply low-risk income strategies on behalf of investors. These may target modest returns in exchange for professional risk management, diversification across counterparties, and operational oversight. These funds can keep exposure to Bitcoin's price and earn yield on top.
- **DeFi via Bitcoin representations:** Bitcoin can be used in decentralized finance through wrapped or bridged versions of BTC. Wrapped or bridged Bitcoin refers to versions of Bitcoin that are locked on the Bitcoin network and represented by a token on another blockchain, such as Ethereum or Solana. This allows Bitcoin to be used in DeFi applications that do not run directly on Bitcoin. These structures rely on smart contracts or custodians to hold the original Bitcoin, which introduces additional technical and counterparty risk compared to holding native Bitcoin. These approaches introduce additional smart-contract and bridge risk and are generally less conservative.
- **Bitcoin-native yield networks:** Ecosystems such as Stacks and Babylon aim to enable Bitcoin-linked yield by using Bitcoin to secure other networks. These models are still evolving and should be evaluated as emerging technologies.

Investor Takeaway:

Bitcoin yield exists, but it is earned, not native. Higher yields usually mean higher complexity and risk. Conservative strategies focus on modest, repeatable income while prioritizing custody, collateral, and counterparty safety.

On-Chain Funds

Some managers run funds entirely on-chain. Instead of using derivatives, prime brokers, or traditional lending desks, these funds earn returns directly through decentralized protocols.

Most on-chain funds focus on yield-based or market-neutral approaches rather than directional bets. Returns often come from lending, providing liquidity, or structured trades designed to earn steady income without relying on prices rising.

As an example, Re7 runs market-neutral strategies that deploy capital across DeFi lending and liquidity protocols. A simple version of the trade looks like this: investor capital is converted into stablecoins and supplied to protocols such as Aave, earning yield from borrowers. The outcome depends far more on protocol design and execution than on whether markets are rising or falling. Over multiple years, Re7's returns have remained largely uncorrelated with broader digital asset price movements, even during periods of market stress.

The appeal is transparency and direct access to returns generated within digital asset markets themselves. The trade-off is a different risk profile. Performance depends on the reliability of the underlying software, the design of the protocols used, and operational discipline. Losses can result from coding flaws, malicious attacks, or sudden changes in market conditions.

On-chain funds are not simply digital versions of traditional hedge funds. They represent a distinct approach, with fewer intermediaries, clearer mechanics, and risks that are technical rather than financial in the traditional sense.

Where Liquid Digital Asset Funds Are Headed

Over time, liquid digital asset strategies are becoming part of broader investment portfolios rather than a standalone category. Digital assets are increasingly traded alongside stocks, commodities, and other assets, while more traditional financial activity is moving onto blockchain systems. That shift is showing up in fund allocations. According to a 2025 joint AIMA–PwC survey of 122 hedge fund managers overseeing nearly $1 trillion in assets, 55% now report some exposure to digital assets, up from 47% the year before.[7]

As this convergence continues, digital asset-focused managers will need to operate across tokens, derivatives, and digital-asset-related equities, and eventually across real-world assets traded on blockchain platforms. Opportunities remain, but they are becoming more competitive. The advantage will belong to managers who can adapt, manage risk carefully, and operate across multiple markets in DeFi and CeFi as digital assets become a standard part of global investing.

Investors, Expectations, and Due Diligence: Buyer Beware

As digital asset markets have matured, expectations have changed. Early investors once demanded very high returns to justify the risks. Today, many institutions are comfortable targeting 15–20% over a full market cycle, reflecting better custody, stronger oversight, and more reliable market infrastructure. Some investors are even willing to accept lower returns in exchange for steadier performance and fewer surprises.

With lower return targets has come tighter scrutiny. Investors now focus less on bold promises and more on basics: who controls the assets, where they're held, and what happens if something goes wrong. This also includes how performance is reported, specifically whether returns are shown before or after fees, financing costs, and losses elsewhere in the portfolio. For on-chain strategies, that means paying close attention to how protocols are designed, how risks are monitored, and what protections exist when systems fail. These priorities often vary more by investor type than by strategy itself.

Due diligence matters across every corner of the market—venture funds, fund-of-funds, and liquid hedge funds alike. The ecosystem still includes many small or inexperienced managers, and not all of them operate at an institutional standard. That makes "buyer beware" more than a cliché. Some funds have failed because of excessive leverage or weak controls. Others were undone by counterparties, most notably during the collapse of FTX. In many cases, managers came from crypto-native backgrounds and had never run institutional funds before.

To help raise the bar, L1D Research published an open-source guide outlining best practices for running a digital asset hedge fund. It offers a useful reference point for what investors should expect.[8]

Using that framework, investors tend to focus on a few core questions:

- Does the fund clearly explain what it does? The strategy, sources of return, risks, limits, and how it's expected to behave in different markets should be easy to understand.

- Is the team experienced and properly structured? Investment, risk, and operations should all have real authority, not just advisory roles.
- Are the systems reliable? Trading, risk monitoring, accounting, valuation, and reporting should work smoothly and consistently.
- Is the legal setup sound? Fund structures, disclosures, and compliance should match what's being offered to investors.
- How are assets protected? Investors should understand where assets are held, how they're separated, and what happens if a counterparty fails.
- Are security controls strong? This includes cybersecurity, key management, access controls, and backup plans.
- Do liquidity terms make sense? Lockups and redemptions should reflect how easily the underlying assets can be sold, especially during stress.
- Is leverage used carefully? Any borrowing should be limited, monitored, and tested against downside scenarios.
- Are fees fair and aligned? Incentives should reward long-term results, not short-term risk-taking.
- Is reporting clear and regular? Investors should receive detailed updates on performance, exposures, and risks, ideally backed by independent administrators and audits.

In this market, the biggest blow-ups usually come from structure and oversight, not just bad trades. If you're allocating to a liquid manager, you're underwriting how they hold assets, who they rely on, what happens in stress, and whether the reporting is real. The case studies below show what can go wrong when those basics aren't in place.

Major Liquid Fund Blow-Ups in Digital Assets

Virgil Capital (2020)

A quantitative fund whose founder admitted to faking performance after losing most of the capital—about $90 million. There was no independent oversight, no third-party administration, and no reliable reporting. False results went unnoticed until it was too late.

Three Arrows Capital (2022)

Once one of the largest funds in the market, Three Arrows Capital collapsed after heavy borrowing and concentrated bets unraveled during a downturn. When prices fell, it couldn't meet margin calls, triggering losses across the ecosystem.

Galois Capital (2022)

A market-neutral fund that shut down after roughly half its assets were trapped on FTX following the exchange's bankruptcy. The failure wasn't bad trading—it was reliance on a single counterparty.

Asymmetric (2025)

A discretionary fund that suffered deep losses after directional bets went wrong in fast-changing markets. Liquidity and timing proved unforgiving.

Common Thread

Different strategies, same lesson. These failures weren't caused by market swings alone. They were made worse by weak controls, poor transparency, too much borrowing, or reliance on the wrong counterparties. For investors, the takeaway is simple: solid oversight and conservative structure matter as much as performance.

INVESTOR TAKEAWAY

Private market digital asset investing is about choosing the right structure and understanding the trade-offs that come with it:

- Venture funds = early-stage upside, but expect a 7–10-year lockup.
- Liquid funds = active management with periodic liquidity, but outcomes depend on discipline and controls.
- Fund-of-funds = diversified access to managers and strategies, at the cost of an extra fee layer.

This chapter focused on accessing digital assets through professional managers and intermediaries. The next chapter covers the other path: self-custody and decentralized infrastructure—what it enables, what can go wrong, and how responsibility shifts when you hold the assets yourself.

CHAPTER SIX

ACCESSING DIGITAL ASSET INVESTMENTS VIA SELF-CUSTODY AND DECENTRALIZED INFRASTRUCTURE

"Wallets are the user's interface to sovereignty in Web3—they are how individuals own assets, identity, and access directly, without intermediaries."

—Joseph Lubin, CEO of ConsenSys, Chairman of Sharplink, Co-founder of Ethereum

Public market products offer convenience, regulation, and familiarity, but they also distance investors from the underlying networks. This chapter explores the alternative: direct ownership through self-custody and interaction with decentralized infrastructure.

In this chapter you will learn:

- What self-custody means
- How wallets, private keys, and seed phrases establish ownership
- The most common self-custody mistakes—and how to avoid them

WHY SELF-CUSTODY MATTERS

At the center of digital asset investing is a simple but consequential question: *Who controls the keys?*

Self-custody means holding digital assets in a wallet where the investor—not a bank, broker, or exchange—controls the private keys. Private keys are cryptographic credentials that authorize transactions and determine who can move the assets. In digital assets, control of the keys is control of the asset. If you do not control the private keys, you are relying on someone else to hold it for you.

This idea is often summarized by the phrase "not your keys, not your coins," meaning ownership depends on direct control rather than an account balance.

This differs sharply from traditional finance. In conventional markets, ownership is mediated by institutions and enforced through legal systems.

Assets are held in custody, transfers can be reversed, and access can often be restored through formal processes. In digital assets, ownership is enforced by software. Transactions are final. If access is lost, there is no intermediary that can undo a mistake or recover funds.

For Marcos C. Veremis, a managing partner at venture capital fund of funds, Accolade Partners, this distinction became tangible long before he worked in digital assets. In 2015, during Greece's financial crisis, the government imposed strict capital controls. Bank withdrawals were capped, transfers were restricted, and accounts could be frozen without warning. Members of his family, including his mother, were suddenly unable to access their own money freely.

Self-custody, however, shifts responsibility. Security, access, and recovery depend entirely on how keys are stored and managed. There is no customer support desk for lost credentials. For some investors, this level of responsibility is a feature. For others, it is a risk they prefer not to take.

Most investors encounter digital assets through custodial models, where a third party holds the private keys on their behalf. Exchanges and regulated custodians manage security, transactions, and compliance, offering convenience and familiarity. This approach lowers the operational burden but introduces counterparty risk. Access to assets depends on the custodian's systems, policies, and financial health, and withdrawals can be delayed or restricted in periods of stress.

Neither approach is inherently better. Custody trades control for convenience. Self-custody trades convenience for control. Understanding where responsibility—and risk—resides is essential before deciding how to hold digital assets. How that control is exercised in practice is determined by wallets.

ACCESSING PUBLIC BLOCKCHAINS THROUGH WALLETS

Owning a digital asset requires using a wallet to exercise control over a private key.

If custody answers who controls an asset, wallets explain how that control is exercised. A wallet is the interface between an investor and a public blockchain. It is not an account held with an institution, and it does not store assets in the traditional sense. Instead, a wallet manages cryptographic credentials that allow the owner to prove control and authorize transactions on the network.

Every wallet has two core components:

- A public key (or public address), which is what others use to send you assets. Think of it like a mailing address: it's safe to share and shows where assets should go.
- A private key, which is what lets you move assets out. Think of it like the key to a locked safe: whoever has it controls the funds.

At the center of ownership is the private key. When an investor sends Bitcoin, Ether, or another digital asset, the wallet uses the private key to approve the transaction. The blockchain verifies that approval mathematically and updates ownership. No name, password, or institution is involved. Control is proven, not granted.

The technical details in this chapter may feel unfamiliar at first, but they explain the practical risks and responsibilities investors face and are essential to understanding how the ecosystem actually works. Early cryptocurrency infrastructure and applications were built primarily for developers rather than investors, consumers, or businesses. As wallet design and user experience improve, much of this complexity is being hidden behind simpler interfaces. That shift lowers barriers to entry, makes digital assets easier to use, and helps explain how adoption can move from early specialists to broader, everyday participation.

Software Wallets vs. Hardware Wallets

Not all wallets manage private keys in the same way. The most common distinction is between software wallets and hardware wallets, each reflecting a different balance between convenience and security.

Software wallets run on a phone, computer, or web browser. They manage private keys digitally, usually in encrypted form on the device or through built-in security features. This design makes them easy to use and well suited for frequent transactions, but it also means their security depends on the safety of the device they run on. Browser-based wallets such as MetaMask,[1] as well as mobile wallets like Phantom and Trust Wallet,[2] are typical examples.

Hardware wallets, by contrast, store private keys inside a dedicated physical device. The keys never leave the device and are never exposed to the internet. When a transaction is initiated, it must be physically approved on the device itself. This added friction significantly reduces the risk of remote theft and is often preferred for long-term holdings or larger portfolios. Common examples include Ledger and Trezor devices.

Both wallet types enable self-custody. The difference lies in where the keys live and how transactions are approved, not in ownership itself.

Private Keys and Seed Phrases: A Practical Example

Most investors never see their private key directly. Instead, when a wallet is created, it generates a seed phrase—typically a list of 12 or 24 common words.

That seed phrase is not a password. It is a master backup. Using those words, the wallet can recreate every private key and address associated with it. For example, entering the seed phrase into a compatible wallet on a new device instantly restores full control over the assets.

This leads to a simple but unforgiving rule: anyone with the seed phrase can take the assets. They do not need the original phone, computer, or permission. The words alone are sufficient.

Traditional self-custody wallets operate on this model. They offer full independence and full ownership—but also full responsibility. If the seed phrase is lost, access may be lost permanently. If it is shared, control is transferred.

Modern Wallet Design and Social Recovery

To reduce the risk of a single point of failure, newer wallets use smart-contract wallets and social recovery.

Rather than relying on one seed phrase, control is distributed. A wallet might require approval from multiple devices, trusted contacts, or recovery services. Transactions are still signed normally, but recovery does not depend on a single secret written on paper.

For example, when setting up a wallet with MetaMask, users can choose between a traditional seed-phrase wallet and a smart-contract–based option with built-in recovery rules.

The key distinction is important: no seed phrase does not mean no keys. The keys still exist, but they are managed collectively rather than entrusted to a single secret.

Loss, Theft, and Finality

If a private key is lost, the assets it controls are locked permanently. If it is stolen, assets can be moved instantly and irreversibly.

There is no password reset, no customer support desk, and no chargeback. Finality is a feature of self-custody, not a bug—and it is the primary source of risk.

Does Crypto Have a User-Experience (UX) Problem?

Digital assets do have a user-experience problem, but not because the technology fails. Many early products were built by geeks for geeks—a business-to-geek model focused on technical infrastructure rather than on how people actually interact with and use financial services.

From the beginning, digital assets emphasized individual control. Users were expected to manage their own keys, understand transaction fees, choose between networks, and accept that mistakes could be permanent. While this level of control is powerful, it also places a heavy burden on users who are not accustomed to managing the underlying mechanics of financial systems. In traditional finance, apps hide settlement, custody, and reconciliation behind simple interfaces. Early digital asset products exposed all of it.

That exposed complexity makes errors easy and costly. Sending funds to the wrong address, approving the wrong transaction, or interacting with a fraudulent application can lead to permanent loss, often with no customer support or way to reverse the mistake. For most users, this creates friction and anxiety—not because digital assets are inherently unsafe, but because the tools require technical understanding that most people do not have and should not need in order to participate in everyday financial activity.

This is now beginning to change. New wallets and platforms increasingly hide technical complexity behind simpler designs, improved security defaults, and recovery options that reduce the consequences of human error. As these layers mature, interacting with digital assets shifts from "understand the system" to "use the product."

When Self-Custody Makes Sense

Self-custody is not a requirement for participating in digital asset markets. It is a tool.

For long-term holdings, on-chain participation, or investors seeking maximum control, self-custody can be essential. In other cases, such as small balances, frequent trading, or situations where speed and simplicity matter, custodial platforms may be more practical.

Many investors adopt a hybrid approach, keeping some assets in self-custody for long-term security while using trusted platforms for liquidity and execution. The decision is less about ideology than alignment: matching custody choices to investment goals, risk tolerance, and operational comfort.

Setting Up Your First Wallet

Setting up a digital asset wallet is a one-time decision with long-term consequences. Most irreversible losses stem from mistakes made at this stage.

Begin by downloading wallet software only from an official website or a verified app store. For example, browser-based wallets such as MetaMask should be installed directly from the Chrome Web Store or Apple App Store, while mobile wallets like Trust Wallet should be downloaded only from official app stores. Hardware wallets such as Ledger or Trezor should be purchased directly from the manufacturer and set up using software downloaded from the official domain.

When a wallet is created, it generates a seed phrase, typically 12 or 24 words. This phrase can recreate the entire wallet and restore full control on any compatible device. At this moment, ownership is established. There is no account, no password reset, and no customer support.

The seed phrase must be backed up securely and offline—written on paper or another physical medium and stored safely. It should never be photographed, saved digitally, or stored in the cloud. Anyone with this phrase controls the assets.

Private keys authorize transactions and move assets on the blockchain. Seed phrases simply regenerate those keys, which means they carry the same power. Losing them can permanently lock you out; exposing them allows assets to be moved instantly and irreversibly.

For larger holdings, advanced setups such as hardware wallets, multi-signature wallets,[3] or social-recovery wallets reduce single-point-of-failure risk. In self-custody, key management is not a technical detail—it is the foundation of ownership.

Funding the Wallet and Choosing Exchanges and On-Ramps

Most wallets allow investors to buy digital assets directly through an in-app "Buy" feature. When used, the wallet connects to regulated third-party payment providers such as Coinbase Pay, MoonPay, Ramp, or Transak. These services typically support bank transfers, debit cards, and sometimes mobile payments, depending on location. Identity verification may be required. Once the purchase is completed, the digital assets are delivered directly to the wallet.

Another common approach is to purchase digital assets on a centralized exchange and then transfer them to your wallet. In this case, you buy assets such as ETH or USDC on an exchange like Coinbase, Kraken, or Binance, then withdraw them to your wallet. This involves copying your wallet address, selecting the correct network, and confirming the transfer. After the transaction is processed, the assets appear in your wallet.

The choice between buying directly in a wallet or using an exchange is largely about convenience and control. Wallet-based purchases are simple but often come with higher fees. Exchanges generally offer better pricing and liquidity, but they temporarily hold your assets until you withdraw them. Understanding this trade-off helps investors decide how much responsibility they want to take on from the start.

Centralized exchanges handle both sides of the transaction: moving money from your bank into digital assets and converting digital assets back for withdrawal. For most investors, this happens on a single platform. Examples include Coinbase, Kraken, Gemini, and Binance.

Decentralized exchanges like Uniswap and Curve, by contrast, operate through smart contracts and allow users to trade directly from their own wallets. Custody remains with the user, but smart-contract risk, variable liquidity, and operational responsibility increase.

Navigating Decentralized Infrastructure

Once you have a wallet, you can move money directly, without asking permission from a bank or payment provider.

Sending digital dollars or other assets can be fast and inexpensive. Moving $1,000 in USDC, for example, often costs a few cents to a few dollars and settles in seconds or minutes, even across borders. Sending the same amount through a bank wire or money transfer service can take days and cost far more, especially internationally.

A wallet also lets you buy and sell assets directly. You can add money using payment services that connect to wallets, then move or exchange assets on your own. If you want to swap one asset for another—say, Ethereum for Solana—you can do that directly from your wallet, without sending funds to an exchange. You can also move assets between different blockchain networks when needed, making the same funds usable in more places.

Beyond payments and swaps, wallets enable basic financial activity that will be explored in greater detail in Chapter 7. Users can swap assets, lend them to earn income, or borrow against them. For example, someone holding $10,000 worth of Solana might borrow roughly $5,000 in USDC while still keeping exposure to Solana's price. These arrangements are automated and settle on-chain.

Wallets also give access to a wide range of applications. Users can stake assets to earn rewards, provide liquidity to trading platforms, vote on protocol decisions, buy and sell digital collectibles, participate in prediction markets, or use payment and gaming apps.

In practice, a wallet acts like a global financial tool. It combines payments, savings, trading, and access to financial services in one place—without relying on traditional intermediaries.

What Is a Crypto "Super App"?

In the digital asset world, a super app is the idea of managing most financial activity through a single interface, centered on a digital wallet. Rather than moving between separate apps or intermediaries for trading, payments, banking, and investing, the wallet becomes the financial hub.

At the center is a self-custody or hybrid wallet. A self-custody wallet gives users full control of their assets and private keys. A hybrid wallet blends that control with selected services typically offered by financial institutions, such as account recovery, compliance checks, fiat on-ramps, and card access, making the experience easier to use without fully giving up ownership.

In practice, this setup allows users to get paid, hold stablecoins, swap tokens, stake or lend, trade tokenized stocks or ETFs, make payments, and move funds back to a bank—all from one app with a unified view of balances and permissions.

This vision is being pursued from different directions. Platforms like Robinhood are extending traditional finance apps to include crypto, cards, and cash management, while MetaMask, Coinbase, and Kraken are expanding wallets into broader financial services.

The long-term goal is simplicity: with an optimized user experience, the wallet replaces the bank login, the card allows you to pay for everything without separate banking accounts and replaces the exchange withdrawal, and a single app replaces multiple financial intermediaries including brokerage, crypto exchanges, payment apps and banks, allowing capital to move fluidly across crypto, traditional markets, and payments, with ownership and portability built in.

Friction Points: Gas Fees, Swaps, and Bridges

On a single blockchain like Ethereum or Solana, exchanging one token for another is fairly simple. A swap uses software to trade one token for another at the current market price.

Many well-known swap venues run directly on individual networks, including Uniswap and Curve on Ethereum, and Raydium and Orca on Solana. Other tools, such as 1inch and Jupiter, don't run markets themselves. Instead, they route trades across multiple venues to find better prices. Today, many wallets include this functionality directly, so users may not even notice which platform is being used.

The bigger complication appears when the tokens being swapped live on different blockchains.

Blockchains don't naturally talk to each other. A token on Ethereum can't be used on Solana, and assets on a main network can't automatically move to its scaling networks. To move value between them, users rely on bridges, which are systems that lock or remove an asset on one network and recreate it on another.

This extra step introduces most of the friction.

First, bridging adds complexity. Instead of one transaction, users depend on multiple systems working together. Second, bridges have historically been one of the weaker points in decentralized finance, with several high-profile losses tied to bridge failures, including Nomad and Ronin. Tools like Wormhole and LayerZero are widely used, but the added moving parts still matter. Third, liquidity gets split across networks, which can lead to worse pricing or limited availability. Finally, cross-network swaps often cost more and take longer than trades done entirely on one chain.

Fees add another small but common hurdle. Most networks require their own native token to pay transaction costs. For example, holding

USDC on Ethereum and swapping it to buy Aave tokens also requires holding some Ether to cover the transaction cost.

That means a user can hold assets on a network but still be unable to move them without a small balance of the network's token. Some newer networks and tools, including routing systems on chains like Sui, try to smooth this out, but it remains a frequent source of failed transactions.

Importantly, many risks come from user actions rather than broken systems. Swaps can go wrong if permissions aren't reviewed carefully. Bridges add timing and execution risk. Every on-chain action requires approving a transaction that spells out what will happen and which assets are involved. Skipping those details is where mistakes usually occur.

The good news is that usability has improved significantly. Modern wallets preview transactions more clearly, highlight permissions, and warn users before risky approvals. Smart wallets like Safe add limits and safeguards, while better design continues to reduce simple errors.

With a basic understanding of fees, permissions, and cross-network movement, these systems become manageable. The friction hasn't disappeared, but it's steadily shrinking.

What Is Maximal Extractable Value (MEV)?

When you send a transaction on a blockchain, it doesn't happen instantly. It waits in a queue. The party responsible for assembling the next block, typically a block producer, such as a validator or miner, decides which transactions go first and which ones wait.

MEV is the extra profit that can be made from controlling that order.

A simple example: you place a large trade that will move a token's price. Someone sees it coming, buys the token first, lets your trade push the price up, then sells. The profit comes from going first, not from taking risk.

MEV also shows up in arbitrage trades, liquidations, and other situations where timing and order matter. Some of this activity helps markets stay in line. Other times, it raises costs or causes trades to fail.

In short, MEV is about who controls transaction order—and who benefits from it. As on-chain markets grow, reducing the impact of harmful MEV has become an important focus for wallets and trading platforms.

SECURITY BEST PRACTICES

Self-custody and decentralized infrastructure remove intermediaries, but they also remove safety nets. Once assets are controlled directly, security becomes an ongoing practice rather than a one-time setup. The risks are real, but they are familiar—largely the same social engineering tactics used in online banking, email, and social media scams.

Common Mistakes and How to Avoid Them

Most losses in digital asset markets are not caused by market movements or protocol failures, but by avoidable operational mistakes. Self-custody shifts responsibility to the investor, and small errors can be permanent.

Sending Funds to the Wrong Address or Chain

Blockchain transactions are irreversible. Sending assets to the wrong address or the wrong network is one of the most common—and costly—mistakes.

This typically happens when:

- A correct address is used on the wrong blockchain[4]
- Addresses are copied from compromised devices
- Similar address formats across chains are confused

How to reduce risk:

- Always confirm the blockchain and token standard
- Send a small test transaction first
- Use saved address books or human-readable naming systems where available
- In crypto, accuracy matters more than speed

Phishing, Wallet Drainers, and Impersonation Scams

The most common way people lose their digital assets is by signing the wrong transaction. This is not a new or crypto-specific problem. It is the digital-asset version of online banking fraud, email phishing, and account takeover scams that have existed for decades. The tactics target behavior, not technology.

Attacks usually begin with messages that look legitimate and urgent—fake airdrops, security alerts, wallet upgrades, or "support" responses. These tactics closely resemble familiar bank and online scams that rely on urgency, authority, and imitation to pressure users into acting quickly. This mirrors familiar bank and internet scams that rely on urgency, authority, and imitation to push users into acting quickly. Links lead to cloned websites or malicious contracts. Once a wallet is connected and a transaction is signed, assets can be drained.

A SIM card swap, also known as SIM hijacking, is a form of identity theft in which a criminal takes control of a victim's phone number. By impersonating the victim with a mobile carrier, the attacker transfers the number to a new SIM card under their control. The victim's phone typically loses service, while the attacker begins receiving calls and text messages, including one-time security codes. Because many financial and digital asset platforms still rely on SMS-based verification, a successful SIM swap can allow attackers to reset passwords and take over accounts. Risk can be reduced by avoiding SMS authentication when possible, using authenticator apps or hardware security keys, and placing additional protections on mobile accounts, such as a SIM or port-out PIN or a requirement for in-person verification.

Criminals are highly adaptive. Tactics range from long-running "pig butchering" schemes, where starting with a random text or social media message, romantic or business trust is built over weeks or months before funds are solicited, to fake job interviews that direct candidates to malicious links including on Zoom or wallet connections. These are the same social-engineering techniques used in credit card fraud, wire transfer scams, and identity theft—only the interface is different. Impersonation of well-known platforms, including exchanges like Coinbase, is common, and the goal is always the same: to rush the user into approving a transaction they don't fully understand, sharing their seed phrases or private keys, or sending funds to a fake enterprise.

Real-world examples documented by TRM Labs[5] and blockchain forensics firms include:

- Phishing emails and fake login portals: Scammers send emails or messages that closely mimic popular cryptocurrency wallet or exchange services, coaxing victims to enter seed phrases or credentials into fraudulent sites. These tactics are a classic example of phishing, designed to steal private keys and access wallets directly.
- Wallet drainers: These malicious smart contracts ask users to approve seemingly harmless transactions, like claiming a "free airdrop," but the approval actually grants spending rights. Once granted, automated drain scripts empty the wallet instantly. In 2023 alone, phishing-linked wallet

drainer attacks reportedly siphoned nearly $300 million from victims' wallets.[6]

- Impersonation scams: Scammers pose as legitimate support agents, executives, legal authority, or well-known figures to pressure users into signing transactions or transferring funds. In one widely reported case, a fraudster in the United States posed as a representative of a major exchange to trick over 100 victims into sending crypto into wallets he controlled, ultimately netting millions.[7]

Common failure patterns include:

- Entering seed phrases into fake wallet apps or websites
- Granting unlimited token approvals that allow later withdrawals
- Interacting with new or unaudited protocols under time pressure
- Responding to private messages impersonating support, founders, or exchanges

All of these scams share the same root cause: they rely on social engineering to get users to authorize an on-chain action that transfers control. Once a transaction is signed on the blockchain, it is final and irreversible.

By understanding how these schemes operate and why they succeed, investors can better protect themselves through vigilance, verification, and cautious interaction with links, contracts, and unexpected requests.

There are many security best-practice guides available, including detailed checklists from leading wallet providers.[8,9] At a minimum, investors who choose to self-custody should follow these core principles:

- Never share private keys or recovery phrases. Anyone who has them can take full control of your assets.
- Spread assets across multiple wallets to reduce the risk of a single point of failure.

- Use hardware wallets to keep private keys offline and protected from online attacks.
- Enable two-factor authentication on all accounts, including email and social media, to add protection beyond passwords.
- Keep wallet software and apps up to date so you benefit from the latest security fixes.
- Verify before you trust. Confirm that emails, messages, or calls truly come from official sources before taking action.
- Be cautious of urgency. Pressure to act immediately is a common feature of scams.
- Avoid clicking links or scanning QR codes unless you have verified their source independently.
- Protect your phone number by blocking SIM swaps or adding a password with your mobile provider.
- Only enter login credentials on official websites you navigate to directly—never through links in emails or private messages.

This is not an exhaustive list, but it represents the minimum standard for anyone choosing to manage their own digital assets.

RECORD-KEEPING FOR TAXES AND COMPLIANCE AND SUCCESSION PLANNING

Every action on the blockchain leaves a permanent record. Translating that activity into usable tax and compliance records requires structure.

Key items to track include:

- Purchase dates and cost basis
- Trades, swaps, and realized gains or losses
- Income events such as staking, lending, or airdrops
- Transfers between personal wallets

While centralized exchanges often provide transaction summaries, wallet activity must usually be tracked separately. Specialized tools can aggregate data across exchanges and wallets and generate reports aligned with local tax rules. Some of the most popular tools for tracking digital asset transactions for tax purposes include Koinly and CoinTracker.

Record-keeping also matters in the event of death. Unlike traditional financial accounts, digital assets held in self-custody do not automatically pass to heirs. If private keys or recovery phrases are not properly documented and shared through a secure estate plan, assets may become permanently inaccessible after death, even when ownership is legally established. Clear records, access instructions, and succession planning are therefore essential.[10]

INVESTOR TAKEAWAY

Self-custody means holding digital assets in a wallet you control, rather than leaving them with an exchange, broker, or fund. That control determines what you can do with your assets and who is responsible when something goes wrong.

Investors who hold assets through custodial platforms or public-market products benefit from simplicity. They do not need to manage wallets or private keys, and operational risk is shifted to regulated intermediaries. The trade-off is limited access. These products are designed mainly for price exposure and generally do not allow investors to stake assets, lend them on-chain, trade on decentralized exchanges, or interact directly with blockchain applications.

Self-custody enables those activities. Investors who want to earn yield through staking or lending, provide liquidity, or use decentralized trading platforms must control their assets through a wallet. There is no intermediary that can perform these actions on an investor's behalf.

That access comes with responsibility. In self-custody, there is no password reset, no transaction reversal, and no customer support desk. Security, access, and recovery depend entirely on how keys are stored and how transactions are approved. Mistakes can be permanent.

For many investors, the right approach is not all-or-nothing. Custodial platforms may make sense for trading, short-term positions, or smaller balances. Self-custody may be better suited for long-term holdings and on-chain activity. The key is to match how assets are held to what the investor wants to do with them and how much responsibility they are willing to take on.

This chapter focused on how investors access and control digital assets. The next chapter focuses on what that access enables. Chapter 7 examines yield opportunities in digital assets—how income is generated through staking, lending, and liquidity pools, how returns differ across assets, and the risks involved in earning yield on-chain.

CHAPTER SEVEN

YIELD OPPORTUNITIES IN DIGITAL ASSETS

GENERATING INCOME THROUGH STAKING, LENDING, AND LIQUIDITY POOLS

"The biggest advantages of DeFi is that its permissionless to participate (no KYC, credit score, etc.), same rules apply to everyone, liquidity is 'borderless' (you can access the market from anywhere and anytime as long as you have internet), and it's non-custodial so you have full control over your money and you can use it however you want."

—Stani Kulechov, Founder and CEO, Aave Labs[1]

Yield in digital asset markets looks familiar, but it is not interest or dividends. It exists because networks need security, liquidity, and participation—and must pay for them. In this chapter, we focus on what is often called on-chain yield: returns generated by protocols themselves.

This is different from yield created through financial engineering in traditional markets. For example, an investor can lend Bitcoin through an intermediary and earn a return. While that serves a similar economic purpose, the source of the yield is fundamentally different. On-chain yield comes from the operation of the network, not from a balance sheet or a derivative structure.

By the end of this chapter, you will gain a clear understanding of:

- The core sources of on-chain yield in digital asset markets, including staking, lending, and liquidity provision
- How yield differs across stablecoins and volatile digital assets, and how to distinguish sustainable yield from incentive-driven returns
- The risks embedded in staking, lending, and DeFi strategies, and how those risks show up in different market conditions

WHAT YIELD MEANS ON-CHAIN

On-chain yield is not the digital equivalent of a savings account or a dividend check. It is compensation for specific behaviors that decentralized networks require in order to function. Specifically, on-chain yield represents the return earned from activities recorded directly on a blockchain, such as staking to secure a network, lending assets through smart contracts, or providing liquidity to trading pools. The yield comes from protocol rules, user fees, or incentives, not from a company's balance sheet or a traditional intermediary.

Traditional finance generates yield through centralized balance sheets. Banks pay interest because they lend deposits. Companies pay dividends from profits. Participation is mandated through contracts, regulation, and intermediaries.

Digital asset networks operate differently. They have no centralized treasury that can compel participation or absorb losses. Instead, they rely on economic incentives to secure the network, attract liquidity, and allocate capital. Yield is the primary mechanism networks use to pay participants who perform those functions.

Yield compensates participants for securing networks and supplying liquidity, and it helps allocate capital toward areas of greatest demand. In proof-of-stake networks, validators and delegators lock capital to validate transactions and protect the network. In return, they earn staking rewards and transaction fees.[2] Without yield, there would be little incentive to lock assets or accept risks such as slashing, downtime, or opportunity cost.

Yield also compensates liquidity. Decentralized markets require assets to be available for trading, lending, and settlement at all times. They cannot rely on internal balance sheets or designated market makers. Yield, through lending rates, trading fees, or liquidity incentives, encourages capital to remain active within decentralized markets, even during periods of stress.

Finally, yield is a coordination tool. Digital asset networks use incentives to direct capital toward specific needs. Higher yields reflect increased demand for security or liquidity and encourage participants to respond accordingly. In practice, yield directs capital toward where the system needs it.

COMPARING YIELD IN DIGITAL ASSETS AND TRADITIONAL FINANCE

Dimension	Digital Asset Yield (DeFi/CeFi)	Traditional Finance Yield
Sources of Return	Earned through activities such as staking, lending, providing liquidity, protocol incentives, and on-chain trading strategies.	Generated from interest on deposits, bond coupons, equity dividends, and income-producing real assets.
Market Volatility	Returns are exposed to sharp price swings in underlying assets, which can materially affect realized outcomes.	Asset prices tend to fluctuate less, producing more predictable return profiles over time.
Role of Intermediaries	Often relies on smart contracts and blockchain protocols, reducing reliance on traditional financial middlemen.	Heavily intermediated through banks, brokers, custodians, and clearing institutions.
Regulation and Protection	Regulatory frameworks are still developing; investor protections vary and losses are typically not insured.	Operates within established regulatory systems that include oversight and formal investor protections.
Typical Yield Levels	Can be meaningfully higher, especially on stablecoins or riskier strategies, but returns are variable and carry higher risk.	Generally lower but more stable, reflecting lower risk and tighter regulation.
Liquidity and Access	Markets operate continuously and are accessible globally to anyone with an internet connection.	Trading occurs during set market hours and usually requires access through a bank or brokerage account.

THE THREE MAIN SOURCES OF ON-CHAIN YIELD

At a high level, there are three main sources of yield on-chain: staking, lending, and liquidity provision.

Staking generates yield by securing blockchain networks. In proof-of-stake systems, investors lock assets to help validate transactions and maintain network integrity. In return, they earn rewards funded by network issuance and transaction fees. The yield exists because the network requires capital to be committed to its security.

Lending generates yield by supplying capital. Stablecoins are commonly lent because they function as the settlement layer for digital markets. Investors earn yield because borrowers are willing to pay to access dollar-denominated liquidity without relying on banks. Lending can be done directly on-chain or through centralized platforms that pool deposits and manage counterparties. In all cases, yield compensates lenders for credit risk, liquidity risk, and market stress.

Liquidity provision generates yield by enabling trading. Decentralized markets rely on users to supply assets into trading pools rather than on internal balance sheets. Liquidity providers earn trading fees and, in some cases, additional incentives. This yield reflects compensation for providing continuous liquidity while absorbing price volatility.

These yields can be accessed directly from a wallet or indirectly through centralized platforms that offer products such as yield on USDC balances. While the interface may differ, the underlying economics do not. The critical question is always the same: Where does the yield come from, and what risks are being taken to earn it?

Not all yield in digital asset markets is created equal. Some models are designed to compensate for real economic activity, while others rely on subsidies, leverage, or constant inflows of new capital.

Real Yield vs. Inflationary (Subsidized) Yield

Not all yield is equal. The key distinction is who is paying it.

Real yield comes from actual usage. In digital asset markets, "real" yield does not mean inflation-adjusted. It refers to yield generated from fees or interest paid by actual users through economic activity, rather than from the issuance of new tokens.

Borrowers pay interest, traders pay fees, and networks pay for security. That income is passed to lenders, liquidity providers, or validators. Examples include lending interest on Aave, trading fees on Uniswap, or transaction fees earned by stakers. Real yield can fluctuate, but it is funded by users and can persist as long as demand exists.

Subsidized yield is paid through incentives, usually by issuing new tokens. This approach is common in early-stage protocols trying to attract capital before real usage develops. These yields can look attractive, but they dilute holders and typically decline as incentives are reduced.

Over time, successful protocols shift from incentives to fee-based economics. Yields fall, but they become more durable.

Yield Type	What Pays the Yield	Typical Use Cases	Examples
Real Yield	Fees paid by users for on-chain services	Mature networks and established protocols	Ethereum (staking rewards increasingly funded by transaction fees), Uniswap (trading fees paid to liquidity providers), Aave (interest paid by borrowers to lenders)

Yield Type	What Pays the Yield	Typical Use Cases	Examples
Subsidized/ Inflationary Yield	Newly issued tokens or incentive rewards	Early-stage networks or growth phases	Early validator rewards on Solana and Avalanche; liquidity mining programs on new DeFi protocols

Ultimately, yield is compensation, not a free lunch. The most important question is not how high the yield looks today, but where it comes from. Yield funded by users can last. Yield funded by token emissions is temporary by design.

Across public markets, private funds, and DeFi, the principle is the same: higher yield usually reflects higher risk or less mature economics. Once you understand the source of return, the remaining decision is sizing—how much exposure fits your portfolio and risk tolerance.

Why Yield Matters Most in Sideways or Bear Markets

Yield matters most when prices stop doing the work for you.

In bull markets, returns are dominated by price appreciation and income feels almost irrelevant. In sideways or declining markets, that illusion fades. When prices stagnate, yield becomes a primary source of return, and a test of whether a strategy can stand on its own.

Sustainable yield can soften drawdowns and keep capital productive without relying on timing the market. Unsustainable yield tends to vanish at exactly the wrong moment, when conditions tighten and liquidity matters most.

On-chain yield is compensation for risk, not free income. When a yield appears unusually high, the real question is not how it is generated, but where the risk—or dilution—ultimately resides.

STAKING: YIELD FROM NETWORK SECURITY

Staking is a direct source of yield because it pays participants for securing the network.

In proof-of-stake networks such as Ethereum, Solana, Cosmos, and Avalanche, transactions are processed by independent operators called validators. Validators run network software and verify transactions. To do that job, they lock up the network's native token as collateral. This locked collateral is the stake.

Validators earn rewards for correctly validating transactions and remaining online. Validators that go offline or violate network rules can be penalized, including the loss of a portion of their staked tokens.

Over time, staking yields usually compress. More tokens are staked, issuance schedules decline, and rewards are spread across more participants. Staking is best understood not as a fixed-income substitute but as variable compensation for providing network security under evolving conditions.

Types of Staking

At a high level, staking approaches fall into three broad categories. Each step adds flexibility and potential yield but also introduces additional layers of risk.

Native and Delegated Staking

Staking is the core way investors earn yield on proof-of-stake networks. Tokens are locked on the network to help validate transactions and secure the system, and rewards are paid in return. These rewards are generated by the network itself, not by individual applications.

There are two ways investors participate. With native staking, investors stake tokens directly and, in some cases, run their own validator infrastructure. With delegated staking, which is more common, investors delegate tokens to a validator who performs the validation work on their behalf. Ownership of the tokens remains with the investor, and rewards are shared after the validator's fee.

Staking rewards come from two sources. The first is new token issuance, where the network creates and distributes new tokens according to preset supply rules. The second is transaction fees paid by users, which are shared with stakers and can grow as network activity increases.

The main risks are operational rather than financial. Rewards depend on validator performance and adherence to network rules. In most networks, staked assets are not immediately liquid. When staking is stopped, tokens typically enter an unbonding period lasting days or weeks during which they cannot be moved or sold and usually stop earning rewards.

Delegated staking is accessible directly from wallets or through platforms that simplify participation. The trade-off for simplicity is reliance on validator performance and lock-up terms set by the network.

Liquid Staking Tokens (LSTs)

Liquid staking improves flexibility by removing the need to wait through unbonding periods. When assets are staked through a liquid staking protocol such as Lido, Rocketpool, Marinade Finance or Jito, investors receive a token that represents their staked position and continues to earn rewards. That token can be traded or used elsewhere, allowing capital to remain mobile. It can be borrowed against, lent out, or placed into liquidity pools, as described later in this chapter.

Examples of the token that represents the staked position include stETH on Ethereum, mSOL on Solana, and rETH through Rocket Pool. The trade-off is added complexity and reliance on protocol software and smart contracts, which introduces risks beyond the base network itself.

Restaking

Restaking extends liquid staking by allowing staked assets to secure additional services beyond the base network in exchange for higher yield. On Ethereum, platforms such as EigenLayer enable this model, often using liquid staking tokens.

While restaking can increase returns, it also layers risk across multiple systems. Yield becomes dependent not only on the base network, but also on the design, incentives, and governance of secondary protocols. Issues in any layer can affect the original stake, even if the underlying network remains stable. Restaking is best suited for experienced participants.

Today, investors can access basic staking through exchanges such as Coinbase, Kraken, and Binance. Liquid staking is typically accessed through wallets and protocols like MetaMask, Phantom, Lido, and Ether.fi. Restaking, by contrast, is still primarily available through EigenLayer-based DeFi platforms and remains a more complex, higher-risk option best suited for experienced participants.

Examples of Yield

Below are yield opportunities across major proof-of-stake networks, with ranges based on late-2025 on-chain and protocol data.

Network	Staking	Liquid staking	Restaking
Ethereum (ETH)	~3–5% annualized network rewards	Tokenized staked ETH ~3–4% net	Additional ~1–8% for extended validation or service layers
Solana (SOL)	~6–8% native network participation	Tokenized SOL staking instruments ~6–8%	Incremental yield from transaction ordering and block-value capture
Avalanche (AVAX)	Variable, typically mid-single-digit rewards	Tokenized AVAX staking ~3.5–4.5%	Emerging integrations; returns depend on DeFi adoption
BNB (BNB)	APY up to 2.81%	APY between 3% and 7%	N/A
Cosmos (ATOM)	~12–16% gross	Limited, ecosystem-specific	Minimal

APY vs. APR: Reading Yield Correctly

Staking returns are usually quoted as APY (Annual Percentage Yield) or APR (Annual Percentage Rate).

APY includes the effect of compounding, meaning rewards are reinvested and generate additional rewards over time. APR measures the simple annual return without assuming rewards are reinvested.

The distinction matters. A staking program offering 5% APR provides a 5% annual return if rewards are left uninvested, while 5% APY already includes the effect of compounding. In some cases, a lower APR can produce a higher total return than a higher APR if rewards are automatically compounded more frequently. For this reason, most consumer platforms highlight APY, while institutional providers often disclose both metrics.

What Investors Mean by "Risk-Free Yield" in Digital Assets

In digital assets, the term "risk-free yield" is often used to describe the baseline return earned from staking on large, established proof-of-stake networks. It is loosely analogous to a government bond yield or risk-free rate in traditional finance, but it is not truly risk-free.

In practice, this yield comes from native staking rewards, where validators earn returns for locking tokens and participating honestly in network security, without taking directional trading risk. Because these rewards represent the lowest expected risk within the system, they are sometimes treated as a reference rate for evaluating other digital asset strategies.

The analogy has limits. Staking still carries protocol risk, slashing risk, liquidity constraints, and exposure to the underlying token's price. For that reason, professionals increasingly refer to staking returns as a "protocol base rate" or "crypto-native yield" rather than a true risk-free rate.

The key idea is simple: staking yield represents the minimum return required to secure a blockchain. All other digital asset strategies are expected to exceed this base yield in exchange for taking additional risk.

Understanding Staking Returns and Risk

Staking is not free money. It is compensation for helping secure a blockchain network, and returns depend on how that network is used.

Staking rewards are variable, not fixed. They change based on network activity, how many participants are staking, and protocol rules. As more assets are staked, returns tend to decline. As activity increases, transaction fees can raise returns. Staking should be viewed as a source of variable income tied to network conditions, not a guaranteed yield.

Most staking risks are operational and tend to be modest. When using established providers, issues typically show up as lower yields or temporary delays rather than permanent losses. Liquid staking adds some complexity, but the underlying assets remain tied to the network.

Staking rewards compensate investors for providing network security. Returns are generally modest and should be evaluated as part of a broader portfolio, not as a high-risk, high-reward strategy.

PUTTING IT ALL TOGETHER

At a high level:

- Native and delegated staking emphasize simplicity and alignment with network security, but involve illiquidity due to unbonding periods, meaning investors must wait days or weeks to fully exit a position.
- Liquid staking emphasizes flexibility and capital efficiency.
- Restaking emphasizes higher potential yield, with greater complexity and shared risk.

LENDING AND BORROWING

> *"I chose the lending market to build Morpho because it's the largest addressable market in finance."*
>
> —Paul Frambot, Founder of Morpho

Lending is the largest market in global finance because nearly all economic activity ultimately relies on credit. Sovereign bonds, corporate debt, mortgages, bank loans, and consumer credit together exceed $300 trillion in outstanding value.[3] That's several times larger than global equity markets, which total roughly $120 trillion.[4] Credit underpins housing, corporate investment, trade, leverage, and system-wide liquidity.

The same structure carries over to digital asset markets. Lending provides the foundation for leverage, liquidity, and yield. It allows traders to borrow against assets, market makers to operate efficiently, and capital to stay productive rather than idle.

Most advanced on-chain activity depends on lending in some form. Trading strategies, arbitrage, and liquidity provision all rely on the ability to borrow or deploy assets flexibly. As a result, lending protocols have consistently been among the largest and most heavily used parts of decentralized markets, remaining relevant across multiple market cycles even as other sectors rise and fall.

Figure 7.1 shows that lending has remained one of the most durable segments of digital asset markets. Aave's Total Value Locked (TVL), which

Figure 7.1 Aave protocol.

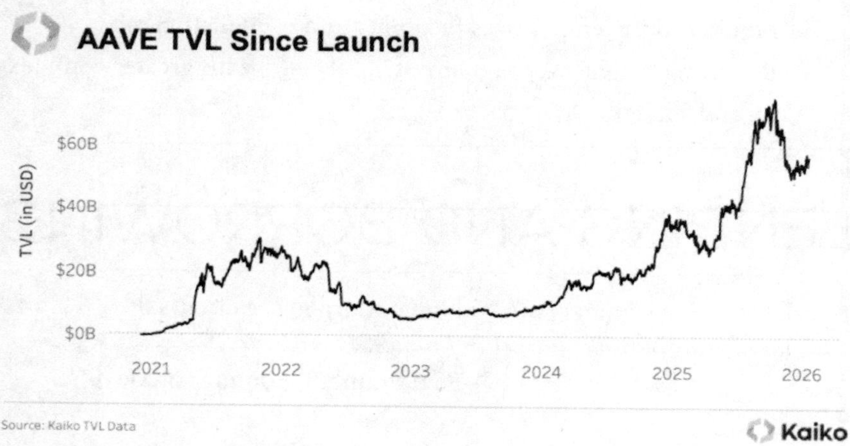

measures the total assets held on the protocol, is used as a proxy for overall lending activity. Activity surged during the 2020–2021 cycle, contracted sharply after the 2022 downturn, and then rebuilt steadily through 2023–2025. While prices and narratives come and go, lending repeatedly returns because it sits at the core of leverage, liquidity, and yield in both centralized and on-chain markets.

Yield, Leverage, and Digital Asset Lenders

"If you don't know where the yield is coming from, you are the yield." This aphorism captures a hard-earned truth that often reveals itself only after the fact. Like many lessons in finance, it sounds obvious in hindsight, but easy to ignore in moments of optimism.

Centralized digital asset lenders such as Celsius Network and BlockFi marketed themselves as low-risk platforms for retail investors by offering interest on customer deposits, presenting their services as a way for investors to put idle digital assets to work.[5] They generated that yield by lending customer assets to hedge funds and trading firms, using them as collateral for loans, and deploying them into leveraged trading and arbitrage strategies.

When digital asset prices fell and borrowers failed to repay, these firms could not recover the assets they had lent out. Withdrawals were frozen, and customers became unsecured creditors in long bankruptcy processes. In the case of Celsius, its founder, Alex Mashinsky, was later sentenced to 12 years in prison and ordered to forfeit millions of dollars in assets.

Lesson: Yield offered by centralized platforms often reflects credit and counterparty risk. Counterparty risk means trusting someone else with your assets. If that person or company fails, your assets may be lost or frozen, even if the market or technology itself is still working. When customer assets are reused and leveraged, liquidity can disappear quickly.

How Lending Works

DeFi lending is built on a simple rule: borrowers must lock up more value than they borrow. This structure is similar to a Lombard loan, a traditional form of lending where securities are pledged as collateral in exchange for cash, without relying on income or creditworthiness.

In DeFi, there are no credit checks, no applications, and no human judgment. The rules are set in advance and enforced automatically by software.

This is fundamentally different from traditional consumer lending.

The core difference is that DeFi lending is based on collateral you already own. Bank lending is based on trust in your future income.

DeFi Lending

On DeFi platforms such as Aave, Euler, or Morpho, loans are over collateralized.

A simple example:

- You deposit $150 worth of ETH
- You borrow $100 of USDC
- If the value of ETH falls too far, the position is automatically closed and liquidated to repay the loan

The system does not assess who you are. It only checks whether the collateral is sufficient.

Key features of DeFi lending:

- Loans are typically overcollateralized (often 120–200%)
- No credit score or income checks
- No identity required
- Loans are enforced automatically by smart contracts
- Access is global and available at all times

Because enforcement is automatic, losses are limited by design. If collateral drops below required levels, liquidation happens without negotiation or delay.

Banks approach lending from the opposite direction. Instead of focusing on existing assets, banks lend based on who the borrower is and what they are expected to earn in the future.

For example:

- You borrow $100,000
- You may provide little or no collateral (as with a credit card or personal loan)

The bank relies on:

- Credit history
- Employment and income
- Legal contracts and enforcement if you default

When you borrow from a bank, you are borrowing against future cash flow. When you borrow in DeFi, you are borrowing against assets you already own.

Banks create credit by taking risk on borrowers. DeFi limits risk by requiring collateral upfront.

Side-by-side Comparison

DeFi Lending	Bank Lending
Overcollateralized	Often under-collateralized
No credit score	Credit score is central
Instant, automated	Slow, manual approvals
Automatic collateral sale	Enforcement via courts
Global and permissionless	Local and regulated
No maturity mismatch	Fractional reserve system

How Interest Rates Are Set

Interest rates for these are not fixed. They move as borrowing demand changes. Markets are not fixed. They adjust automatically based on supply and demand.

When many borrowers want to access funds and available capital is limited, rates rise. When borrowing slows, and cash sits idle, rates fall. During market rallies, traders often borrow stablecoins to buy assets, which pushes lending rates higher. When markets cool, borrowing drops and yields come down.

Most lending platforms adjust rates based on how much of the available capital is already in use. As pools become heavily used, borrowing becomes more expensive and lending more attractive. This keeps capital available when it is most needed.

Rates vary by asset and platform. On Aave V3, recent lending returns have typically been around 3–4% for USDC, about 2–3% for USDT, and lower for ETH unless additional incentives are offered.

Some platforms deliver higher returns by matching lenders and borrowers more directly. Morpho, for example, has recently shown lending returns around 6% per year on ETH in certain markets, though rates change with demand.

More specialized platforms can show even wider ranges. Euler offers asset-specific lending pools where common assets may earn mid-single- to low-double-digit returns, while smaller or more volatile markets have at times paid much higher returns.

The key point is straightforward: lending returns rise when capital is in demand and fall when it is not. Higher yields are available, but they reflect tighter conditions or higher risk, not free income (see Figure 7.2).

Figure 7.2 DeFi lending has rebounded since 2023, with total value locked surging, led by Aave's rapid growth.

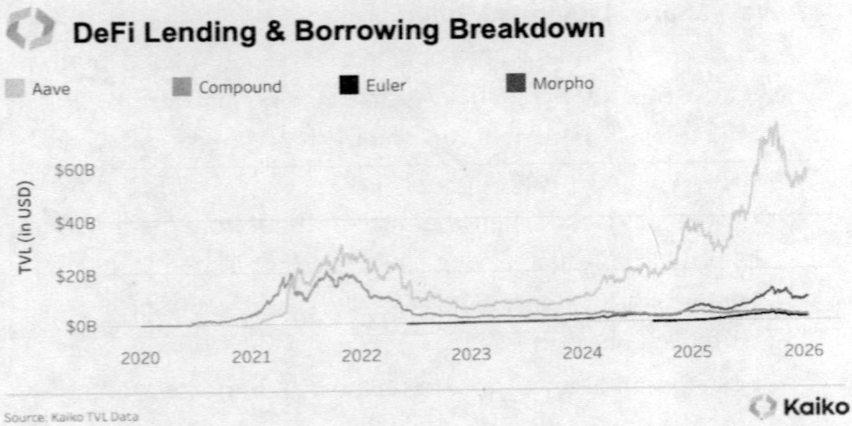

Why Platform Yields Change

The yield shown on Defi platforms moves because the underlying conditions change.

Yields rise when demand for liquidity increases, network rewards temporarily grow, or platforms offer incentives to attract capital. They fall when borrowing slows, activity declines, or rewards normalize.

Platforms also adjust yields as they change fees, manage risk, or limit exposure during volatile periods.

Yield levels are signals, not promises. Some products offer variable rates that change continuously, while others lock in a rate for a defined period. Even when a rate is locked, access to funds may be restricted, and reinvestment will occur at prevailing rates once the term ends. Sudden yield increases often reflect tighter conditions or temporary incentives. Declines usually indicate lower demand or reduced rewards. Yield should be evaluated as compensation for changing conditions, not as a guaranteed return.

DeFi Lending Models: Three Different Approaches

Aave—Shared Liquidity Model

- Built on shared liquidity pools that aggregate user deposits into standardized, widely accessible lending markets
- Structure: Users deposit assets into shared pools, which are then used for lending
- How lending works: Borrowers access funds from these pools by posting collateral
- Interest rates: Adjust automatically based on supply and borrowing demand
- Risk oversight: Key parameters are set and updated through on-chain governance
- Design emphasis: Broad access, standardized markets, and conservative risk settings
- Typically used by: Participants seeking a widely used and established lending protocol

Aave has also expanded its institutional offerings through Horizon, an Ethereum-based lending market launched in 2025 that enables institutions and qualified investors to borrow stablecoins against tokenized real-world assets. By combining decentralized lending infrastructure with permissioned access and compliance controls, Horizon reflects the growing convergence of traditional finance and DeFi.

Morpho—Separate Risk Management Pools

- Structure: Isolated lending markets, each with a single collateral asset, loan asset, oracle, and immutable risk parameters; curated vaults allocate lender deposits across selected markets
- How lending works: Borrowers access funds from a specific market by posting the required collateral

- Interest rates: Set independently for each market, while vault yields reflect a blended return from their underlying markets
- Risk oversight: Liquidation thresholds and risk parameters are fixed at the market level, while vault curators determine how depositor capital is allocated across markets
- Design emphasis: Greater flexibility, customizable risk management, and capital allocation across isolated lending markets
- Typically used by: Participants seeking tailored risk exposure and curated lending strategies

Euler—Modular and Customizable Markets

- Structure: Separate markets are created for individual assets or strategies
- How lending works: Each market operates with its own parameters rather than sharing a single pool
- Interest rates: Set independently for each market
- Risk oversight: Market-level isolation limits the impact of issues in one market on others
- Design emphasis: Flexibility, customization, and support for less common assets

How These Approaches Differ

- Aave emphasizes pooled assets and standardized markets for broad participation
- Morpho uses isolated markets to optimize capital efficiency and manage risk per market
- Euler prioritizes flexible, customizable markets built around isolated pools

Common Lending Uses

Lending exists because it solves real problems for different participants:

- Stablecoin lending for income:
    - Investors supply USDC, USDT, or similar assets to earn interest from borrowers who need liquidity for trading, payments, or short-term financing.
- Lending tokens:
    - Assets such as ETH or SOL can also be lent to traders who want to hedge exposure or run specific strategies. Lenders earn interest but remain exposed to price movements in the underlying asset.
- Borrowing without selling:
    - Investors often borrow stablecoins against assets they want to keep. This allows access to liquidity without selling and triggering taxes or giving up future upside. The risk is liquidation if prices fall too far.

Together, these use cases create consistent demand for lending and underpin the yields earned by lenders. They allow digital assets to function not just as investments, but as usable financial collateral, enabling borrowing and income generation in ways that are often limited or inaccessible in traditional banking and brokerage systems.

The Core Trade-Off

Lending is efficient and transparent, but it is not risk-free. It works best when markets are orderly and collateral remains liquid. During sharp moves, automated liquidations can accelerate quickly, and liquidity can dry up.

Yields rise during these periods because liquidity becomes more valuable—not because risk disappears.

Key Risks to Understand

Lending risks tend to be systemic rather than personal. Even careful participants can be affected by:

- Software risk: Bugs or exploits in lending platforms can freeze or drain funds.
- Price feed risk: Incorrect price data can trigger unnecessary liquidations.
- Liquidation cascades: Rapid market moves can force simultaneous collateral sales, amplifying losses.
- Correlation risk: When many loans rely on similar collateral, stress can spread quickly.

Lending yield is compensation for supplying liquidity when others need it. Higher yields usually signal tighter conditions and higher risk. Understanding collateral, utilization, and liquidation dynamics is essential to deciding how much capital to allocate and when caution matters most.

Today, investors can access lending yield either directly from their own wallets by interacting with on-chain protocols, or through centralized exchanges such as Coinbase and Kraken, which have begun offering lending products built on protocols like Morpho and Aave.

Can Insurance Help Cover the Risk?

Insurance exists in digital asset markets, but it works very differently from insurance in traditional finance and has clear limits.

In decentralized finance, a small group of digital-asset-native insurers, such as Nexus Mutual and InsurAce, offer optional coverage for specific technical failures. These policies typically cover events like smart-contract bugs or protocol exploits. In some cases, coverage is built directly into a product, such as a lending vault that includes protection against contract failure. However, this insurance is narrowly defined, capped in size, and does not cover market losses, price volatility, or user error. It functions as a supplement to risk management rather than a comprehensive safety net.

For individuals, protections remain limited. Some centralized platforms carry insurance against theft or operational failures, but this coverage generally protects the platform itself rather than guaranteeing individual balances. Losses caused by hacks, phishing, or user mistakes are often excluded. Unlike bank deposits, there is no government-backed insurance for holding digital assets, and any protection in decentralized systems is typically optional and user-funded.

Institutional investors have more coverage options, but these are still incomplete. Funds and custodians rely on traditional policies such as crime insurance, professional liability coverage, and operational insurance, sometimes combined with custodial insurance for key management. Large platforms may also maintain internal insurance funds to absorb losses from liquidations or operational failures. These measures provide some protection, but they are discretionary, opaque, and not backed by public guarantees.

Today, insurance in digital asset markets should be viewed as a way to reduce certain risks, not eliminate them. Broader and more reliable coverage will likely require clearer regulation, better separation of different risk types, and deeper involvement from traditional insurers and reinsurers. Until then, insurance can help in specific cases, but careful risk management remains essential.

LIQUIDITY PROVISION, YIELD FARMING, AND ADVANCED YIELD

Beyond lending and staking, yield can come from supporting trading itself via Automated market makers (AMMs) or Decentralized exchanges (DEXs) and liquidity pools.

Liquidity provision means supplying assets so others can trade and getting a fee for it. Instead of buyers and sellers meeting through an order book, decentralized markets rely on shared pools of assets. When you contribute to a pool—say Ether and USDC—you make it possible for others to trade between them.

In return, you earn a share of the trading fees paid by every user who uses that pool. Fees accrue continuously and are paid automatically, in proportion to how much liquidity you provide.

The trade-off is that your asset mix changes as prices move. If one asset rises or falls sharply relative to the other, your position can end up worth less than if you had simply held the assets. Higher trading volume or additional incentives can offset this, but the risk remains.

Over time, these strategies have become more complex. Some pools focus only on stablecoins to reduce price swings. Others allow providers to earn fees only within chosen price ranges. Many add extra rewards on top of trading fees. These approaches can increase returns, but they also make outcomes more sensitive to market conditions and timing.

Instead of matching buyers and sellers, automated market makers (AMMs) use pools of assets.[6] Each trade pays a fee, which is shared with liquidity providers.

- Stablecoin pools (e.g., USDC–DAI): lower volatility, lower risk, modest fees
- Token pools (e.g., ETH–USDC): higher fees, but exposed to price swings

The main trade-off is impermanent loss: if one asset moves sharply relative to the other, the value of the pool position can underperform simply holding the assets.

Liquidity provision works best when:

- Trading volume is high
- Prices move within a range
- Fees compensate for volatility

How Uniswap Works

Uniswap, one of the first AMMs, lets people trade digital assets without a central exchange or order book.

Instead of matching buyers and sellers, Uniswap uses liquidity pools. Each pool holds two tokens—for example, ETH and USDC. People who deposit both tokens into the pool are called liquidity providers.

When someone wants to trade:

- They send one token into the pool
- They receive the other token from the pool
- The price adjusts automatically based on how much of each token remains
- There is always a price and always liquidity, even if no other trader is active

Each trade pays a small fee. Those fees are distributed to liquidity providers as compensation for supplying capital and accepting price risk. If prices move sharply between the two tokens, liquidity providers may end up with less value than if they had simply held the assets.

Uniswap succeeded because it is permissionless[7] and always on:

- Anyone can trade directly from a wallet
- Anyone can create a trading pool
- Anyone can provide liquidity

Today, Uniswap is one of the most active decentralized exchanges. While centralized exchanges still handle most global trading volume, Uniswap processes significant activity on-chain and serves as core infrastructure for decentralized trading.

In short:

- Traders trade against pools, not people
- Liquidity providers earn fees for supplying capital
- Prices move automatically based on supply and demand

How DeFi Vaults Are Built

DeFi vaults are automated products that manage yield strategies on an investor's behalf. Instead of manually lending, trading, or staking assets across multiple protocols, investors deposit funds into a vault that executes a predefined strategy automatically.

Vaults operate through smart contracts that execute these strategies automatically. In their simplest form, they are open-access: anyone with a compatible wallet and the required asset can participate, and strategy rules are enforced by code rather than by a central manager. This structure removes manual decision-making while allowing capital to be deployed continuously as market conditions change.

As DeFi has matured, vaults have expanded beyond retail use. Professional investors are increasingly accessing structured vaults designed for regulated participation. Asset managers such as Bitwise have launched conservative, yield-focused vault strategies, while protocols including Maple, Centrifuge, and Euler support permissioned environments with Know Your Customer (KYC) and compliance controls. These designs allow institutions to access on-chain lending through familiar guardrails, preserving the core mechanics of DeFi while meeting regulatory requirements.

Behind every vault are two distinct roles: Strategy Designers (Vault Curators) and Risk Manager.

Vault curators design how the vault operates. They decide:

- Which assets the vault accepts
- Which protocols it uses
- How capital is allocated across opportunities
- When and how the strategy rebalances

Their role is to define a clear, repeatable approach so investors do not have to manage positions themselves. Examples of active vault curators include Gauntlet, Steakhouse Financial, Edge Capital, and vault delegates on platforms like Drift, such as Neutral Trade and Elemental.

Risk managers focus on limits and controls. They:

- Stress-test strategies under adverse market conditions
- Set constraints on leverage, exposure, and concentration
- Adjust parameters to reduce the chance of large losses

Their job is not to eliminate risk, but to keep it within defined bounds. Once a strategy and its risk limits are coded into a smart contract, the vault operates automatically. Investors deposit assets, and the vault executes the strategy according to predefined rules.

Common Types of Vaults

In practice, the curator–risk manager model shows up in a few common structures:

- Lending vaults: Stablecoins or other assets are deployed into lending markets. Curators decide where capital is placed, while risk managers limit exposure to any single borrower or market. Investors earn lending yield without managing loans directly. Examples include Morpho vaults curated by Steakhouse Financial, Gauntlet-managed stablecoin vaults.
- Liquidity vaults: Vaults provide liquidity to trading pools within defined price ranges. Curators select token pairs and positioning, while risk managers monitor exposure to price swings. Investors earn trading fees with controlled parameters. Examples include Uniswap liquidity vaults; Drift Vault strategies on Solana.
- Staking and restaking vaults: Assets are staked, and sometimes restaked, across multiple services. Curators manage allocation, and risk managers cap exposure to slashing or protocol risk. Investors receive combined staking yield without handling each step themselves. Examples include ETH staking and restaking vaults using EigenLayer-based strategies.

Why Vaults Are Accessible

Once deployed on-chain, vaults are permissionless and anyone with a wallet can access them:

- No applications or minimums
- No discretionary approval
- No manual intervention

Investors connect a wallet, deposit supported assets, and the vault follows its rules automatically.

STABLECOIN YIELD: THE FOUNDATION OF ON-CHAIN INCOME

Stablecoins are sometimes described as "yield-bearing," but that phrasing is misleading. Simply holding a stablecoin does not generate income. Any yield comes from how the stablecoin is used or from separate arrangements layered on top of it.

In practice, there are two ways investors encounter stablecoin yield:

- Directly, by choosing to lend or deploy stablecoins into yield-generating strategies
- Indirectly, through platforms that share rewards or incentives funded by other revenue sources

It is also important to distinguish between yield earned by stablecoin issuers and yield earned by users. Dollar-backed stablecoin issuers typically invest reserves in cash or US Treasuries and earn interest on those assets. That issuer income is generally not distributed to stablecoin holders. Any yield a user receives comes from a separate, opt-in product or strategy.

Not all stablecoins are structured the same way. How a stablecoin is backed determines how it behaves under stress and what risks investors are taking.

Types of Stablecoins

1. Dollar-Backed Stablecoins (USDC, USDT)
   These stablecoins are issued by companies that hold dollar-denominated reserves such as cash and US government bonds. The goal is to maintain a one-to-one peg with the dollar. USDC is

generally viewed as more conservative and transparent. USDT is the most widely used for trading but has historically disclosed less detail about reserves. The main risks are issuer trust and regulation. Despite this, dollar-backed stablecoins are widely used and typically considered the lowest risk option for liquidity and payments.

2. Digital-Asset-Backed Stablecoins (DAI)
   These stablecoins are backed by locked digital assets rather than cash. More than one dollar of collateral is required to issue one dollar of stablecoin. DAI is a common example. It is governed by smart contracts, and collateral is automatically sold if values fall too far. This reduces reliance on an issuer but introduces market and liquidation risk.
3. Algorithmic or Hybrid Stablecoins (Higher Risk)
   These stablecoins rely on incentives and market behavior rather than hard backing. They can fail quickly when confidence breaks, as seen with LUNA/UST. Newer designs add complexity and tend to be most fragile during stress. Higher yields reflect higher risk.

Terra and the Limits of Algorithmic Stability

Terra collapsed in May 2022 after its stablecoin, UST, failed to hold its $1 peg. UST was not backed by dollars or hard collateral. Instead, it relied on an algorithm that linked its value to a related token, LUNA.

When confidence weakened and large withdrawals began, the mechanism broke. Attempts to restore the peg required minting large amounts of LUNA, which drove its price toward zero and destroyed the remaining support for UST. Tens of billions of dollars in value were wiped out within days. The project's founder, Do Kwon, was later sentenced to 15 years in prison.

Lesson: Stability without hard collateral depends on confidence. When confidence breaks, these systems can fail quickly.

When yield becomes disconnected from sustainable demand, it tends to fail abruptly. The examples below illustrate how and why that happens.

Category	Project	What Was Promised	What Actually Happened	Core Lesson
Algorithmic/ Ponzi-Like Yield	Ponzi-Like Yield Terra (Anchor Protocol)	~20% "stable" yield on UST	Yield was subsidized and required constant new capital; when confidence broke, UST depegged and the system collapsed	Subsidized yield is not sustainable long term
Leverage & Recursive Yield	Celsius	High yield on customer deposits	Used leverage, rehypothecation, and opaque strategies; withdrawals were frozen and the company went bankrupt	Yield came from hidden balance-sheet risk
Leverage & Recursive Yield	BlockFi	Attractive yields on "safer" digital asset deposits	Depended on counterparty risk and leverage; collapsed during market stress	CeFi yield often mirrors hedge-fund risk

Putting It Together

- USDC/USDT → backed by dollar-denominated reserves (simpler, lower risk)
- DAI → backed by over-collateralized digital assets (more decentralized, more complex)
- Algorithmic or hybrid designs → rely on incentives and market behavior (higher risk, higher potential yield)

Not all stablecoins are equal. The closer the backing is to dollars held in reserve, the more stable the system tends to be. The more it relies on financial engineering and incentives, the more carefully risks must be evaluated.

Case Study: Stream Finance—When High Yield Breaks

Stream Finance was a DeFi project that promised unusually high returns on stablecoin deposits through complex yield strategies and yield-bearing tokens such as xUSD.[8] Rather than relying on simple lending or staking, Stream used leveraged strategies, recursive borrowing, and external fund managers to amplify returns.

In November 2025, Stream disclosed that an external manager had lost approximately $93 million of protocol assets. Confidence collapsed almost immediately. The stablecoin xUSD, designed to trade near $1, fell sharply and withdrawals were frozen as operations were paused.

Because Stream's strategies were intertwined with multiple lending and yield platforms, losses spread beyond the protocol itself. As positions unwound, liquidity dried up and stress rippled through connected DeFi markets. Subsequent reporting suggested legal action against the external manager, though investigations remain ongoing.

What kind of yield was being offered:

Stream marketed itself as a "yield optimizer," advertising high double-digit yields—around 18% APY on USDC—well above prevailing rates on established platforms like Aave or Compound. These returns were driven by leveraged strategies, including incentive farming, arbitrage, and recursive reinvestment. When a single loss occurred, the structure unraveled.

Lesson:

High yields funded by leverage and opaque strategies can collapse quickly. When returns appear meaningfully higher than the market, risk is often embedded in ways that are not immediately visible.

Sources of Stablecoin Yield

Stablecoins do not earn yield on their own. Any return comes from allowing someone else to use them. That use can take several forms. Centralized platforms pay yield by lending or trading with customer funds, which is simple but requires giving up control and relying on the platform's financial health. In some cases, platforms advertise "rewards" for holding stablecoins, which are typically paid by the platform itself and not generated by the stablecoin token.

On-chain lending markets pay interest from borrowers who need digital dollars, with rates rising and falling based on demand. Trading pools generate yield from transaction fees as stablecoins are exchanged for settlement. Some products share revenue from actual usage, while others offer structured or fixed returns that involve lockups and additional risk.

Across all cases, stablecoin yield is compensation for providing capital, not free income. Returns are typically lower than those on volatile assets, reflecting a trade-off between steadier income and risk. The key questions are straightforward: Who is paying the yield, what stands between you and your money, and what happens under stress?

What matters most:

- Stablecoins themselves do not pay yield
- Yield comes from lending, trading, or balance-sheet risk
- Higher yields reflect higher risk
- These products are not substitutes for holding stablecoins for payments or liquidity

Simple Rule of Thumb

If a stablecoin is earning yield, it is being used for something—and that use carries risk.

Holding stablecoins in your own wallet provides stability and liquidity. Earning yield means opting into an on-chain yield investment strategy with trade-offs.

Stablecoin issuers earn interest on the assets backing their coins, but this income is not paid to holders of the stablecoin itself. Any yield sharing happens through separate, opt-in products offered by platforms—not through the stablecoin token.

Who Gets the Yield on Stablecoins?

For dollar-backed stablecoins, users often assume that if the issuer earns interest, holders should too. That is usually not how stablecoins work.

How dollar stablecoins make money

When a stablecoin issuer receives dollars, it typically invests those funds in cash, US Treasury bills, or other low-risk assets. These investments generate yield. That yield generally belongs to the issuer, not the stablecoin holder.

Regulation and the "no-interest" rule

Under US frameworks such as the GENIUS Act, payment stablecoins are treated as non-interest bearing. Issuers may earn yield on reserves, but they are generally prohibited from paying interest to users simply for holding the stablecoin. This has shifted the policy debate toward what counts as "interest" vs. what can be labeled as third-party "rewards," a distinction banks and regulators are actively scrutinizing.

Tether vs. Circle: Current models

Tether (USDT): Tether earns yield on reserves, primarily from Treasury bills and cash equivalents. That yield is retained by the issuer and its shareholders and is not shared with USDT holders.

Circle (USDC): Circle also earns reserve yield. Simply holding USDC, whether on-chain or in a wallet, does not entitle users to that yield. The economics largely accrue to Circle and its distribution partners.

Why Coinbase advertises "USDC rewards"

When Coinbase promotes rewards for holding USDC, those payments are not inherent yield from USDC itself. They are rewards paid by Coinbase under its own program. Coinbase can offer them because it receives a share of USDC reserve economics as a major distributor. This structure sits at the center of current regulatory debates, as some policymakers argue it closely resembles issuer-paid interest.

Investor Takeaway

Stablecoins like USDC can earn yield in decentralized markets, but that yield is market-driven, variable, and not guaranteed. Issuer reserve yield from Treasury bills is a separate stream, and US policy momentum is toward preventing stablecoins from functioning like interest-bearing bank deposits. Investors should not assume stablecoin issuers will be allowed to directly "share the yield" with holders going forward.

YIELD FARMING: INCENTIVES ON TOP OF FEES

Yield farming refers to actively combining multiple DeFi activities, such as lending, trading, and staking, to increase returns, often by earning additional incentive tokens on top of fees or interest.

Unlike single-purpose activities like staking, lending on Aave, or providing liquidity on Uniswap, yield farming usually involves moving assets between protocols to chase higher returns. This added complexity can increase returns in the short term, but it also increases risk and often involves leverage. Yield farming is generally best suited for experienced participants who are comfortable navigating DeFi systems.

Incentive tokens can materially boost returns at first. Over time, those incentives tend to decline as more capital enters and rewards are reduced. When incentives fall, capital often exits quickly and yields drop sharply.

A simple rule applies: if most of the return comes from incentive tokens, the yield is likely temporary by design.

INVESTOR TAKEAWAY

On-chain yield exists because networks need security and markets need liquidity. Staking pays investors for helping secure a network. Lending pays investors because borrowers need stablecoin liquidity. Liquidity provision pays investors because traders need continuous markets. In every case, yield is compensation for a job being done—not a dividend or "free interest."

The most important question is not how high the yield looks, but who is paying it. Returns funded by users—borrowers paying interest, traders paying fees, networks paying for security—tend to be more durable. Returns funded mainly by incentives or token issuance are temporary and usually decline as conditions change.

Yields also move. They rise when capital is scarce or demand is high, and they fall when liquidity is abundant. Even when a rate appears fixed for a period, access to funds and reinvestment terms can change. Yield should be viewed as variable compensation for providing capital under changing conditions, not as a guaranteed outcome.

Most investors do not need to maximize yield. The real decision is sizing: how much exposure to on-chain yield fits within a broader portfolio, given liquidity needs, volatility, and risk tolerance.

A practical way to apply this chapter is to size yield exposure like a tool, not a bet:

- Consider staking as a baseline yield on assets you already want to hold.
- Consider stablecoin lending and liquidity only if you understand where returns come from and how quickly conditions can change.
- Treat high headline yields as a prompt for deeper diligence, not a conclusion.

This chapter explained how yield is generated and what trade-offs come with earning it. The next step is deciding how it fits inside a broader portfolio. Chapter 8 focuses on portfolio diversification—why digital assets can play a role in a modern portfolio and how to think about sizing and allocation.

CHAPTER EIGHT

PORTFOLIO DIVERSIFICATION

WHY DIGITAL ASSETS BELONG IN A MODERN PORTFOLIO

"Investing in crypto is risky. Not investing in crypto is also risky."
—Changpeng "CZ" Zhao on the opportunity cost of not investing in one of the most disruptive technologies of our time.[1]

Portfolio construction is not about finding the single best-performing asset. It is about combining assets so the portfolio behaves better over time—growing capital while limiting drawdowns, preserving flexibility, and reducing the risk of catastrophic mistakes.

For decades, investors achieved that balance with stocks, bonds, real estate, and cash. Digital assets do not replace those building blocks. They add a new one.

By the end of this chapter, you will clearly understand:

- How digital assets have performed historically relative to traditional asset classes, including their volatility and drawdowns
- Why modest allocations to digital assets can improve long-term portfolio outcomes, even when prices are volatile
- How to decide how much to allocate to digital assets, and how to structure those allocations to manage risk and reduce emotional decision-making

WHY DIGITAL ASSETS MATTER FOR DIVERSIFICATION

Diversification works when different parts of a portfolio are driven by different forces. If everything is responding to the same shock, diversification fails.

For years, many portfolios relied on a simple balance: stocks for growth, bonds for stability. But that relationship has not been reliable in every period. When inflation rises quickly, rates jump, or liquidity tightens, both stocks and bonds can fall at the same time, leaving investors more exposed than they expected.

Digital assets can help because their long-term results have been shaped by a different set of drivers. Instead of earnings, dividends, or central bank policy, returns have been tied more closely to network adoption, usage, and the pace of technological development. When an asset is driven by different forces, it has a better chance of adding true diversification rather than simply adding "more of the same."[2]

That said, diversification is not a permanent feature—it is a pattern that changes. Digital assets have often shown lower average correlation to major traditional asset classes over multi-year periods, which is one reason they are increasingly evaluated in diversified portfolio frameworks.[3] But correlations can rise during stress, especially when investors rush to sell anything risky at the same time. In other words: digital assets may diversify over time, but they may not protect in every short-term drawdown.

Diversification also has a "within-crypto" limitation. Bitcoin and Ethereum tend to move together more than many investors expect, meaning that holding both does not automatically diversify digital asset exposure. The bigger diversification benefit usually comes from how digital assets relate to the rest of the portfolio, not from owning multiple large tokens.

Over the past decade, digital assets have at times outperformed traditional asset classes, led primarily by Bitcoin and Ethereum. Smaller networks have sometimes produced even higher returns, but typically with sharper drawdowns.

Franklin Templeton studied this by looking at annual returns from 2014 through 2024 and comparing digital assets with traditional investments like stocks, bonds, and commodities. Their data show that digital assets were the best-performing asset class in 8 of those 11 years, despite experiencing sharp declines along the way.[4] Figure 8.1 compares Bitcoin's performance against a range of assets, including precious metals and equities.

The key takeaway from Franklin Templetone's work is not that digital assets are "safe" or predictable. It is that even a small allocation can materially affect long-term results. When exposure is kept modest and portfolios are rebalanced over time, strong years can meaningfully lift overall returns, while losses remain contained at the portfolio level. This is why Franklin Templeton frames digital assets as a portfolio tool, not a stand-alone bet.

Research from Bitwise Asset Management reaches a similar conclusion when looking at how digital assets perform over longer periods. Using its Bitwise 10 Large Cap Crypto Index, which tracks the most established digital assets, Bitwise found that the index delivered more than 800%

Figure 8.1 Asset performance rotates year to year: Bitcoin leads in boom years but posts the deepest drawdowns, while gold and silver deliver steadier gains across cycles.

2020	2021	2022	2023	2024	2025
BTC 301.43%	BTC 61.11%	SILVER 4.53%	BTC 156.88%	BTC 119.69%	SILVER 142.28%
SILVER 46.44%	REIT 30.81%	Gold 1.23%	NDX 54.90%	Gold 27.47%	Gold 62.47%
NDX 45.27%	SPX 28.79%	SPX −19.95%	SPX 24.73%	NDX 27.01%	NDX 20.38%
Gold 24.17%	NDX 28.56%	REIT −21.17%	Gold 12.16%	SPX 24.01%	SPX 16.65%
SPX 15.29%	Gold −5.83%	NDX −33.71%	REIT 10.34%	SILVER 22.16%	REIT −3.20%
	SILVER −14.59%	BTC −64.86%	SILVER −0.89%	REIT 2.60%	BTC −5.79%

Source: Kaiko Fair Market Value, Stooq

cumulative returns over a five-year period, equivalent to roughly 56% per year (see Figure 8.2). Nearly 90% of the index is made up of Bitcoin and Ethereum, reinforcing that long-term performance in the digital asset market has been driven primarily by a small number of large, established networks rather than by constant rotation into smaller tokens.

Figure 8.2 Digital assets dominate over the long-term: The Bitwise 10 Large Cap Crypto Index shows outsized cumulative returns over three and five years, even as shorter-term performance remains volatile.

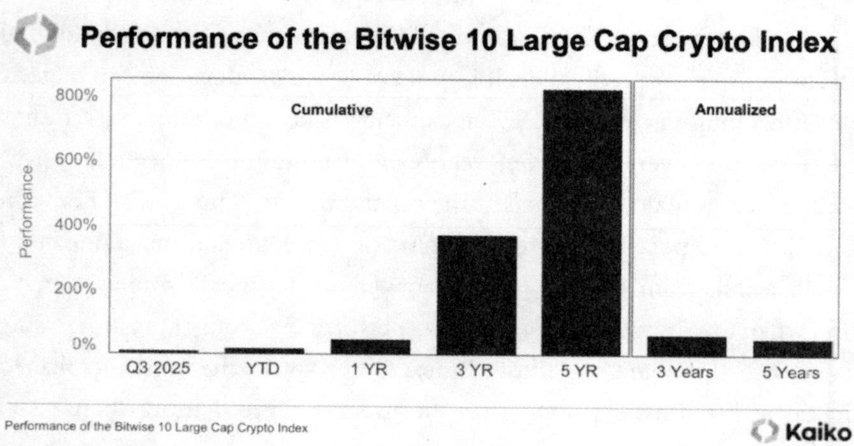

Uncorrelated Assets

Diversification only works when the things you own behave differently. Holding many assets that rise and fall together doesn't reduce risk—it just spreads it around. Figure 8.3 shows how major asset classes have moved in relation to one another in recent years, helping clarify which combinations actually smooth returns and which tend to break down at the same time. By comparing stocks, defensive assets, and digital assets, the data highlights where diversification is meaningful and where it only looks that way on paper.

Figure 8.3 reveals a clear structural pattern in how different asset classes move relative to one another, with direct implications for portfolio construction. The percentages in the table measure correlation, which indicates how often two assets move in the same direction.

First, traditional risk assets tend to move together. US equities, technology stocks, emerging market equities, and real estate all show relatively high correlations, generally ranging from the mid-50% to the high-70% range. This means these assets frequently rise and fall at the same time. A portfolio spread across these assets may appear diversified, but in practice it is still driven by a single underlying risk: global equity markets. When equities sell off, these assets often decline at the same time, limiting the protection diversification is meant to provide.

Second, long-term US Treasuries and gold stand apart as genuine diversifiers. Treasuries show much lower average correlations with risk assets—around the low-20% range—while gold exhibits the lowest correlations in the table, near the low teens. Lower correlations indicate that these assets often move differently from equities, which reinforces their long-standing role as defensive assets that can help stabilize portfolios during periods of equity stress, even if their long-term returns are more modest.

Third, digital assets occupy a distinct middle ground. Bitcoin and Ethereum are strongly correlated with each other, indicating that holding both does little to diversify digital asset exposure. However, their correlations with traditional assets, particularly Treasuries, gold, and emerging equities, are meaningfully lower. This suggests that digital assets introduce a return driver that is not simply another form of equity risk.

What Happens When Digital Assets Are Added to a Portfolio

The question investors care about is not whether digital assets can generate high returns in isolation. It is what happens when they are added to an existing portfolio.

Several large asset managers have tested this directly.

Bitwise Asset Management analyzed a simple 60/40 stock-and-bond portfolio and compared it to the same portfolio with a small Bitcoin allocation added and rebalanced periodically. Over long test periods, portfolios with a 1–5% Bitcoin allocation produced meaningfully higher cumulative returns than the traditional portfolio, while overall volatility increased only modestly (see Figure 8.3).[5]

In one representative study, the traditional portfolio generated cumulative returns of roughly 55%. When a 5% Bitcoin allocation was introduced and rebalanced, cumulative returns rose into the 75–80% range. Drawdowns during market stress were slightly deeper, but not dramatically so, and portfolio volatility remained within ranges that long-term investors already experience.

WisdomTree examined smaller allocations. Their research showed that adding just 1% Bitcoin improved long-term returns while having little impact on overall portfolio volatility. The portfolio did not become meaningfully harder to hold, even though Bitcoin itself was volatile.[6]

VanEck extended this analysis by examining allocations to both Bitcoin and Ethereum. Portfolios that included a modest mix of the two generally outperformed portfolios holding Bitcoin alone, without a meaningful increase in portfolio-level risk. The benefit came from diversification *within* digital assets themselves.

Figure 8.3 Small Bitcoin allocations boost long-term returns: Portfolios with even modest Bitcoin exposure show higher returns and Sharpe ratios over time, with gains rising as allocations increase despite higher volatility.

Source: Wisdomtree.

Figure 4: Historical performance of example portfolios, including increasing proportions of bitcoin

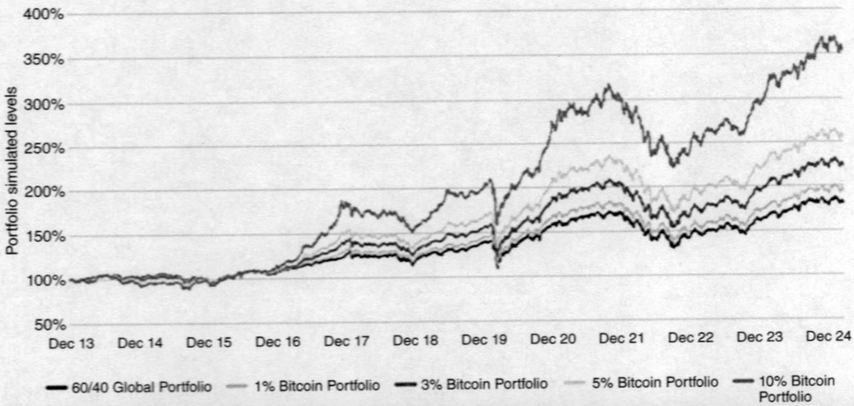

	60/40 Global Portfolio	1% Bitcoin Portfolio	3% Bitcoin Portfolio	5% Bitcoin Portfolio	10% Bitcoin Portfolio	MSCI AC World	Bloomberg Multiverse	Bitcoin
Annualised return	5.41%	6.06%	7.36%	8.66%	11.85%	8.43%	0.58%	51.91%
Volatility	8.76%	8.83%	9.12%	9.59%	11.38%	13.89%	5.03%	66.73%
Sharpe ratio	0.43	0.50	0.62	0.73	0.89	0.49	–0.21	0.75
Information ratio		0.97	0.96	0.96	0.96			
Beta	70%	71%	73%	75%	81%	100%	24%	182%
Max drawdown	–24.4%	–24.9%	–26.1%	–27.3%	–30.2%	–33.7%	–25.3%	–83.1%
Up capture	67.9%	70.4%	75.4%	80.2%	92.1%	100.0%	18.8%	241.2%
Down capture	69.5%	69.3%	69.0%	68.7%	68.3%	100.0%	24.9%	97.8%

Source: Bloomberg, WisdomTree. From 31 December 2013 to 31 March 2025 in US dollars. Based on daily returns. The 60/40 Global Portfolio is composed of 60% MSCI AC World and 40% Bloomberg Multiverse. **You cannot invest directly in an index. Historical performance is not an indication of future performance and any investment may go down in value. For illustrative purposes only.**

Figure 8.4 Bitcoin's volatility fades as prices rise: Rolling volatility has trended lower over time, even as Bitcoin's price has climbed to new highs, pointing to a maturing market.

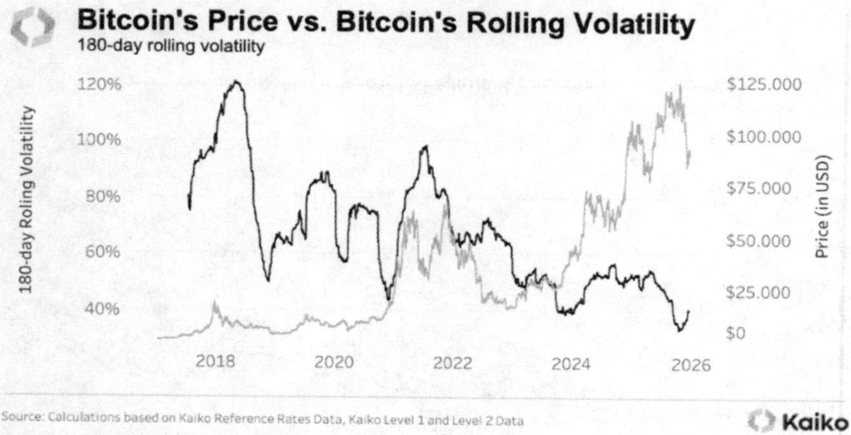

Across these studies, the pattern is consistent. Volatility at the asset level does not translate directly into volatility at the portfolio level when exposure is kept small and rebalanced. Figure 8.4 illustrates the relationship between Bitcoin's price and its volatility.

VOLATILITY IS A SIZING PROBLEM, NOT A PORTFOLIO PROBLEM

Digital assets are volatile. That is not in dispute. What matters is how much of the portfolio they represent.

A volatile asset held at 1%, 3%, or even 5% simply cannot dominate a diversified portfolio in the same way it would if held at 20% or 30%. Even large price declines remain contained at the portfolio level, while strong performance can still move long-term results.

Using this approach, risk is shaped more by position size than by price forecasts. Allocation determines impact. Prediction does not.

Liquidity also matters. Bitcoin and Ethereum have historically remained liquid during sharp market declines, allowing portfolios to rebalance or reduce exposure if needed. Smaller assets may not offer the same flexibility, reinforcing why most institutional portfolios concentrate exposure in the largest, most established networks.

WHERE DIGITAL ASSETS FIT IN A PORTFOLIO

From a construction standpoint, digital assets fit most naturally alongside other alternatives—assets that fall outside traditional stocks, bonds, and cash.

Like commodities, real estate, or private investments, digital assets respond to different forces than public equities. They introduce a return stream driven by adoption and innovation rather than by corporate cash flows.

In practice, digital assets tend to serve two functions:

- Diversification, by altering portfolio behavior
- Growth, by providing exposure to emerging financial infrastructure

Used intentionally, they complement existing holdings rather than compete with them.

Lessons from Institutions on Allocation

Large institutions and professional investors approach digital assets with the same discipline they use for any other risk asset, and those principles translate directly to individual portfolios. They do not allocate based on excitement or headlines. By "allocation," they mean deciding how much of a total portfolio to expose to digital assets—whether that is 1%, 3%, or more—not which coin to buy or when to trade.

Many institutions treat digital assets as part of the alternatives bucket, alongside commodities and real assets, rather than as a replacement for stocks or bonds. Individual investors can apply the same mindset. The guiding question is not "How high could this go?" but "How much risk does this add to my overall portfolio?"

For example, Morgan Stanley's Global Investment Committee classifies crypto alongside commodities and real assets. Based on volatility and risk contribution, their guidance has generally fallen into clear ranges[7]:

- Up to 2% for balanced portfolios
- Up to 3% for growth-oriented portfolios
- Up to 4% for aggressive, opportunistic portfolios
- 0% for investors focused purely on income or capital preservation

These ranges are not prescriptions for individuals, but they provide useful reference points. Because digital asset prices move more than most traditional assets, small allocations can still have a meaningful impact—both positive and negative.

Some prominent investors take a more forceful macro view. Billionaire hedge fund manager Ray Dalio has argued for holding a significant allocation to either Bitcoin or gold as protection against what he describes as a US government "debt doom loop." He views Bitcoin as a form of alternative money—scarce by design, globally traded, and increasingly adopted.[8]

BlackRock approaches the question differently. Rather than focusing on expected returns, they emphasize risk budgeting, a framework that can be useful for individuals as well. Because Bitcoin is volatile, a 1–2% allocation can contribute roughly the same amount of portfolio risk as a much larger position in equities.[9] In other words, a small allocation can meaningfully improve diversification without dominating the portfolio.

Other firms, including Bitwise Asset Management, VanEck, and WisdomTree, have published research showing that allocations in the 1–6% range historically improved risk-adjusted returns across many market environments. The consistent lesson is not to copy institutional portfolios but to adopt their discipline: start small, measure risk, and size exposure intentionally.

THE PSYCHOLOGY OF INVESTING IN DIGITAL ASSETS

The hardest part of investing in digital assets is not the technology. It is managing your reaction to volatility.

The volatility can be difficult to handle for many investors. Sharp declines often lead to selling at the worst moments, while strong rallies can create pressure to buy after prices have already moved higher. Because digital asset markets trade continuously, it can feel like prices demand constant attention, which makes emotional decision-making more likely.

The reason is that prices move quickly. Losses can happen fast. Gains can disappear just as fast. Feedback is constant. Decisions that take years to play out in traditional markets can feel compressed into days or weeks.

Before allocating capital, investors need to be honest about their own tolerance. Can you handle seeing sharp declines shortly after investing? Can you hold through temporary losses without reacting? Can you stay disciplined when markets feel chaotic?

If the answer is no, digital assets are not off-limits. The approach simply needs to change. Smaller allocations, diversified funds, or strategies that aim to reduce exposure to broad market swings may be more appropriate.

Successful investors do not eliminate volatility. They design portfolios so volatility does not control their behavior.

BUILDING EXPOSURE BASED ON RISK TOLERANCE

Not all digital asset exposure needs to look the same.

Conservative investors tend to focus on Bitcoin and Ethereum, often through ETFs or more defensive strategies that emphasize liquidity and risk control.

Moderate investors may combine Bitcoin and Ethereum with diversified funds, limited venture exposure, or strategies that generate income while maintaining flexibility.

Aggressive investors may include smaller networks and early-stage investments, balanced with strict position sizing and clear rules.

There is no single correct allocation. The most common mistake is not choosing too little but choosing more risk than one can comfortably hold through market cycles.

Choose Your Risk Profile

A simple self-check before investing real money

Risk tolerance is not about conviction. It is about behavior. Before deciding how much to allocate to digital assets, it helps to be honest about how you actually respond when markets move. This approach aligns with traditional risk assessments used by financial advisors, such as time horizon, liquidity needs, and tolerance for losses.

Asking Yourself the Right Questions

Start by asking yourself a few simple questions:

- How would you react if part of your portfolio fell 30–40% in a short period?
- Could you stay invested through a year or more of weak performance?
- Do you rely on this portfolio for near-term income or expenses?
- During past downturns, did you stay invested or feel pressure to sell?
- Do you follow markets daily, or only check in occasionally?

These questions focus on drawdowns, time, and behavior, not abstract measures of volatility. Your answers matter more than any return forecast.

Lower Risk Profile

- You may fit this profile if preserving capital matters more to you than maximizing growth, if large drawdowns would cause meaningful stress, if you rely on your portfolio for income or liquidity, and if you prefer simplicity and stability.

- This usually means digital assets play a small, supporting role. Exposure is focused on established assets and designed to limit portfolio-level volatility.

Medium Risk Profile

- You may fit this profile if you want growth but still value stability, if you can tolerate temporary losses as long as the long-term plan remains intact, if you believe in diversification across asset types, and if you are comfortable rebalancing through market cycles.
- This usually means digital assets are a meaningful but controlled allocation, balanced with traditional assets and diversified strategies.

Higher Risk Profile

- You may fit this profile if you have a long-time horizon and stable income, if volatility does not drive emotional decisions, if you accept that some investments may fail entirely, and if you prioritize long-term growth over short-term comfort.
- This usually means digital assets play a larger role, with exposure to innovation and emerging networks. Discipline and position sizing become more important than avoiding volatility.

If you are unsure which profile fits you best, choose the more conservative one. You can always increase exposure later. The cost of moving too slowly is usually smaller than the cost of moving too fast and being forced to sell at the wrong time.

The goal is not to take as much risk as possible. The goal is to build a portfolio you can stay invested in through full market cycles.

Why Rebalancing Is Essential

Rebalancing is central to making digital assets work inside a portfolio.

When prices rise sharply, rebalancing requires trimming exposure and locking in gains. When prices fall, it encourages modest additions at lower levels. Over time, this discipline controls risk and reduces emotional decision-making.

Most long-term portfolio studies assume rebalancing occurs quarterly or annually. That cadence is realistic and sufficient. Constant monitoring is unnecessary.

Without rebalancing, volatility becomes a source of stress. With rebalancing, it becomes a tool.

How to Enter a Position Without Bad Timing

One of the biggest concerns new investors have is buying at the wrong moment. That concern is reasonable—and largely avoidable.

The simplest way to reduce timing risk is dollar-cost averaging. Instead of investing all at once, capital is deployed in equal amounts on a regular schedule, such as monthly or quarterly, regardless of price. This spreads entry points across different market conditions and removes the pressure to predict short-term moves.

Institutions use this approach routinely. It works just as well for individuals.

If the long-term goal is a 3% allocation to digital assets, there is no requirement to reach that level immediately. Building toward it gradually over 6 to 12 months lowers timing risk and makes it easier to stay disciplined if prices move sharply along the way.

No matter how an investment is made, whether through centralized exchanges, decentralized platforms, or public-market products, there are costs involved. Fees, spreads, and execution differences vary by venue and should be considered as part of any entry plan.

Beyond dollar-cost averaging, investors can build positions in several ways, including investing all at once, spreading purchases across multiple tranches, using price-based rules, adjusting position size based on volatility, rebalancing over time, or using options. Each approach balances timing risk and opportunity cost differently.

Why Some Investors Go Higher

Not all investors have the same constraints.

Some have long-time horizons, stable income, and the ability to tolerate significant volatility. For these investors, higher allocations to digital assets can be reasonable, particularly if they view digital networks as long-term financial infrastructure rather than short-term trades.

Many early investors have also seen their digital asset holdings grow to represent a much larger share of their portfolios over time. Some choose to maintain that exposure, either because gains elsewhere would not materially change their financial position or because they have a strong conviction in the asset class and a high tolerance for risk. This approach is not about balance or diversification. It reflects comfort with volatility and a willingness to accept large swings in value.

That does not mean everyone should do this.

Allocation should match three things: time horizon, financial stability, and emotional resilience.

The most important rule: you should never size digital assets so large that they cause you to panic-sell.

Successful portfolio construction is not about maximizing upside. It is about staying invested long enough for upside to matter.

PUTTING IT ALL TOGETHER: PORTFOLIO EXAMPLES

So far, we've talked about why digital assets can belong in a portfolio and how professionals think about sizing and risk. The next step is seeing how this looks in real life.

There is no single "correct" portfolio. What works depends on three things: how long you can stay invested, how much volatility you can tolerate, and whether you rely on your portfolio for income or growth.

Below are three example portfolios, each built around a different risk tolerance. These are not prescriptions. They are illustrations meant to show how digital assets fit alongside more familiar investments.

High Risk Tolerance Portfolio (Growth-Focused)

Objective: Maximize long-term growth while accepting significant volatility.

Who this is for: Investors with long-time horizons, stable income, and the ability to hold through large drawdowns without reacting.

Allocation (100%):

- US & Global Equities (growth-tilted): 60%
- Digital Assets: 10%
- Bonds (short/intermediate duration): 15%
- Real Assets/REITs: 5%
- Cash: 10%

This portfolio is designed to prioritize growth. Equities and digital assets are the primary return drivers, while bonds and real assets provide partial ballast during periods of stress. Cash is kept modest to avoid diluting long-term returns. The structure assumes the investor can tolerate sharp fluctuations and remain invested through periods of volatility without changing course.

Medium Risk Tolerance Portfolio (Balanced Growth)

Objective: Grow capital while moderating portfolio volatility across market cycles.

Who this is for: Investors who want exposure to innovation and long-term growth but with greater emphasis on stability and diversification.

Allocation (100%):

- US & Global Equities: 50%
- Bonds: 25%
- Digital Assets: 5%
- Real Assets/REITs: 5%
- Alternatives/Hedge-Style Funds: 5%
- Cash: 10%

What Bitcoin does here:

- Adds a diversifying growth asset alongside equities
- Has historically improved risk-adjusted returns at modest allocation sizes
- Contributes limited downside risk at this level

This portfolio balances growth and resilience. Equities remain the foundation, while bonds anchor stability and provide liquidity during downturns. Real assets and alternatives help smooth returns across different environments. Bitcoin is included as a satellite allocation, meaning a smaller, complementary position added around the core portfolio to provide additional growth potential without dominating overall risk. The structure closely resembles a modernized 60/40 portfolio and can be implemented using traditional brokerage platforms.

Lower Risk Tolerance Portfolio (Capital Preservation)

Objective: Preserve capital and limit drawdowns while maintaining long-term optionality.

Who this is for: Investors who prioritize stability, income, and liquidity over maximizing returns.

Allocation (100%):

- Bonds: 40%
- US Equities: 35%
- Real Assets/REITs: 10%
- Digital Assets: 2–3%
- Other Alternatives: 2–3%
- Cash: 10%

What Bitcoin does here:

- Provides asymmetric upside without destabilizing the portfolio
- Maintains exposure to digital asset innovation over long horizons
- Functions as optionality rather than a return driver

The emphasis is on protection first. Bonds, income-oriented equities, and cash reduce the need to sell assets during market stress. Digital asset exposure is intentionally small, allowing participation in long-term upside without materially increasing volatility or drawdown risk.

DIVERSIFYING A DIGITAL-ASSET ALLOCATION

After deciding how much exposure to digital assets makes sense, the next question is what that exposure should look like.

At small allocation sizes, the exact mix often matters less than people expect. Research looking at modest allocations, such as 5% of a portfolio, shows that both a concentrated position in Bitcoin and a diversified basket of large digital assets have historically improved overall portfolio outcomes. Returns increased, risk-adjusted performance improved, and volatility rose only modestly relative to traditional portfolios.

For most investors, simplicity works. A focused allocation is easier to understand, easier to monitor, and easier to hold through periods of stress. Diversification within digital assets can make sense as exposure grows, but it should be added deliberately rather than by default.

The goal is not to trade digital assets actively or optimize short-term returns. It is to integrate them into the portfolio in a way that supports long-term discipline, aligns with overall risk tolerance, and allows the investor to stay invested when markets inevitably become volatile.

Within a digital-asset allocation, there are a few ways to get exposure. ETFs and ETPs are often the simplest starting point. They offer regulated access to major digital assets or broad indices and fit easily into traditional portfolios. Direct ownership, whether through a custodian or self-custody, offers more flexibility and control. For investors who want to engage more deeply, self-custody opens the door to on-chain activity like staking, governance, and decentralized finance, without relying on intermediaries.

Managed funds provide another option. These range from long-only strategies to more defensive approaches and are designed for investors who want professional oversight and diversification without managing positions themselves. Venture investments sit at the other end of the spectrum, offering exposure to early stage blockchain projects with higher upside potential, but less liquidity and longer time horizons. Separately, yield strategies using cash or stablecoins can be used selectively to generate income or build exposure gradually.

For investors looking beyond a single asset, indices like the Kaiko 10 Index offer a simple benchmark (see Figures 8.5 and 8.6). It tracks 10 of the most established and liquid digital assets, aiming to broaden exposure while avoiding excessive concentration. Because of its focus on liquidity and maturity, it's increasingly used as a reference point for funds and structured products.

Figure 8.5 The Kaiko 10 Index balances exposure across ten established digital assets, with caps on individual weights to reduce concentration while maintaining liquidity.

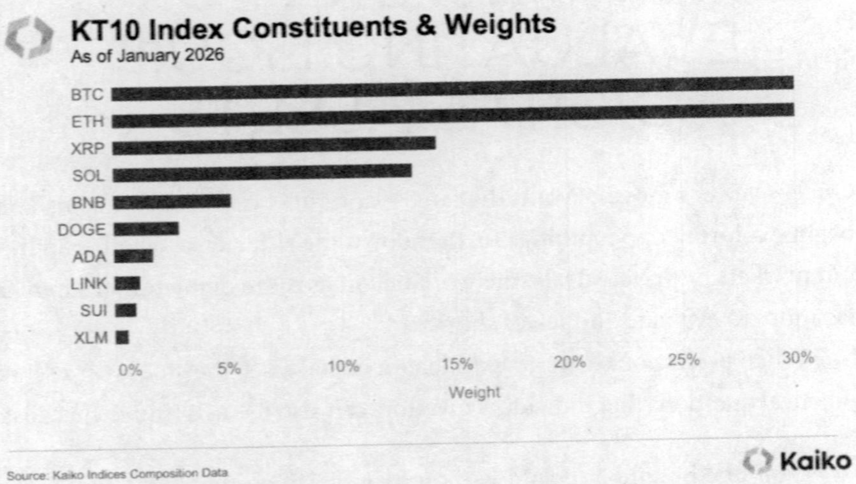

Figure 8.6 The index captures the long-term growth of a diversified basket of large, liquid digital assets, while reflecting the pronounced cycles and drawdowns typical of the asset class. Over time, it highlights how digital assets have delivered substantial gains.

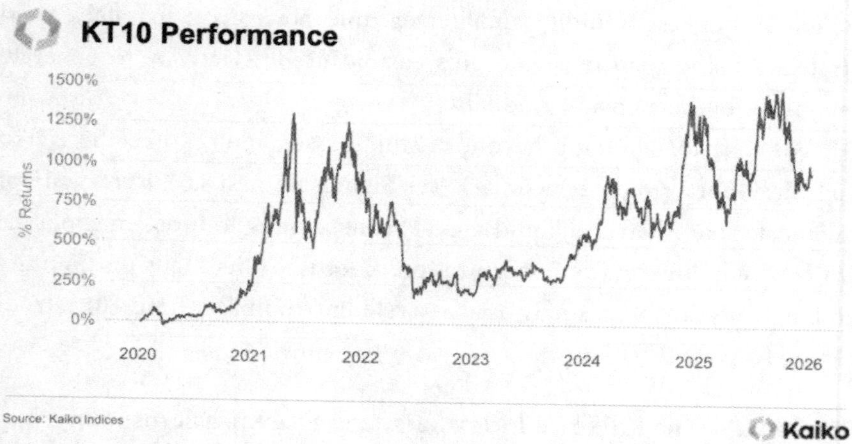

FRAMEWORK FOR EVALUATING LIQUID DIGITAL ASSETS

Once investors move beyond the largest and most established tokens and begin exploring opportunities further down the risk curve, whether in liquid markets or private deals, the work becomes more demanding. There is far more to evaluate and fewer shortcuts.

When professional investors evaluate a digital asset, they focus on a set of practical questions that individual investors can also use as a simple checklist:

Can it be bought and sold without trouble? Liquidity is the first filter. Investors want to know whether they can enter and exit a position without moving the price too much. This means looking at daily trading volume, how deep the order books are, and how many reputable exchanges the asset trades on. The presence of futures or options matters because it allows risk to be managed. If an asset is hard to trade or only available on obscure venues, it carries extra risk regardless of how promising the project sounds.

Does the valuation make sense given actual use? Instead of focusing only on today's market price, experienced investors look at what a project could be worth if all tokens were in circulation, known as the fully diluted valuation (FDV). They compare that figure to real usage: Are people actually using the network or projects building on the protocol? Is there revenue, growth, or clear demand? Assets with very high theoretical valuations but limited real activity are vulnerable if new tokens enter the market faster than demand grows. What is the business and revenue model, and how do the token's economics convert real network activity into value? Investors look at where revenue comes from, who pays for the product or service, and whether fees, usage, or growth accrue to the protocol itself. They also assess how new tokens are issued, how existing tokens are used, and whether the design rewards long-term participation or simply subsidizes short-term activity.

How much supply is still coming? Token supply matters as much as token price. Investors pay close attention to how many tokens are already circulating and how many will be released in the future. This is mainly informed in the token economics which are public documents. Large unlocks for founders,[10] early investors, or foundations can create selling pressure even if the project itself is strong. Concentrated ownership or unclear disclosure around supply schedules is a warning sign.

Why does the token need to exist? A simple question often reveals a lot: What role does the token actually play? Strong tokens are tied directly to the network's function—used for fees, staking, or governance that genuinely matters. If a network grows, demand for the token should grow as well. Tokens that exist mainly for branding or speculation tend to move with sentiment rather than fundamentals.

Is the activity real or artificially boosted? Not all growth is equal. Investors look beyond headline metrics to see whether usage is sustainable or driven by short-term incentives. They pay attention to trends in users, transactions, and fees, and whether activity holds up once rewards or subsidies decline. Healthy ecosystems show consistent use, developer participation, and user retention over time.

Who is in control, and how can the system change? Finally, governance matters. Investors want to know who can change the rules, pause the system, or upgrade the protocol. Early-stage projects may be more centralized, but that control should be transparent and gradually reduced over time. Clear governance processes and a track record of responsible decision-making increase long-term confidence.

Evaluating digital assets is complex, and for professional investors it is a full-time job. Anyone willing to go down that path needs to be prepared to spend the time and do the deeper work. The good news is that much of the necessary information is widely available online and often free, if you are willing to look for it. You do not need paid analyst reports to get started, and the appendix includes a list of websites and resources to help guide further research.

INVESTOR TAKEAWAY

This chapter is not an argument for chasing returns or for treating digital assets as a separate category of speculation. It is about portfolio behavior. When digital assets are sized appropriately and combined with traditional investments, they can improve how a portfolio grows and how it holds up during stress.

The evidence across multiple market cycles is consistent. Digital assets are volatile on their own, but volatility does not automatically translate into portfolio-level risk. Allocation size, diversification, and rebalancing matter far more than short-term price movements. This is why professional investors focus on sizing and structure, not on timing or narratives.

What follows are the practical principles that matter most:

- Digital assets work best as a complement to existing holdings, not as a replacement for stocks or bonds.
- Small allocations can meaningfully improve long-term returns without overwhelming portfolio risk.
- Risk is managed through position sizing and rebalancing, not through price prediction.
- The right allocation depends on time horizon, financial stability, and emotional tolerance for drawdowns.
- Simpler structures are easier to hold through volatility than complex or aggressive strategies.
- The objective is not maximizing upside in any single year but building a portfolio that can be held through full market cycles.

If an allocation causes stress, second-guessing, or panic during market declines, it is too large. The right exposure is one that allows an investor to stay invested long enough for diversification and compounding to work.

CONCLUSION

THE FUTURE OF DIGITAL ASSETS AND WHY IT MATTERS

Over the next decade, digital assets are likely to become a normal part of many investment portfolios. Not as a novelty or a side bet, but as a category investors expect to hold, much like equities, bonds, alternatives, and real estate. As the market matures, exposure will move beyond simply owning volatile tokens and toward more refined options, including income-generating strategies, diversified funds, and products that behave more like growth or technology investments.

This shift is already underway. Global adoption continues to expand, new use cases keep emerging, and the broader macro environment has made investors more open to alternatives. At the same time, infrastructure has improved. Custody, liquidity, and investment vehicles are becoming more familiar and easier to access. Together, these changes are making digital assets a more durable part of the financial system.

What matters most for investors is not predicting which asset or protocol will succeed, but understanding *how* digital assets behave and how they can be used to build a diversified portfolio. They operate continuously, settle quickly, and place more responsibility on the holder than traditional financial products. Decisions around custody, wallet design, collateral, and counterparty exposure are not technical details—they directly affect risk, liquidity, and outcomes. The tools discussed in this book are the building blocks for navigating those trade-offs deliberately.

Getting involved does not require big bets or perfect timing. It starts with understanding how digital assets fit within a portfolio and sizing exposure in a way that feels manageable. Starting early, even with a small allocation, gives investors time to learn how these assets behave and how they affect the rest of the portfolio, rather than feeling rushed later.

This book only scratches the surface of what digital asset investing can look like. The strategies, products, and structures will continue to evolve. The investors who tend to do best are not the ones chasing the next trend, but those who approach the space thoughtfully, manage risk carefully, and stay focused on long-term portfolio outcomes.

LIST OF RESOURCES

CRYPTO NEWS

- Bankless https://www.bankless.com
- Blockworks https://blockworks.co
- Bloomberg Crypto https://www.bloomberg.com/crypto
- Decrypt https://decrypt.co
- CoinDesk https://www.coindesk.com
- Cointelegraph https://cointelegraph.com
- FT https://www.ft.com/crypto
- Forbes Crypto https://www.forbes.com/crypto-blockchain
- Reuters https://www.reuters.com/technology/cryptocurrency
- Messari Crypto News https://messari.io/news
- The Block https://www.theblock.co
- The Defiant https://thedefiant.io
- Wall Street Journal—Crypto https://www.wsj.com/news/type/cryptocurrency

CRYPTO PODCASTS

- Bankless Podcast https://www.bankless.com/podcast
- Bell Curve https://blockworks.co/podcast/bell-curve
- Empire (Blockworks) https://blockworks.co/podcast/empire
- Epicenter https://epicenter.tv
- Forward Guidance (Blockworks) https://blockworks.co/podcast/forward-guidance
- Odd Lots—Crypto episodes (Bloomberg) https://www.bloomberg.com/oddlots
- On the Brink (Nic Carter & Matt Walsh) https://onthebrink-podcast.com
- The Breakdown (NLW / CoinDesk) https://www.coindesk.com/podcasts/the-breakdown
- The Defiant Podcast https://thedefiant.io/podcast
- The Market Structure Podcast https://cumberland.io/market-structure-podcas
- The Pomp Podcast https://anthonypompliano.com/podcast
- Macro Voices (*frequent crypto episodes*) https://macrovoices.com
- Unchained (Laura Shin) https://unchainedcrypto.com
- What Bitcoin Did https://www.whatbitcoindid.com
- Zero Knowledge https://zeroknowledge.fm

CRYPTO RESEARCH FIRMS

- Blockworks Research https://blockworksresearch.com
- Delphi Digital https://www.delphidigital.io
- Galaxy Research https://www.galaxy.com/research
- Messari https://messari.io

ASSET MANAGER RESEARCH FIRMS

- 21Shares https://21shares.com/research
- ARK Invest https://ark-invest.com/research/
- Bitwise Research https://www.bitwiseinvestments.com/research
- BlackRock Investment Institute https://www.blackrock.com/insights
- Coinbase Institutional https://www.coinbase.com/institutional/research
- CoinShares Research https://coinshares.com/research
- Fidelity Digital Assets https://www.fidelitydigitalassets.com/research
- Franklin Templeton Digital Assets https://www.franklintempleton.com/digital-assets
- Grayscale https://www.grayscale.com/research
- Invesco https://www.invesco.com/us/en/solutions/invesco-etfs/digital-assets.html
- Northern Trust Digital Assets https://www.northerntrust.com/europe/insights-research/asset-servicing/digital-assets-financial-markets
- State Street Global Advisors Digital Assets https://www.ssga.com/us/en/institutional/capabilities/digital-asset-etfs
- VanEck https://www.vaneck.com/us/en/insights/
- WisdomTree Digital Assets https://www.wisdomtree.com/investments/digital-assets

TRADITIONAL FINANCE (TRADFI) RESEARCH

- BlackRock Investment Institute https://www.blackrock.com/insights
- BNY Mellon (Digital Assets) https://www.bny.com/corporate/global/en/solutions/platforms/digital-assets.html
- Citi Research https://www.citigroup.com/global/insights
- CME Group https://www.cmegroup.com/markets/cryptocurrencies.html
- Fidelity Digital Assets Research https://www.fidelitydigitalassets.com/research
- FTSE Russell—Digital Assets & Blockchain https://www.ftserussell.com/research
- Goldman Sachs Global Investment Research https://www.goldmansachs.com/insights
- HSBC Global Research https://www.gbm.hsbc.com/insights
- J.P. Morgan Onyx https://www.jpmorgan.com/insights/payments/blockchain-digital-assets
- Morgan Stanley Research https://www.morganstanley.com/ideas
- MSCI—Digital Assets https://www.msci.com/our-solutions/digital-assets
- S&P Dow Jones Indices https://www.spglobal.com/spdji/en/indices/digital-assets/

EXCHANGES

- Coinbase Institutional Research https://www.coinbase.com/institutional/research
- Coinbase Learn https://www.coinbase.com/learn

- Kraken Intelligence https://blog.kraken.com/kraken-intelligence
- Kraken education https://blog.kraken.com/category/crypto-education
- Kraken Learn https://www.kraken.com/learn
- Binance Research https://research.binance.com
- Binance Academy https://academy.binance.com
- Binance Blog https://www.binance.com/en/blog

CONSULTING & ADVISORY (DIGITAL ASSETS FOCUS)

- BCG (Crypto & Digital Assets) https://www.bcg.com/industries/financial-institutions
- Deloitte (Blockchain & Digital Assets) https://www2.deloitte.com/global/en/pages/financial-services/topics/blockchain.html
- McKinsey (Digital Assets & Tokenization) https://www.mckinsey.com/industries/financial-services/our-insights
- PwC (Crypto & Digital Assets) https://www.pwc.com/gx/en/industries/financial-services/fintech/crypto.html

DATA

- Chainalysis https://www.chainalysis.com
- CoinMetrics https://coinmetrics.io
- DefiLlama https://defillama.com
- Dune analytics https://dune.com
- Glassnode https://glassnode.com
- Kaiko https://www.kaiko.com
- Nansen https://www.nansen.ai
- Token Terminal https://tokenterminal.com

ONLINE EDUCATION

- Blockchain and Bitcoin Fundamentals (Princeton University) https://www.coursera.org/learn/bitcoin-and-cryptocurrency
- Blockchain Basics (edX) https://www.edx.org/course/blockchain-basics
- Bitcoin & Cryptocurrency Technologies (Stanford) https://www.coursera.org/learn/crypto
- Blockchain Strategy (Oxford/Saïd) https://www.sbs.ox.ac.uk/programmes/oxford-blockchain-strategy
- Crypto and Blockchain Executive Education (MIT) https://executive.mit.edu/crypto

DeFi, SMART CONTRACTS & TECHNICAL SPECIALIZATIONS

- Alchemy Full Stack Web3 Bootcamp https://www.alchemy.com/bootcamp
- Bankless Academy (Ethereum + DeFi) https://banklessacademy.xyz
- CoinDesk Learn + Insights https://www.coindesk.com/learn
- Consensys Academy https://consensys.net/academy
- Messari Academy https://messari.io/academy
- Shefi https://www.shefi.org/

NOTES

CHAPTER ONE

1. Kraken (July 28, 2011). "Kraken is Born." *Kraken Blog.*
2. Brian Armstrong (August 10, 2017). "Coinbase raises $100M Series D led by IVP." *Coinbase Blog.*
3. Silk Road was an online marketplace founded by Ross Ulbricht that used Bitcoin for payments and operated outside traditional legal frameworks. While it demonstrated Bitcoin's ability to function as digital money, it also contributed to early public and regulatory associations between cryptocurrency and crime.
4. A stablecoin is a digital asset designed to maintain a stable value, typically one U.S. dollar. It allows investors to move cash within digital asset markets without relying on traditional banks and is intended to remain firmly pegged at $1 rather than rise or fall in price.
5. See: Keynote Address by Commissioner Brian D. Quintenz before the DC Blockchain Summit (March 7, 2018).
6. A DAO, or Decentralized Autonomous Organization, is an organization governed by software rules rather than managers. Decisions are made through voting by token holders, and outcomes are enforced by smart contracts instead of traditional corporate structures.
7. Dirk A. Zetzsche, Ross P. Buckley, Douglas W. Arner, Linus Fohr (Summer 2019). "The ICO Gold Rush: It's a Scam, It's a Bubble, It's a Super Challenge for Regulators." *Harvard Law.*

8. Sabrina T. Howell, Marina, Niessner, David Yermack (September 2019). "Initial Coin Offerings: Financing Growth With Cryptocurrency Token Sales." *NBER*.
9. Automated market makers are trading systems that use software and shared pools of assets to set prices and execute trades, rather than matching buyers and sellers through a traditional order book.
10. See generally: Remarks of Chairman J. Christopher Giancarlo to the ABA Derivatives and Futures Section Conference, Naples, Florida, CFTC PUBLIC STATEMENTS & REMARKS (January 19, 2018), https://www.cftc.gov/PressRoom/SpeechesTestimony/opagiancarlo34
11. See: Alessandro Aimone (December 5, 2017). "CFTC approves CME and Cboe Bitcoin Futures." *FX Markets*.
12. Brian Armstrong (November 16, 2017). "Announcing Coinbase Custody: A Digital Currency Custodian For Institutions." *Medium*.
13. Kate Rooney (October 15, 2018). "Fidelity just made it easier for hedge funds and other pros to invest in cryptocurrencies." *CNBC*.
14. Enterprise Ethereum Alliance (February 28, 2017). "Enterprise Ethereum Alliance Launches".
15. A layer-1 blockchain is a base network with its own security and transaction processing, rather than an application built on top of another blockchain. Bitcoin and Ethereum are layer-1 blockchains.
16. See: Evelyn Cheng (December 6, 2017). "Meet CryptoKitties, the $100,000 digital beanie babies epitomizing the cryptocurrency mania." *CNBC*.
17. See: Block Fang (December 7, 2021). "PAK's NFT Artwork 'The Merge' Sells for $91.8 Million." *Barron's*.
18. EVM is the software environment that executes smart contracts on Ethereum and compatible blockchains.
19. Bittensor is a decentralized network that uses blockchain-based incentives to coordinate the training and share of AI models. Developers contribute AI models to the network and are rewarded based on their usefulness, creating an open network for machine intelligence.
20. Sam Bourgi (July 2, 2025). "SEC ends 'regulation through enforcement,' calls tokenization 'innovation.'" *Cointelegraph*.
21. See Texas Senate Bill 21 (89th Legislature), which establishes the Texas Strategic Bitcoin Reserve and authorizes the state comptroller to acquire and hold Bitcoin as a reserve asset; and Wyoming House Bill 0201 (2025), which authorizes the state to invest a portion of certain public funds in Bitcoin,

reflecting legislative exploration of digital assets as part of state investment and reserve strategies.

22. California Public Employees' Retirement System gained indirect exposure to Bitcoin by investing in shares of Strategy, a digital asset treasury company that holds Bitcoin.
23. The State of Wisconsin Investment Board has invested in BlackRock's iShares Bitcoin Trust.
24. Melinda Huspen (January 30, 2026). "Fidelity plans to Launch a stablecoin." *American Banker.oc*
25. Visa has expanded support for stablecoin settlement and blockchain networks on its payment platform; Mastercard has developed infrastructure supporting stablecoin payments and blockchain payment capabilities that integrate digital assets into traditional payment rails; PayPal's Pay with Crypto feature allows merchants to accept cryptocurrencies (with automatic conversion to stablecoins or fiat).
26. Jamie Dimon acknowledged the real-world utility of blockchain technology at the Future Investment Initiative (FII9) in Riyadh, Saudi Arabia. *Crypto Briefing, 2025.*

CHAPTER TWO

1. The Enterprise Ethereum Alliance was launched in 2017 as a consortium of financial institutions and technology companies aimed at developing blockchain standards and use cases based on Ethereum technology. See "Consortium launches Enterprise Ethereum initiative," *Markets Media,* 2017.
2. In 2025, the GENIUS Act clarified rules for custody and tokenized products, while the CLARITY Act was being drafted to establish standards for asset classification, oversight, and consumer protection. In parallel, the SEC shifted toward clearer guidance on listings and custody, and the President's Working Group expanded coordination across key financial regulators.
3. See: Alexander Osipovich and Dylan Tokar (March 4, 2026). "Kraken Becomes First Crypto Firm to Win Access to Fed's Core Payments System." *The Wall Street Journal.*
4. Jenny Johnson praises blockchain's value in financial infrastructure. *LinkedIn.*

5. Alex Chriss described stablecoins as "the next evolution of payments," highlighting their role in improving the speed and efficiency of digital transactions. See: Lynne Marek (September 12, 2025). "PayPal CEO rejects stablecoin threat." *Payments Dive.*
6. In September 2025, Citigroup revised its outlook, projecting the stablecoin market could reach $4 trillion by 2030. See: Vince Quill (September 26, 2025). "Citi raises stablecoin market cap forecast to $4T by 2030." *Cointelegraph.*
7. Larry Fink discusses the future of asset markets and blockchain, noting how tokenization is becoming integral to finance. *CNBC, 2025.*
8. See: Agencies clarify the capital treatment of tokenized securities (March 5, 2026). Board of Governors of the Federal Reserve System.
9. Carlos Domingo speaks about tokenizing funds and real-world assets. See: Investcorp (June 26, 2024). Investcorp and Securitize Form Partnership to Tokenize Funds.
10. See Krisztian Sandor (December 15, 2025). "JPMorgan Launches Tokenized Money Market Fund on Ethereum as Wall Street Moves Onchain." *CoinDesk;* Sandy Kaul (June 9, 2025). "Tokenized money market funds: The bridge to a new financial infrastructure." *Franklin Templeton.*
11. Vlad Tanev discussing the transformative impact of tokenized assets at the Token2049 conference in Singapore in October 2025. See: Sam Reynolds (October 3, 2025). "'Tokenization Is Going to Eat the Entire Financial System' Says Robinhood CEO." *CoinDesk.*
12. Jamie Redman (January 19, 2026). "NYSE Joins Tokenization Race With New Digital Trading Venue." *Bitcoin.com.*
13. Frank La Salla discusses DTCC's push to tokenize real-world assets and modernize financial infrastructure after the SEC issued a No-Action Letter allowing a DTCC subsidiary to provide tokenization services for traditional securities. See: DTCC (December 11, 2025). "DTCC Authorized to Offer New Tokenization Service, Paving the Way to Tokenized DTC-Custodied Assets."
14. JPMorgan's Onyx network and Citi's tokenized deposits are examples of large banks using blockchain technology to modernize core financial infrastructure. These systems allow deposits, payments, and settlement processes to be represented digitally on blockchain-based networks, enabling faster movement of funds.
15. Research suggests that digitizing trade finance documents could reduce processing times by more than 80%. See: McKinsey (October 4, 2022). "The multi-billion-dollar paper jam: Unlocking trade by digitalizing documentation. *McKinsey.*

CHAPTER THREE

1. Emmie Martin (December 4, 2017). "The Winklevoss twins have become the world's first bitcoin billionaires: Report." *CNBC.*
2. David Gura (August 13, 2023). "The future of crypto hinges on a fight between the SEC and a former burger flipper." *NPR.*
3. See: a16z Crypto (October 22, 2025). State of Crypto 2025: The year crypto went mainstream.
4. See: Chainalysis (September 2, 2205). The 2025 Global Adoption Index: India and the United States Lead Cryptocurrency Adoption.
5. Surveys show that 14% to 28% of US adults now own or have used cryptocurrency, up from single digits in 2021. That's somewhere between 36 million and 65 million Americans, with adoption strongest among men aged 18–49, college graduates, and upper-income households. Awareness has become almost universal: while 86% of Americans had heard of digital assets in 2021, today that number is nearly 100%. Sources: Gallup, Texas Comptroller, Security.org
6. Coinbase State of Crypto Q4 2025: Younger investors are rewriting the investing playbook.
7. Charles Yu (December 6, 2023). The Great Wealth Transfer & its Impact on Crypto. Galaxy.
8. Jeffrey M. Jones and Lydia Saad (July 22, 2025). Cryptocurrency Still Has Limited Main Street Appeal. Gallup.
9. Bank of America. Will the 'Great Wealth Transfer' transform the markets?
10. Bitwise (January 2025). The Bitwise/VettaFi 2025 Benchmark Survey of Financial Advisor Attitudes Toward Crypto Assets.
11. CoinShares. Digital assets: what advisors really think.
12. See: Samantha Downes (March 20, 2024). "Wealth managers remain cautious on crypto." *Pwmnet.com*
13. See: Reuters (January 23, 2026). "UBS explores crypto investing for select private banking clients, Bloomberg News reports." *Reuters.*
14. Vivian Nguyen (October 13, 2025). "€2.3 trillion Amundi to launch Bitcoin investment product." *Crypto Briefing.*
15. Big Banks Embrace Bitcoin: Allocations Recommended for Wealth Management Clients, *Markets.com*, 2025.

16. See: Financial Times (July 21, 2025). "JPMorgan explores lending against clients' crypto holdings." *Financial Times;* Krisztian Sandor (December 15, 2025). "JPMorgan Launches Tokenized Money Market Fund on Ethereum as Wall Street Moves Onchain." *CoinDesk.*
17. "Wealth management firms need to adapt to this changing consumer need to provide great service to their customers, and more importantly, market-beating returns," Katharine Wooler told *Professional Wealth Management*, 2024.
18. Siamak Masnavi (July 19, 2025). "Charles Schwab CEO Says Crypto Trading Is Coming Soon, Will Compete With Coinbase for Retail." *CoinDesk.*
19. Spot trading refers to the direct purchase or sale of a digital asset for immediate ownership and settlement. Unlike derivatives, spot transactions involve real assets rather than contracts.
20. See: Zach Pandl (September 11, 2025). The Macro Case for Crypto. *Grayscale.*
21. Ibid.
22. Chris Burniske, Adam White (January 16, 2017). Bitcoin: Ringing the Bell For a New Asset Class. ARK Invest.
23. Dr. Mark Shore (May 21, 2025). "Why Bitcoin's Relationship with Equities Has Changed. *CME Group.*
24. James Van Straten (December 4, 2025). "Bitcoin's Negative Correlation With Nasdaq Persists, and History Suggests a Bottom May Be Forming." *CoinDesk.*
25. CoinMarketCap (January 30, 2025). "Bitcoin Shows Strongest Correlation With Russell 2000 Tech Stocks, Says JPMorgan." *CoinMarketCap, 2025.*
26. Zach Pandl (February 9, 2026). Market Byte: Bitcoin Trading More Like Growth Than Gold. *Grayscale.*
27. See: Sam Bourgi (October 25, 2025). "ISM Manufacturing PMI suggests Bitcoin cycle may extend beyond historical norm." *Cointelegraph;* Sam Bourgi (March 4, 2025). "As Trump tanks Bitcoin, PMI offers a roadmap of what comes next." *Cointelegraph.*

CHAPTER FOUR

1. See: Ben Stack (January 2, 2024). "The decade-long road to (possible) spot bitcoin ETF approval." *Blockworks.*
2. See: Sam Bourgi (August 29, 2025). "Gryphon approves merger with American Bitcoin, Nasdaq ticker ABTC." *Cointelegraph.*

3. See: Sam Bourgi (September 15, 2025). "As digital asset treasury mNAVs collapse, only strong will survive—Standard Chartered." *Cointelegraph.*
4. Joseph Adinolfi (December 31, 2024). "2024 was another record-breaking year for options trading. What's on tap for the industry in 2025." *MarketWatch.*
5. Crypto.com (May 8, 2025). Wall Street On-Chain Part 3: Trading & Liquidity.
6. Helen Braun (October 6, 2025). "Bitcoin Options Market Now Big Enough to Move Spot Prices, FalconX Says." *CoinDesk.*
7. See: CoinShares (October 20, 2025). "Billions in liquidations: what happened?"
8. Christopher Robbins (May 11, 2023). "If Crypto Belongs in Retirement Accounts, Where Are the Assets?" *CoinDesk.*
9. Ezra Reguerra (August 7, 2023). "Trump to allow crypto in 401(k) plans for US workers: White House." *Cointelegraph.*

CHAPTER FIVE

1. Fund of funds is an investment vehicle that allocates capital across multiple venture funds rather than investing directly in individual companies or projects. This structure provides diversification and access to managers that may otherwise be unavailable, but it typically adds an additional layer of fees and reduces direct control over individual investments.
2. Marlize van Romburgh (January 9, 2026). "A16z Raises $15B In New Funds, Its Largest Haul To Date, Promises To Back Startups Advancing U.S. Interests." *Crunchbase News.*
3. Alex Thorn (November 25, 2025). "Crypto and Blockchain Venture Capital—Q3 2025." Galaxy.
4. State Street Investment Management. (November 19, 2025). "Digital Assets: The Next Frontier for Markets and Investors. State Street Investment Management.
5. IRR (Internal Rate of Return) measures the annualized return of an investment over time, accounting for the timing of cash inflows and outflows. See: Sean Duffin. "Unlocking Innovation with Blockchain and Crypto Venture Capital Funds." Cambridge Associates.
6. See: U.S. Securities and Exchange Commission Litigation Release No. 26430.
7. Hedgeweek. (November 7, 2025). "More than half of hedge funds now hold crypto assets, finds AIMA survey."
8. L1D (September 13, 2024). "How to Launch a Liquid Crypto Find." *Medium.*

CHAPTER SIX

1. MetaMask is a widely used browser-based non-custodial wallet that allows users to interact directly with public blockchain networks. MetaMask operates as a browser extension and mobile application, supporting both traditional seed-phrase wallets and newer smart-contract–based wallets with built-in recovery features.
2. Trust Wallet is a mobile-based non-custodial wallet that allows users to store, send, and receive digital assets while interacting directly with public blockchain networks.
3. A multisignature (or multisig) wallet requires approval from multiple private keys to authorize a transaction. Instead of a single point of control, assets are secured by several independent signers, reducing the risk of loss or theft if one key is compromised. Multisig setups are commonly used by institutions, families, and long-term investors to improve security.
4. Sending USDT or USDC to a correct wallet address on the wrong blockchain can result in permanent loss. For example, sending USDC intended for the Ethereum network over the Tron or BNB Chain network may render the funds inaccessible. While the address may appear valid, recovery often depends on whether the recipient supports that network; in many cases, especially with exchanges, the assets cannot be recovered.

5. TRM Team (December 8, 2025). "14 Crypto Scam Types (and How Blockchain Forensics Helps Detect and Disrupt Them)." *TRM Labs*.
6. James Hunt (January 3, 2024). "Crypto phishing attacks drained nearly $300 million in 2023: Scam Sniffer." *The Block*.
7. See: Kyle Schnitzer and Natalie O'Neill (December 19, 2025). "Gen Z NYC crypto crook still living with dad busted for swiping $16M in jaw-dropping digital heist." *New York Post*.
8. Trust Wallet (January 20, 2026). "Best Practices to Increase Your Crypto Wallet Security."
9. Ledger (November 7, 2025). "5 Best Practices to Increase Your Crypto Wallet Security."
10. Vineet Nair (December 24, 2025). "What Happens to Your Crypto When You Die?" Ledger Academy.

CHAPTER SEVEN

1. See: Antonio Madeira (July 20, 2020). "DeFi Vs. Legacy Finance: Solving Old Issues Brings New Complexities." *Cointelegraph*.
2. Proof of stake (PoS) secures a blockchain by requiring participants to lock digital assets as collateral. Validators run the network software, validate transactions, and earn rewards and fees, but can be penalized for errors or downtime. Delegators participate by staking their assets with a validator instead of running infrastructure themselves. For example, on the Ethereum network, investors can stake ETH by delegating to a validator and earn staking rewards while accepting the risk of validator underperformance or slashing.
3. Dhara Ranasinghe (September 14, 2021). "Global debt is fast approaching record $300 trillion - IIF." *Reuters*.
4. Dorothy Neufeld (February 26, 2025). "The $124 Trillion Global Stock Market, Sorted by Region." *Visual Capitalist*.
5. In the digital asset space, centralized lenders take custody of customer assets and try to earn yield by lending them to others. For example, a platform might take customer-deposited Bitcoin and lend it to a trading firm that wants to borrow BTC to make leveraged bets, or take customer-deposited stablecoins and lend them to borrowers who pay interest.
6. Automated market makers are trading systems that use pooled assets and predefined formulas to set prices and execute trades automatically, rather than matching individual buyers and sellers. Users who supply assets to these pools earn trading fees in exchange for providing liquidity.
7. In this context, permissionless means that participation does not require approval from a centralized operator. Users interact directly with publicly available software using a compatible wallet.
8. xUSD is the yield-bearing stablecoin issued by Stream Finance that represented a claim on deposited stablecoins plus accrued yield. Instead of holding USDC directly, users received xUSD, whose value depended on the performance and solvency of Stream's underlying strategies rather than a fixed one-to-one backing.

CHAPTER EIGHT

1. See: "CZ_Binance" X post from May 19, 2025.
2. 21Shares. Portfolio Allocation Primer
3. Alexandre Chau, Ranjit Ramachandran (February 2022). "Evaluating cryptocurrencies as an asset class." Wellington Management.
4. Franklin Templeton. "The compelling case for crypto." Franklin Templeton.
5. Matt Hougan, Gayatri Choudhury, Mallika Kola. (April 1, 2025). "Bitcoin's Role in a Traditional Portfolio." *Bitwise.*
6. WisdomTree Portfolio Insights (November 2025): The Role of Bitcoin in a Portfolio.
7. Jamie Crawley (October 7, 2025). "Morgan Stanley Recommends a 4% 'Opportunistic' Crypto Portfolio Allocation." *CoinDesk*.
8. Daniel Kuhn (July 28, 2025). "Billionaire investor Ray Dalio recommends 15% allocation in long-term assets like bitcoin and gold." *The Block.*
9. Samara Cohen, Paul Henderson, Vivek Paul, and Robert Mitchnick (December 11, 2024). "Sizing bitcoin in portfolios." BlackRock.

10. Large unlocks refer to scheduled releases of previously restricted tokens, often held by founders, early investors, or foundations, that significantly increase the circulating supply over a short period of time. When the amount being released is large relative to daily trading volume, it can create selling pressure even if nothing has changed about the project itself.

ACKNOWLEDGMENTS

This book was shaped not only by research and market experience, but by conversations with the builders, operators, legislators, and investors who are building, investing in, and strengthening the digital asset ecosystem every day. The list would be far too long for this page but most would recognize themselves.

This book was made possible thanks to the direct support and belief of several people. First and foremost my agent, Tim Hays. Tim and I met at a conference called Assets on the Blockchain organized by Suresh Nichani at The Harvard Club of New York. Tim immediately saw the opportunity and the need for such a book and invested considerable time and effort to bring it to life. Secondly, my deep gratitude to Jessica Roy for connecting me to Sam Bourgi whose support and commitment helped take this book to the finishing line. My sincere thanks to J. Christopher Giancarlo whose trust and willingness to write the foreword brings exceptional insight and perspective to this book. Finally, I want to thank Wiley and their team notably Judith Newlin, Delainey Henson, Katherine Cording, Richard Samson and Julie Kerr for their vision and helping bring this book to readers.

I am also deeply grateful to the experts who generously shared their time, insights, and perspectives. Their contributions helped ground this book in real-world experience and informed some of the frameworks presented throughout these pages.

I also want to extend a special thanks to Kaiko and their teams for supplying the market data and charts that helped bring many of the book's insights to life.

Adam Blumberg, Managing Partner and Co-Founder, Protocol Wealth

Ambre Soubiran, CEO, Kaiko

Anthony Scaramucci, Founder, Managing Partner, SkyBridge Capital

Barton Mallon, Managing Partner of Cole-Frieman & Mallon LLP

Carlos Domingo, CEO and Founder, Securitize

Dan Kim, Head of Digital Asset Listings and Services, Coinbase

Donna Redel, Adjunct Professor, Fordham Law School and Gabelli School of Business

Edward Woodford, Founder and CEO, Zerohash

Evgeny Gokhberg, Founder, Re7 Capital

J. Christopher Giancarlo, Attorney, Author, Board Director, Investor, Former Executive and Ex-Chairman, US Commodity Futures Trading Commission

John D'Agostino, Head of Strategy, Institutional, Coinbase

Joseph Lubin, CEO and Founder, ConsenSys

Kyle Samani, Chairman, Forward Industries

Marcos C. Veremis, Partner, Accolade Partners

Martin Green, CEO, Cambrian Asset Management

Matthew Roszak, Chairman, Bloq, Co-Founder, Hemi

Matthew Szilagyi, CIO, Aspen Digital

Dr. Nagendra Bharatula, Founder & Senior Portfolio Manager, G-20 Group

Paul Frambot, Co-Founder and CEO, Morpho

Ray Hindi, CEO, CIO, Co-Founder L1D AG

Sam Bourgi, CEO, Pathway Economics

Sam Gaer, CIO, Directional Fund, Monarq Asset Management

Sean Pattwell, Founder and CEO, CW8

Shiliang Tang, Managing Partner, Monarq Asset Management

William Wolf, Managing Partner, Arche Capital

Jordan Lazaro Gustave, CEO, The Human Dynamics, former COO of Aave

Ruud Smets, Managing Partner, Theta Capital Management

Thanking each of them for contributing to a more informed and thoughtful discussion around digital assets and their role in modern portfolios.

ABOUT THE AUTHOR

Vanessa Grellet is Managing Partner of the multi strategy fund Arche Capital, where she invests in emerging technologies including blockchain, artificial intelligence, and digital financial infrastructure. Her work spans both private and public markets, with a focus on digital asset treasury companies, tokenized finance, and financial networks built on blockchain technology.

She discovered Bitcoin in 2013 and later joined ConsenSys in 2016, where she worked with entrepreneurs building applications on Ethereum during the network's early development.

Her perspective on digital assets is grounded in a background in traditional finance. A native New Yorker, Grellet spent more than 15 years on Wall Street, including at the New York Stock Exchange, where she developed experience in capital markets, financial regulation, and global market structure. Trained as a securities lawyer, she brings a combination of legal, financial, and technological insight to an industry that continues to evolve rapidly.

Over the course of her career, she has also worked with other venture firms, supporting founders building infrastructure for the digital asset ecosystem.

Grellet currently serves on the boards of the Enterprise Ethereum Alliance, Based AI, and the Art and Antiquities Blockchain Coalition. She is a frequent speaker at industry gatherings, including Consensus, SALT, Digital Asset Summit, Crypto Finance Conference in St. Moritz, Digiassets, and Mainnet.

Based in the United States—and often traveling—Grellet works globally with founders and investors, as digital assets continue moving into mainstream finance.

INDEX

A

Aave, 15, 17, 171, 190, 200, 204, 212, 214, 216–219, 221, 231, 235

AI. *See* artificial intelligence (AI)

algorithmic stablecoin, 20, 229, 230

alpha strategies (independent returns), 163–164

altcoin, 6, 94

- seasons, 131
- treasury companies, 117–118

American Bitcoin, 112

AMMs. *See* automated market makers (AMMs)

Annual Percentage Rate (APR), vs APY, 209

Annual Percentage Yield (APY), vs APR, 209

application-layer fund, 152

Arbitrum, 21

Arche Capital, x

ARK Invest, 82, 109

artificial intelligence (AI), x, 23–25, 94, 163, 272

asset class, x, xiii, xiv, xv, xvi, xvii, 2, 28–34, 43, 65, 66, 69, 72, 82, 83, 97, 118, 168, 238, 239, 241, 252, 258, 273

Atkins, Paul, 76

automated market makers (AMMs), 222–224

B

Backed Finance issue, 55

balanced growth portfolio, 254–255

basket products, 110–111, 128, 137, 138

bear markets, 21, 164, 205

BENJI, 53

Bharatula, Dr. Nagendra, 125

Bitcoin, xiv, 2–6, 8–13, 16, 18, 21, 23, 39, 40, 45, 64, 66–68, 71–73, 75, 79–81, 88–93, 95, 97, 98, 117–118, 129–130, 132–133, 143, 146, 162, 164–167, 200, 239–245, 247, 248, 255, 256, 271–273, 275, 276, 279

Bitcoin (*continued*)
asset class correlation matrix, 82–87
derivatives trading, 118–119
derivatives in digital assets, 123–125
futures contracts, 120
US equity options, 120–121
dominance, 130–131
ETFs, 24, 29–31, 109
miners, 111–112
native staking yield, 169–170
Bitcoin: A Peer-to-Peer Electronic Cash System (Satoshi Nakamoto), 2, 10
Bitgo, 11, 71
BitMine Immersion Technologies (BMNR), 117
Bittensor, 25, 272
Bitwise Asset Management, 239, 242, 247
Bitwise 10 Crypto Index Fund (BITW), 110
Bitwise 10 Large Cap Crypto Index, 239, 240
BlackRock, 23, 26, 29–32, 35, 50, 52, 54–56, 71, 109, 143
approaches, 247
Bitcoin ETF, 24
BUIDL Fund, 54–55
BlackRock's USD Institutional Digital Liquidity Fund (BUIDL), 52–55
Blockchain for Social Impact Coalition, x
blockchain technology, x, xiv, xvii, 2, 5–7, 9, 12–18, 20, 21, 24, 33–36, 38–39, 272–274, 278, 279
infrastructure, 25
public blockchains (*see* public blockchains)
use cases, 46
clearing and settlement, 59
payments and stablecoins, 46–50
tokenization of assets and securities, 50–54, 58
tokenized equities, 55–58
trade finance systems and supply chains, 60
BlockFi, 20, 213
Bored Ape Yacht Club (BAYC), 18, 19
bridges, 43, 99, 101, 141, 170, 189–190
broker-dealers, 69–72, 145
browser-based wallets, 181, 185
BTC, 10, 64, 103, 132, 169, 279
bull markets, 81, 148, 164, 205
business-to-geek model, 183

C

capital preservation portfolio, 255–256
Cboe, 15, 32
Celsius Network, 20, 213
centralized digital asset, 20, 213
centralized exchanges (CEXs), 73, 74, 102–106, 186, 196
comparison with decentralized exchanges (DEXS) and, 105, 106

CEXs. *See* centralized exchanges (CEXs)
CFTC. *See* Commodity Futures Trading Commission (CFTC)
Chalom, Joseph, 100
Chicago Mercantile Exchange (CME), 16, 31–32, 84, 109, 120, 125
Chriss, Alex, 46, 274
Christensen, Clayton, 37
Citigroup, 48, 49, 274
CLARITY Act, 26, 76, 273
CME. *See* Chicago Mercantile Exchange (CME)
Coinbase, 3, 9, 11, 16, 33, 53, 58, 67, 71, 73, 100, 102, 105, 113, 114, 123, 146, 148, 186, 188, 193, 208, 221, 234
CoinDesk, 74
CoinDesk Indices CoinDesk Market Index, 110
CoinShares, 70
Commodity Futures Trading Commission (CFTC), 12, 16, 25, 31, 32, 76
compliance records, 195–196
ConsenSys, xiv, 4, 5, 12, 43, 117
correlation, 80, 82–87, 95, 113, 142, 221, 239, 241, 242
  with gold, 87–89
  with Nasdaq, 87
  risk, 221
counterparty risk, 59, 137, 162, 170, 179, 213
cryptocurrencies, ix–xi, xiii, xvi, xvii, 3, 5–7, 10, 18, 41, 44, 67, 77–81, 100, 102–104, 110–118, 120, 121, 123, 128, 129, 134, 180, 193
  assets, 6
  interest rates and risk appetite, 81
  liquidity contracts, 81
  "super app," 188
  winter, 20–21
CryptoKitties, 18
crypto-native exchange is Coinbase (COIN), 113
crypto-native yield, 210
CryptoPunks, 19
curator–risk manager model, 226–227

D

DAI. *See* Digital-Asset-Backed Stablecoins (DAI)
Dalio, Ray, 247
decentralized applications (dApps), 5, 136
Decentralized Autonomous Organization (DAO), 13, 271
decentralized exchanges (DEXS), 27, 73, 74, 104–106, 122, 166, 186, 197, 222, 224
  comparison with centralized exchanges (CEXS) and, 105, 106
decentralized infrastructure, 175, 178, 191
  navigating, 187
  security practice, 191–195

decentralized markets, 201, 203, 212, 223, 234
DeFi, 169–170, 205
advantages, 200
lending, 214–215, 217
models, 218–219
platforms, 208, 217
project, 231
Summer, 17–18
systems, 235
vaults, 225–227
delegated staking, 206, 207, 211
delta-neutral fund, 166–167
derivatives fund, 31–32
derivatives markets, xiv, 23–24, 73, 83, 118
derivatives trading, 3, 73, 105, 106, 118, 119
Bitcoin, 118–119
derivatives in digital assets, 123–125
futures contracts, 120
miners, 111–112
US equity options, 120–121
DEXS. *See* decentralized exchanges (DEXS)
Digital-Asset-Backed Stablecoins (DAI), 47, 48, 229, 230
digital asset-related equities, 172
Bitcoin, 117–118
miners, 111–112
digital asset treasury (DAT) companies, 114–115
exchanges and infrastructure providers, 113–114
MicroStrategy (MSTR), 115–116
digital assets, xiii, xiv, xv, xvi, xviii, xix, 1–2, 41, 63–66, 237–238, 263–264, 271, 273, 275, 276, 278, 279
allocation, 256–258
asset class, 28–29, 97
derivatives and hedge funds, 31–32
gold ETFs and bitcoin ETFs, 29–31
institutionalization, 32–34
avoidable operational mistakes, 191–195
blockchain technology, 38–39
blockchain use cases, 46
clearing and settlement, 59
payments and stablecoins, 46–50
tokenization of assets and securities, 50–54, 58
tokenized equities, 55–58
trade finance systems and supply chains, 60
characteristics of public blockchains, 42–43
comparison with traditional assets and, 96
correlation, 82–87
with gold, 87–89
with Nasdaq, 87
cryptocurrency, 78–81
interest rates and risk appetite, 81
liquidity contracts, 81
derivatives in, 123–125
diversifying exposure, 110–111
example portfolios, 253

high risk tolerance
portfolio, 253–254
lower risk tolerance
portfolio, 255–256
medium risk tolerance
portfolio, 254–255
exposure based on risk
tolerance, 248–249
investors, 252–253
rebalancing, 251
timing risk, 251–252
exposure pathways, 101
financial markets, rewiring of,
60–61
financial services, 43–44
four-year cycle, 90–92
history, 2–3
Bitcoin, 3–4
Ethereum, 4–7, 12–16, 18, 19, 21,
23, 26, 27, 31, 34
innovation, 39–40
investment class, xvi
investments, 69–72
investor, 61–62, 98
investors, 36
lending and borrowing market,
211–213
Defi platforms, 217
interest rates, 216–217
risks, 220–221
trade-off, 220
uses, 219–220
working, 214–215
liquidity provision, 222–223
DeFi vaults, 225–227
liquid markets, 259–261
market cycles and transformative
events, 7–8
artificial intelligence, 25
DeFi Summer, 17–18
early adoption and growing
pains, 11–12
Ethereum and ICO cycle, 14–16
foundational infrastructure, 9
infrastructure, regulation, and
institutional learning, 12–13
institutional participation, 23–26
price discovery, 25–26
stablecoins, 23–24
systemic stress, 20–21
next generation of investors, 67–68
on-chain yield, 201–202
investors, 235–236
real yield vs inflationary
(subsidized) yield, 204–205
sideways/bear markets, 205
sources, 203
portfolio, 245–246
from institutions on allocation,
246–247
investing, 247–248
portfolio diversification, 238–240
adding, 242–244
uncorrelated assets, 241–242
volatile asset, 245
private markets (*see* private markets)
professional investors
principles, 261–262
public blockchains through
wallets, 180–181
friction points, 189–190
funding, 185–186

digital assets (*continued*)
loss, theft, and finality, 183
navigating decentralized infrastructure, 187
private key and seed phrase, 182
sense, 184
setting up, 184–185
smart-contract wallets and social recovery, 182
software wallet vs hardware wallet, 181
public market investment (*see* public market investment)
renewed legal and regulatory framework, 75–77
sector's performance, 92–95
self-custody, 178–179
investors, 196–197
markets by avoidable operational mistakes, 191–195
record-keeping for taxes, 195–196
security practice, 191–195
simple mental model, xvii
stablecoin yield, 227–228
sources, 232–233
types, 228–230
staking yields, 206
APY *vs* APR, 209
returns and risk, 210–211
types, 206–209
technologies, xi
trading and transaction activity numbers, 72–74
users growth, 66–67
yield farming, 235
yield opportunities, 200
comparison with digital asset and traditional finance, 202
examples, 208–209
digital asset treasury (DAT) companies, 114–117
digital scarcity, 18, 39
Dimon, Jamie, 35, 273
direct investments, 143, 145
direct ownership, 30, 58, 72, 74, 98, 104, 107, 117, 118, 137, 178, 257
to public market access, 100–101
direct spot exposure
public market investment, 102–103
exchange-traded products, 107–109
platform custody, 103–104
Distributions to Paid-In Capital (DPI), 158
dollar-backed stablecoin, 228, 233
Domingo, Carlos, 52, 274
DoorDash, 38
double spending, 41
DTCC, 59, 274
due diligence, 142, 156, 172–174

E

ecosystem focused operating companies, 114–115
EigenLayer-based DeFi platforms, 208
Employee Retirement Income Security Act (ERISA), 135, 145

Enterprise Ethereum Alliance, x, xiv, 16, 43, 273
ERISA. *See* Employee Retirement Income Security Act (ERISA)
ETFS, 23, 24, 26, 29–34, 99, 107–109, 131, 248, 257
  futures-based products, 109–110
  index and basket products, 110–111
  spot-based products, 109
ETH. *See* Ethereum (ETH)
Ethereum (ETH), xiv, 4–7, 12–16, 18, 19, 21, 23, 26, 27, 31, 34, 66, 72, 73, 80, 93, 129–130, 132–133, 162, 164, 165, 167, 170, 177, 186, 187, 189–190, 206, 208, 214, 216, 220, 224, 227, 239, 240, 242, 244, 245, 248, 279
Ethereum-focused treasury strategy, 117–118
Ethereum Virtual Machine (EVM), 21, 272
ETPS. *See* exchange-traded products (ETPS)
Euler, 214, 216, 219, 225
EVM. *See* Ethereum Virtual Machine (EVM)
exchange-traded products (ETPS), 107–111, 123, 125, 257

F
Facebook, 64
Federal Reserve, 44, 50, 81
fees/interest, incentive tokens, 235
Fidelity Investments, 31, 71
financial markets, rewiring of, 60–61
financial services, x, xi, 12, 17, 43–44, 183, 187, 188
Fink, Larry, 50, 274
FIT21 Act, 76
Forward Industries (FWDI), 118
four-year cycle, in digital assets, 90–92
Frambot, Paul, 211
Franklin Templeton, 46, 53, 148, 239
FTX, 20, 22, 156, 173, 174
fully diluted valuation (FDV), 259
fund-of-funds, 139–140
  investing through digital asset, 142–144
    direct investments, 145
fund size, 159–160
Future Investment Initiative (FII9), 273
futures-based products, 30, 109–110, 120, 138
futures contracts, 24, 31, 109, 120, 129, 168

G
GAAP, 157
Gaer, Sam, 29, 66
Galois Capital, 174
Gauthier, Pascal, 39
GENIUS Act, 26, 50, 76, 233, 273
Gensler, Gary, 75
Gen Z, 68
Giancarlo, J. Christopher (Chairman), xi, 16, 32
GLD, 29, 30
Global Investment Committee, 246
gold, correlation with, 87–89

Gold ETFs, 29–31, 34, 109
Grayscale Bitcoin Trust, 11, 107
Grayscale Research, 89
Grellet, Vanessa, ix–xi
growth-focused portfolio, 253–254
Gryphon Digital Mining, 112
Gura, David, 275

H

hardware wallet, 185, 195
  software wallet vs, 181
hedge funds, 16, 29, 31–32, 35, 91, 120, 139–143, 161, 162, 165, 171–173, 213, 247
high-frequency trading (HFT), 160–161
high risk tolerance portfolio, 253–254
Hindi, Ray, 142
hybrid stablecoins, 229, 230

I

ICO cycle, 14–16
impersonation scams, 192–194
incentive tokens, on fees/interest, 235
income strategies (carry), 162
index products, 70, 110–111, 128, 132
inflationary (subsidized) yield, vs real yield, 204–205
infrastructure-focused funds, 151
institutional participation, 23–26, 76, 83, 100, 107, 165, 218
insurance, in digital asset markets, 221–222
Intercontinental Exchange, 127
Internal Rate of Return (IRR), 149, 158, 277
Invesco QQQ Trust (QQQ), 120
investments, 69–72
  digital assets (*see* digital assets)
  liquid funds, 161–162, 171–172
    alpha strategies (independent returns), 163–164
    delta-neutral and market-neutral, 166–167
    directional strategies, 165
    due diligence, 172–174
    income strategies (carry), 163
    investor, 175
    market conditions and capacity constraints, 164–165
    market exposure (beta) strategies, 162
    market-neutral funds, 167–168
    on-chain funds, 170–171
    yield-focused bitcoin funds, 169
  portfolios, 263–264 (*see also* portfolios)
  in private markets (*see* private markets)
  public market investment (*see* public market investment)
investors
  digital assets, 36
    investment opportunity, 98
    next generation, 67–68
    on-chain yield, 235–236
    portfolio construction, 261–262
    private market investment, 175

public market investment, 137–138
self-custody, 196–197
technology and use case, 61–62
IPOs, 149, 152, 154, 160
iShares Bitcoin Trust (IBIT), 24, 26, 30, 136

J

Johnson, Jenny, 46, 273
JPMorgan, 16, 29, 33, 35, 48, 49, 53, 59, 71, 85, 130, 274

K

Kaiko 10 Index, 257–258
Katharine Wooller of AssetPass, 70
Know Your Customer (KYC), 200, 218, 225
Kraken, 9, 11, 33, 44, 57, 73, 100, 102, 123, 154, 186, 188, 208, 221

L

large unlocks, 260, 280
La Salla, Frank, 59, 274
layer-1 blockchain, 18, 21, 272
lending and borrowing market, 211–213
Defi platforms, 217
interest rates, 216–217
risks, 220–221
trade-off, 220
uses, 219–220
working, 214–215
liquid funds, 161–162, 171–172
alpha strategies (independent returns), 163–164
blow-ups, 174–175
delta-neutral and market-neutral, 166–167
directional strategies, 165
due diligence, 172–174
income strategies (carry), 163
investor, 175
market conditions and capacity constraints, 164–165
market exposure (beta) strategies, 162
market-neutral funds, 167–168
on-chain funds, 170–171
yield-focused bitcoin funds, 169
liquidity markets, 259–261
contracts, 81
pools, 207, 218, 222, 224
providers, 203, 204, 223–225
provision, 222–223
DeFi vaults, 225–227
staking, 207, 208, 211
venture capital funds, 157–159
liquid staking tokens (LSTs), 207, 208
lower risk tolerance portfolio, 255–256
lquidation cascades, 221
Lubin, Joseph, 4, 177
LUNA, 229

M

macro case, for crypto, 78–81
market-cap weighted indices, 111
market cycles and transformative events
digital assets, 7–8
artificial intelligence, 25
DeFi Summer, 17–18

market cycles (*continued*)
early adoption and growing pains, 11–12
Ethereum and ICO cycle, 14–16
foundational infrastructure, 9
infrastructure, regulation, and institutional learning, 12–13
institutional participation, 23–26
price discovery, 25–26
stablecoins, 23–24
systemic stress, 20–21
market exposure (beta) strategies, 162
market makers, 120, 160–161, 201, 212, 222, 223, 272, 279
market net asset value (mNAV), 116–117
market-neutral fund, 166–167, 174
Martin, Emmie, 275
Mashinsky, Alex, 213
Maximal Extractable Value (MEV), 190–191
medium risk tolerance portfolio, 254–255
memecoins, 27–28
mergers and acquisitions (M&A), xiv, 158
MetaMask, 12, 181, 182, 185, 188, 208, 278
MicroStrategy (MSTR), 33, 115–116
Millennials, 67, 68
Morpho, 211, 214, 216, 218–219, 221, 226
MSCI, 110
Mt. Gox, 11, 12
Multiple on Invested Capital (MOIC), 158
multisignature wallet, 278
multisig wallet, 278

N

Nakamoto, Satoshi, 2, 10
NASCAR, 27
Nasdaq, 84, 86
correlation with, 87
native staking, 169, 206–207, 210, 211
network security, yield from, 206–211
new layer-1 blockchains, 17–18, 21
New York Stock Exchange, xiv, 3, 56, 127
nodes, 41, 45
nonfungible tokens (NFTs), 6, 13, 17–19, 131
NYSE, 3
NYU technology, 3

O

Office of the Comptroller of the Currency (OCC), 25
on-chain funds, 52, 54, 55, 58, 170–171
on-chain income foundation, 227–234
on-chain yield, 201–202
investors, 235–236
real yield vs inflationary (subsidized) yield, 204–205
sideways/bear markets, 205
sources, 203
Ondo Finance, 53, 58
Operation Choke Point, 77–78
2.0, 77–78

Original Program, 77
over-the-counter (OTC), 123, 160–161

P
Panigirtzoglou, Nikolaos, 85
Pantera Capital, 142, 150
Pax Gold (PAXG), 58
PayPal, 33, 39, 46, 47, 273, 274
permissioned blockchain, 44, 59
perpetual futures, 74, 118, 119, 121–123
  decentralized exchanges, 106
phishing emails, 192–195, 222
platform custody, 103–104
Polychain Capital, 142, 150
Polymarket, 125, 127, 152
portfolios, 245–246
  construction, 159–160
  diversification, 238–240
    adding, 242–244
    uncorrelated assets, 241–242
    volatile asset, 245
  example, 253
    high risk tolerance portfolio, 253–254
    lower risk tolerance portfolio, 255–256
    medium risk tolerance portfolio, 254–255
  from institutions on allocation, 246–247
  investing, 247–248
PotCoin, 3
power law, 140, 156, 159–160
prediction markets, 125–128, 187
pre-seed fund, 151
price discovery, 25–26, 32, 118, 120
price exposure, 24, 31, 103–104, 109, 121, 128, 136, 141, 196
price feed risk, 220
private blockchain, 38
  comparison with public blockchain and, 45
private key, 134, 137, 178–183, 185, 188, 193, 194, 196, 278
private markets
  digital assets, 139
    fund-of-funds, 139–140, 142–145
    investor, 175
    liquid fund blow-ups, 174–175
    liquid funds (*see* liquid funds)
    venture capital funds (*see* venture capital funds)
professional investors principles, 261–262
Project Ion, 59
proof of stake (PoS), 201, 206, 208, 210, 279
proof-of-stake networks, 201, 203, 206, 208, 210
ProShares Bitcoin Strategy ETF (BITO), 30, 109
protocol base rate, 210
public blockchains
  characteristics, 42–43
  comparison with private blockchain and, 45
  through wallets, 180–181
    friction points, 189–190

public blockchains (*continued*)
funding, 185–186
loss, theft, and finality, 183
navigating decentralized infrastructure, 187
private key and seed phrase, 182
sense, 184
setting up, 184–185
smart-contract wallets and social recovery, 182
software wallet vs hardware wallet, 181
public market investment, 99–100
Bitcoin derivatives trading, 118–119
derivatives in digital assets, 123–125
futures contracts, 120
US equity options, 120–121
digital asset-related equities
Bitcoin, 117–118
Bitcoin miners, 111–112
digital asset treasury (DAT) companies, 114–115
exchanges and infrastructure providers, 113–114
MicroStrategy (MSTR), 115–116
from direct ownership to, 100–101
direct spot exposure, 102–103
exchange-traded products, 107–109
platform custody, 103–104
exchange-traded products (ETPS), 107–111
investor, 137–138
pathway, 128–129, 133–137
Bitcoin and Ethereum, 129–130, 132–133
ETF sponsors and index, 131
pathways to digital asset exposure, 101
prediction markets, 125–128

R

real yield, vs inflationary (subsidized) yield, 204–205
rebalancing, in digital assets, 251
record-keeping, for taxes, 195–196
registered investment advisors (RIAs), 69–72
regulation-by-enforcement, 25–26
restaking, 208, 211, 227
retail market cycles, 27–28
risk appetite, 28, 81, 89
risk-free yield, 210
risk management, xviii, 20, 24, 32, 65, 100, 118, 120–121, 127, 129, 164, 169, 221, 222
risk manager, 225–2247
risk profile, 171, 219, 249
higher risk profile, 250–251
lower risk profile, 250
medium risk profile, 250
risk tolerance, 98, 184, 205, 236, 257
exposure based on, 248–249
investors, 252–253
rebalancing, 251
timing risk, 251–252
robinhood markets, 55, 56, 58
"rolling" futures, 110

Roubini, Nouriel, 38
rules-based indices, 111

S
Samani, Kyle, 147
Scaramucci, Anthony, 68, 143
Schwab, Charles, 72, 109, 135
Securities and Exchange Commission (SEC), 25, 31, 75–76, 135, 153, 272–275, 277
securitize tokenizes stocks, 56
security practice, self-custody, 191–195
seed funds, 151
seed phrase, 178, 182, 185, 193, 194, 278
self-custody, 103–104, 178–179
  assets, 145–146
  investors, 196–197
    principles, 194–195
  public blockchains through wallets, 180–181
    friction points, 189–190
    funding, 185–186
    loss, theft, and finality, 183
    navigating decentralized infrastructure, 187
    private key and seed phrase, 182
    sense, 184
    setting up, 184–185
    smart-contract wallets and social recovery, 182
    software wallet vs hardware wallet, 181
  record-keeping for taxes, 195–196
  security practice, 191–195
Selig, Michael S., 76
SharpLink Gaming (SBET), 117
Shima Capital, 153
Shore, Dr. Mark, 84
sideways market, 205
Silk Road, 11, 271
SIM hijacking, 192, 193, 195
Simple Agreement for Future Equity (SAFTs), 154
simple rule of thumb, 232–233
SkyBridge, 68, 143
smart-contract wallets, 182
Smets, Ruud, 43
social recovery wallets, 182, 185
software risk, 220
software wallet, vs hardware wallet, 181
Solana (SOL), 6, 18, 21, 28, 31, 45, 55, 58, 108, 109, 114, 117, 132, 140, 151, 152, 162, 165, 167, 170, 187, 189, 220, 227
Solana-focused treasury strategy, 117–118
S&P 500, 84, 85, 92
S&P Dow Jones Indices, 110
SPDR S&P 500 ETF Trust (SPY), 120
spot-based products, 109, 120
spot Bitcoin ETF, 23, 24, 29, 30, 91, 107, 109, 125, 128, 138, 146
spot trading, 73, 74, 102, 104–106, 276
stablecoins, xvii, 6, 11, 15, 20, 23–24, 26, 33, 35, 200, 203, 216, 219, 220, 223, 226, 234–236, 271, 273, 274, 279
  comparison with tokenized deposits and, 48

stablecoins (*continued*)
payments and, 46–50
yield, 227–228
sources, 232–233
types, 228–230
staking yields, 206
APY *vs* APR, 209
returns and risk, 210–211
types, 206–209
Stanley, Morgan, 71, 246
Strategy Designers, 225–226
Stream Finance, 231, 279
subsidized yield, vs real yield, 204–205
succession planning, 195–196
super app, 188
swap venues, 189–190
systemic stress, 20–21

T

Tanev, Vlad, 274
taxes, record-keeping for, 195–196
Tenev, Vlad, 55
Terra, 20, 229
Tether Gold (XAUT), 58
thematic funds, 152
thematic indices, 111
Three Arrows Capital, 174
timing risk, 251–252
tokenization, xiii, xiv, xvi, xvii, 6, 23–24
of assets and securities, 50–54, 58
comparison with stablecoins and tokenization deposits, 48
equities, 55–58
Total Value Locked (TVL), 210, 212, 217
trade finance systems, and supply chains, 60
trading and transaction activity numbers, 72–74
traditional assets, 35, 50, 62, 66, 82–84, 92, 95, 238, 239, 242, 247, 250
comparison with digital assets and, 96
traditional finance yield, comparison with digital asset yield and, 202
Trump administration, 76
Trust Wallet, 181, 185, 278
TVL. *See* Total Value Locked (TVL)

U

Ulbricht, Ross, 271
uncorrelated assets, 241–242
Union Square Ventures, 160
Uniswap, 15, 17, 27, 105, 152, 186, 189, 204, 224–225, 227, 235
USDC, 11, 24, 47, 48, 186, 187, 190, 203, 214, 216, 219, 223, 224, 228, 230, 231, 234, 278, 279
USDT, 11, 47, 48, 216, 219, 228, 230, 234, 278
use cases, 9, 36, 38, 39, 92, 94, 127, 132, 220, 263, 273
blockchain technology, 46
clearing and settlement, 59
payments and stablecoins, 46–50
tokenization of assets and securities, 50–54, 58

tokenized equities, 55–58
trade finance systems and supply chains, 60
US equity options, 120–121
user-experience (UX) problem, 183–184
US Investment Advisers Act, 145
US Securities and Exchange Commission, 25, 31, 75, 76, 135, 153, 272–275, 277

V

validators, 190, 201, 204, 206, 207, 210, 279
VanEck, 56, 109, 244, 247
venture capital (VC) funds, 147–154
digital assets, 150
application-layer and thematic funds, 152
fund structure, 152–154
infrastructure-focused funds, 151
liquidity, 157–159
manager selection, 155–156
portfolio construction, 159–160
pre-seed and seed funds, 151
risks, 156
Veremis, Marcos C., 179
Virgil Capital, 174
volatile asset, 64, 232, 245
volatility management, 120–121

W

wallets
drainers, 192–194
funding, 185–186
public blockchains through, 180–181
friction points, 189–190
funding, 185–186
loss, theft, and finality, 183
navigating decentralized infrastructure, 187
private key and seed phrase, 182
sense, 184
setting up, 184–185
smart-contract wallets and social recovery, 182
software wallet vs hardware wallet, 181
wallet-based purchases, 186
wealth managers, role of, 69–72
Web3 applications, xvii, 5, 7, 13, 177
Winklevoss, Tyler, 2, 64, 275
Winters, Bill, 60
WisdomTree, 244, 247
Wood, Cathie, 82
wrong network, sending assets to, 191–195

X

xUSD, 231, 279

Y

yield-bearing tokens, 227, 231
yield-focused bitcoin funds, 169
yield opportunities, in digital assets, 200
comparison with digital asset and traditional finance, 202
examples, 208–209

yield opportunities (*continued*)
farming, 235
lending and borrowing market, 211–213
Defi platforms, 217
interest rates, 216–217
risks, 220–221
trade-off, 220
uses, 219–220
working, 214–215
liquidity provision, 222–223
DeFi vaults, 225–227
from network security, 206–211
on-chain yield, 201–202
investors, 235–236
real yield vs inflationary (subsidized) yield, 204–205
sideways/bear markets, 205
sources, 203
stablecoin yield, 227–228
sources, 232–233
types, 228–230
staking yields, 206
APY *vs* APR, 209
returns and risk, 210–211
types, 206–209
yield farming, 235

Z
Zhao, Changpeng, 64, 237
zkSync, 20